Violence

Encounters: Experience and Anthropological Knowledge

ISSN: 1746-8175

Series Editor: John Borneman

Encounters: Experience and Anthropological Knowledge is a series that examines fieldwork experiences of contemporary anthropologists. It aims to render into vivid and accessible prose the insights gained from fieldwork on topics such as money, violence, sex and food. These short collections of essays are committed to:

- the subjective quality of sensual experience, tied to a particular time and place;
- curiosity in difference itself, in translating the strange, foreign or unassimilable;
- storytelling that contributes both to the documentary function of the ethnographic encounter and to analytical potential.

Violence

Ethnographic Encounters

Edited by
Parvis Ghassem-Fachandi

Oxford • New York

English edition
First published in 2009
Berg
Editorial offices:
1st Floor, Angel Court, 81 St Clements Street, Oxford OX4 1AW, UK
175 Fifth Avenue, New York, NY 10010, USA

Berg is the imprint of Oxford International Publishers Ltd.

Library of Congress Cataloging-in-Publication Data
Violence : ethnographic encounters / edited by Parvis Ghassem-Fachandi.
    p. cm.
Includes bibliographical references and index.
    ISBN 978-1-84788-416-9 (pbk. : alk. paper) — ISBN 978-1-84788-417-6
(cloth : alk. paper) 1. Violence. 2. Ethnology—Fieldwork. 3. Political
violence. 4. Ethnic conflict. I. Ghassem-Fachandi, Parvis.
    GN495.2.V555 2009
    305.8—dc22   2009021840

British Library Cataloguing-in-Publication Data
A catalogue record for this book is available from the British Library.

ISBN 978 1 84788 417 6 (Cloth)
        978 1 84788 416 9 (Paper)

Typeset by Avocet Typeset, Chilton, Aylesbury, Bucks
Printed in Great Britain by the MPG Books Group, Bodmin and King's Lynn

www.bergpublishers.com

Contents

Notes on Contributors

John Borneman teaches anthropology at Princeton University. He has done field-work in Germany, Central Europe, Syria, and Lebanon and has published widely on issues of kinship, sexuality, nationality, justice and political form. His most recent ethnographic study is *Syrian Episodes: Sons, Fathers, and an Anthropologist in Aleppo* (2007).

Kristen Drybread teaches anthropology at Columbia University, where she recently completed her Ph.D. In addition to studying relationships between incarceration, identity, masculinity and justice among male prisoners in a Brazilian juvenile detention facility, she has conducted research on issues of immigration, nationality, human rights, and childhood socialization. She has conducted ethnographic research in Indonesia, Brazil and, most recently, in New York City. Grants from the Wenner-Gren, Fulbright Hays, Firestone, and Woodrow Wilson Foundations made possible her field research in Brazil.

Parvis Ghassem-Fachandi teaches in the Department of Anthropology at Rutgers University in New Jersey. Born in the divided former West Berlin, he grew up in Germany, France, and Canada. He received his Ph.D. in anthropology from Cornell University in 2006. He taught at Princeton in 2006 and held a post-doctoral fellow at the Center for Religion and Media at New York University in 2006–7. He has completed field research on nationalism, religion and violence in Gibraltar, the United States, and India. He has done research in Gujarat in 1995, 1999, 2000, 2001–3 and 2005. He is currently completing a book on the 2002 anti-Muslim pogrom in Gujarat, India.

Billie Jean Isbell is Professor Emerita and Graduate Professor of Anthropology at Cornell University. She served in the Peace Corps in Colombia during 1963–5. She attended San Francisco State and was awarded a Ph.D. in Anthropology in 1973 from the University of Illinois. Her expertise is in the Andean region of South America. She was the director of the Andean program for Cornell International Institute for Food, Agriculture and Development from 1990 until 2002. She served as director of the Latin American Program at Cornell from 1987 to 1993 and again in 2001–2. She has been a Fellow at the Woodrow Wilson

Center, and Chercheur Associée de L'École des Hautes Études, Paris. She received grants and fellowships from Woodrow Wilson, Fulbright, Mac Arthur, NEH, and A Ford Training Grant for Interdisciplinary Training of Graduate Students. The most recent grants include an Institute for the Social Sciences grant (2006) and two Faculty Innovation in Teaching grants from the office of the Provost (2005, 2007) and a grant from Olin library to create a digital website (2005) resulting in the following sites: (1) A Virtual Tour through Time and Space: Lessons from Vicos, Peru (http://instruct1.cit.cornell.edu/courses/vicosperu/vicos-site/, accessed 5 December 2008) and (2) a grant from Olin Digital Collection to create a site for Isbell's work (http://isbellandes.library.cornell.edu/, accessed 5 December 2008).

Diane E. King teaches in the Department of Anthropology at the University of Kentucky. She completed her Ph.D. at Washington State University in 2000. Her main research site is the Kurdistan Region of Iraq and she has also worked in Southeast Asia and among Kurdish communities in the United States. Her topical interests include kinship, gender, migration and the state. Previously she taught at American University of Beirut (2000–6, except during two research leaves), was a research fellow in the Department of History at the University of Kentucky (2001–2) and carried out fellowships sponsored by the William and Flora Hewlett Foundation (at UCSD, Spring 2004) and the George A. and Eliza Gardner Howard Foundation (at Washington State University, 2006–7).

Brenda Maiale teaches in the Department of Anthropology at Hobart and William Smith Colleges. She completed her Ph.D. at Cornell University in 2008. In her work she examines how recent changes in fiesta practices are transforming gender subjectivities in southern Mexico and uses the Zapotec fiesta as a lens to examine the ways in which local configurations of gender articulate with the global market, the national imagination, and the contentious body politic of the Oaxacan state. Her research in Oaxaca City and the Isthmus of Tehuantepec was funded by the National Science Foundation, the Mario Einaudi Center for International Studies at Cornell University, and the Tinker Foundation.

Annarose Pandey teaches anthropology, philosophy and global studies at Westview High School in Portland, Oregon. She has found that working in a large public high school is a kind of fieldwork in and of itself. Anna's research fieldwork took place in Sidi Ifni, Morocco during 2001–2 through a Fulbright Grant. Her dissertation is on the politics of nostalgia in formerly Spanish colonial Morocco. She is completing her graduate study at Cornell University.

Bilinda Straight (Ph.D., University of Michigan 1997) is the editor of *Women on the Verge of Home* and author of *Miracles and Extraordinary Experience in Northern Kenya* and numerous articles and book chapters on gender, sexuality, religion, material culture, and interethnic violence in northern Kenya. She is the recipient of a Fulbright and two National Science Foundation grants. The latter are generously supporting her recent and current work on violence affecting the Samburu pastoralists with whom she has conducted research since 1992. She is an associate professor in anthropology at Western Michigan University.

Natasha Zaretsky (Ph.D., Princeton University 2008), is a cultural anthropologist who studies political violence, social change, and citizenship. Her recent work examines the significance of memorial practices to social movements that developed in the wake of violence in Argentina and how Jewish Argentines engage memories of violence in redefining their relationship to their state and one another as they negotiate for belonging. Zaretsky's current research focuses on the emerging Argentine diaspora in Europe and the United States, investigating transformations to Argentine citizenship and sovereignty in response to political and economic uncertainty. She currently holds a postdoctoral lectureship in the Princeton Writing Program, where she teaches a seminar on political violence and social change. Her research in Argentina was funded by a Fulbright grant (2001–2) and research grants from Princeton University's Program in Latin American Studies, Council on Regional Studies, and Program in Judaic Studies.

Foreword

Modern anthropology is different from the other human sciences because it takes the intimate experiences of fieldwork to be a primary source of knowledge. Anthropological and ethnographic knowledge is most often produced through "fieldwork," a form of long-term experiential study that brings the researcher into direct contact with an "Other." Anthropologists have, of course, incorporated into their own craft methods and techniques of other disciplines – history (archival work), literature (reading texts), linguistics (discourse transcriptions), and psychology (controlled experimentation); and scholars in a wide range of disciplines have made use of ethnographic techniques. But while ethnography has become an important tool in many disciplines, its success has come with more than a few vexing questions. Is *any* place a field site? Should reading in the archives or in one's own office be regarded as an encounter with an Other who speaks back to the researcher through the text? Are all field sites and encounters equally valuable or productive?

The popularization of ethnography beyond its original context and use challenges assumptions of anthropologists about their own unique contributions to the understanding of culture and about the relative value of the risks they take in ethnographic encounters. To the extent that anthropologists have succumbed to a professionalization and standardization in style of presentation, their accounts are often dismissed as obsessed with the everyday or, alternately, as overly ambitious theoretical renderings of simple things. They all too frequently sacrifice the specific cultural texture of person and place for a more streamlined theoretical account that focuses solely on a particular question or problem. Moreover, since the disappearance of "the primitive" as an object of study, the public tends to be confused about what it is, exactly, that ethnographers do.

This series on anthropological encounters responds to this contemporary situation with accounts of actual fieldwork experiences focused around selective themes. Such personal encounters during fieldwork betray an experience with difference that makes for good reading and can be highly productive theoretically, but nonetheless tends to be omitted from standard academic accounts. In addition to individual essays of encounters in a wide range of societies, each volume includes an introduction that draws out the particular questions of theoretical significance that such accounts pose and suggestions for further reading on the theme.

Violence: Anthropological Encounters, edited by Parvis Ghassem-Fachandi, is the second volume of this series. The first, *Money: Anthropological Encounters*, edited by Stefan Senders and Allison Truitt, took up the many ways in which the experience anthropologists have with money shapes the fieldwork experience and the kinds of insights generated from research on a broad variety of topics. In this second volume, anthropologists depict an experience of violence during fieldwork and then demonstrate how this shapes the anthropological encounter – both delimiting and generating particular kinds of insights about it. In nine different chapters, contributors explores some of the forms violence takes, the processes by which they learn of these forms, and the social life – mental and physical – of the experience in South Asia, Latin America, Africa, and the Middle East. Their essays include encounters with: Shining Path and governmental anti-insurgency campaigns in Peru, an RSS member during an anti-Muslim pogrom in India; fear among Iraqi Kurds near the end of Saddam Hussein's rule; how familiarity with the warrior ethos of Samburu pastoralists in Kenya leads the (American) son of one anthropologist to consider volunteering for the war in Iraq; brutality and affinity in a youth detention center in Brazil; violence in relations with a transgendered fieldwork assistant in Mexico; local security measures following the bombing of a Jewish community center in Buenos Aires; dreams and memories of punishment and collaboration in South Lebanon and Syria; and rumors and sexual molestation in fieldwork in Morocco.

Authors were asked to write with a particular concern in mind: to focus on stories of their own encounters with violence in fieldwork and to show how these encounters lead to particular kinds of engagements with cultural difference. They were asked to resist the temptation to subsume their writing under theoretical concerns. Hence contributors have elaborated their specific interactions and eschewed most of the conventions that today authorize ethnographic accounts, such as extensive historical contextualizing, footnoting, long bibliographies, or dense theoretical language. Our wish is that the reading of these essays awaken an appreciation for the subjective quality of experiential encounters (personal, tied to a particular time and place); for curiosity in difference itself, in translating the strange, foreign or unassimilable; and for a kind of storytelling that contributes both to the documentary function of the ethnographic encounter and to its theoretical potential.

John Borneman

Acknowledgements

This book grew out of an interest in affirming the singularity of face-to-face field-work experience, especially experience of events that fundamentally lack closure. The essays in this volume by Natasha Zaretsky and Parvis Ghassem-Fachandi were initially presented as papers at a panel in a session titled "Security, Crisis, Violence," at the 2004 Spring Meetings of the American Ethnological Society (AES) in Atlanta, Georgia. Most of the other papers were written for a panel that would have built on the AES one, "Ethnographic Encounters with Violence in the Field," planned for the American Anthropological Association (AAA) Meetings in San Francisco in late 2004. Alas, these meetings were canceled due to a labor dispute between service workers and the host hotel. I want to thank the anonymous reviewers, as well as those many thinkers and lovers, who contributed to this volume in their own respective ways.

Introduction

Parvis Ghassem-Fachandi

In *Violence: Ethnographic Encounters* anthropologists offer first-hand accounts of fieldwork experiences with violence in Peru, India, Iraq, Kenya, Brazil, Mexico, Argentina, Lebanon and Syria and Morocco. Written in a decidedly descriptive style, the stories depict how personal experience with violence made insight into the phenomenon of violence possible. However, by foregrounding the contingency of fieldwork experiences, the unexpected and unassimilable, these essays also elucidate where the anthropological project of producing knowledge about other peoples and places ultimately finds its limits: in the body and mind of the ethnographer.

We follow diverse writing strategies and our emphasis is on narrative description in lieu of impatient rendering of experience into concepts and theoretical paradigms. Especially in the U.S., where popular culture openly cultivates a bias against things "intellectual," an emphasis on history and theory in academic settings is understandable, even laudable. But in much contemporary anthropological writing, historical texts and "high theory" are often deployed as substitutes for a thicker descriptive exposition of what happens during research in the fieldwork setting and elides working through our uncomfortable experiences on paper.

Our descriptions rely on creative and theoretically informed methods and strategies that never allow for a passive harvesting of facts for disinterested presentation. They elucidate the authors' field experiences *in* and *through* the act of writing. By struggling with the adequate expression of experience, the authors insist on holding on to a difference between their own discourse and a conceptual apparatus, holding on to a relation of astonishment and surprise. Our narrative descriptions hope to *show* insights gained through theory, submitting neither to theory nor substituting theory in its exposition. They focus on moments during fieldwork that haunt later memory and which betray an intimacy with difference – a *difference* that is not merely external to the experiencing subject. In this way, we hope, the reader will be brought into the text, completing the promise of expository writing.

Although the authors of this volume are regional specialists, they do not offer systematic analyses for the causes of violence in their own locations. In any case, the phenomenon of violence tends less to unify subjects than to fragment them. Rather, we offer insight into varied forms of violence in diverse locations by situating violence in the intersubjective experiences of fieldworkers in encounters with a place. As in the first volume of this series *Money: Ethnographic Encounters* (edited by Allison Truitt and Stephan Senders), this book does not, then, suggest a general theory of our object of inquiry—violence. There is a large literature on violence that precisely tries to systematize individual accounts into a general theory, which has much to offer the discipline of anthropology. Hence, a select annotated bibliography for further reading on theories and ethnographies on violence concludes the book.

Our focus on the experience of violence in fieldwork hopes to contribute not only to a general awareness of conflict studies throughout the world but also tries to show in which specific ways the intimate encounter with a particular place in a limited amount of time can have heuristic value. How can our encounters transcend the act of gathering data, or the strategies of gaining access to information in order to produce what social scientists often refer to as "explanation"? Anthropological contributions drawn out of fieldwork experience produce knowledge that is refracted by social relationships in concrete contexts of human interaction in which the researcher partakes intimately. Fieldwork experiences remain open to interpretation and are a necessary prelude to more rigorous forms of theorization/explanation. We hope that in this way the desire to understand violence and thus the attempt to control the meaning of it is led on to a detour of *Verstehen* (understanding). This detour can both lead us to better understand, and to acknowledge our limits in comprehending the causes, effects, and forms of violence.

We write at a moment when military strategists have started turning toward the social sciences for insights and methods in intelligence work and counter insurgency operations. Military strategists now evoke "ethnographic intelligence" and have initiated a "cultural turn" to minimize what analysts call "friction" in military parlance – all newly employed buzzwords (cf. Gusterson 2006, Gonzalez 2007, Tyrell 2007). It is disturbing to realize that due to the problems faced by American troops in the occupation of Iraq and Afghanistan, military intelligence agencies conceive of their own miscalculations now as a failure to employ ethnographic field methods. In the age of the "phraselator," when young anthropologists might be recruited into the C.I.A. and military in order to facilitate "nonkinetic solutions" to tensions on the ground, it is important to intervene and correct naïve misconceptions of what is at stake in contemporary fieldwork encounters.

The U.S. military now attempts to operationalize ethnographic knowledge in order to make up for past policy mistakes. But if they had taken ethnography seriously beforehand, they would have been cautioned against misguided adventures such as the Iraqi occupation in the first place. The new deployment of ethnographic methods is supposed to improve the relationship between American soldiers and Iraqi civilians in their everyday encounters, to remove obstacles to the successful social engineering of occupation. Ethnographic knowledge is merely supposed to mitigate tension, to provide the lubricant that will make occupation run more smoothly.

However, as this volume shows, the very thing military logic renders as "friction" and tries to minimize – the unexpected and incalculable – is precisely the stuff that makes for ethnographic insight. What makes the ethnographic encounter essentially different – in intent and outcome – from the military one is that it allows for an encounter with a reality that does not behave and act as expected. In the fieldwork encounters of anthropologists, the other is not predicated or dependent upon one's own expectations and demands: the native does not execute acts and thoughts that a theoretically informed fieldworker might be waiting and wishing for. Hence, the problem with the military encounter is not that it lacks insights into "native culture" (as embarrassing and revealing as that may be). A lack of knowledge of local ways, desires and complaints, might lead to misunderstandings, but it is not an obstacle for encounter the way we conceive of the concept. Rather, by minimizing "friction" the military forecloses a specific possibility of interaction with the other in order to avoid the incalculable risk that comes with it.

In other words, the military attempts to control the encounter by foreclosing certain experiences that might challenge its authority – the opposite behavior of the contemporary ethnographer, who usually has to submit to the authority of the other as a condition of access. For the military the possibilities for a project of *Verstehen* (understanding) are irretrievably lost. In this the military remains its own biggest obstacle because by default it has to deny itself the unexpected and incalculable moments of encounter. This would essentially mean that the other freely assumes a position, leaves an imprint, inclusive of expressing opposition and resistance. The reasons for this fact are as vital, as they are banal: a military operation does not invest in understanding for its own sake, but only insofar as new insights promise strategic results and advantages. Thus using ethnographic methods as mechanical tools employed to achieve preconceived ends, even if infused by "cultural sensitivity," guards against the very insights that might lie in an ethnographic encounter. The result of this muted and asymmetrical exchange between the U.S. military and foreign subjects, even if informed by ethnographic method, will be violence, regardless of the degree of cultural competency brought into the encounter.

Eight Observations on Violence and the Anthropological Encounter

The focus on violence is no longer a novelty within anthropology. For more than twenty-five years, detailed studies on violence – its social forms, causes, and functions – have pervaded the discipline, some of which are mentioned in Chapter 10. A decade ago, Krohn Hansen (1997) even argued that the study of violence "typifies the current moment in anthropology" in North America. But whereas anthropologists have become eager to engage – and skilled in engaging – modern theorists of violence and conflict (e.g., Georg Simmel, Walter Benjamin, Hannah Arendt, Georges Bataille, Jacques Derrida, Pierre Bourdieu, Michel Foucault, René Girard, Hans Magnus Enzensberger, Giorgio Agamben), they usually avoid incorporating into analyses their own personal encounters with violence in the field. Entry into the fieldworker's own experiences with violence in the field leads to eight observations. First, *to the degree that during fieldwork anthropologists are confronted with serendipitous, unsettling violence, violence in fieldwork is always also a violent experience.* Such encounters not only threaten the ethnographer's physical integrity but also damage the integrity of the inquiry by casting doubt on the possibility for understanding. When we seek to integrate the ethnographic experience into the reasons and effects of violence, an understanding of what happens seems either generally impossible, or all too banal. In witnessing violence, the researcher becomes a part, often intimate, of what is being studied, and therefore complicit in the further unfolding of events. This holds true for all contributions of this volume. As Feldman (1995: 228) has put it, violence never stands in a "relation of pure externality" to the consciousness of the researcher. The inability to extricate oneself from what one studies is fundamental in any experience but holds particularly true for an encounter with violence, where the moral or physical integrity of the researcher is put at risk. Yet, at the same time, such extrication remains a necessary moment in order to arrive at some degree of objectification.

Second, *a descriptive exposition of personal experience with violence always begs the question of the desire of the ethnographer.* Why do researchers not leave such scenes? Or stay? Why do they participate in situations of heightened physical and moral risk when they have the option of leaving and later reading the reports of others? Behind such questions lurk more difficult ones, reaching back into the biographical past of the researcher, his or her emotional state of being, forms of naiveté or cynicism, as well as personal levels of tolerance of and investments in violence. How much violence one can bear is closely related to the researcher's own domestic experiences of abuse or shelteredness, the sense of self derived from them and the degree to which professional responsibility has been internalized. Each of these factors has its own complex relation to class, gender and the cultural background of the researcher.

But these are only sociological indices. The more pertinent question for the ethnographer is how the subjective experience of violence brings about, or allows for, an insight about the realities in a particular place. The subjective experience of violence is peculiar in that it tends to overwhelm other daily experience. Violence humiliates. The victim is humiliated by being reduced to an object; the witness by being reduced to impotent bystander and the perpetrator, in retrospect, by an inability to ever adequately redress the violence perpetrated. Or, in turn, all participants are humiliated because it is frequently difficult to delineate clearly between victim, bystander, perpetrator or analyst. Moreover, researchers are often plagued ethically in pursuing an academic career on the basis of other people's suffering, or alternatively, they feel guilt for having abandoned the violent scene – its victims and perpetrators alike – to work on other issues. Even if such themes are not always addressed explicitly by these contributors, they do become apparent in the interstitial spaces of the individual narratives of this volume. It is here where descriptive exposition is a precondition for theoretical renderings of accounts, as will become evident below.

Third, *to personally witness violence, even if one remains physically unharmed, burdens the listener with a debt, which often finds its way into the body of the researcher.* This debt is transmuted into the physical body as a wound and ailment – or mentally into dreams, obsessions, neuroses and repetitions. The experience of violence enters the researcher's unconscious and has thus effects beyond what one is consciously aware of, as Isbell (this volume) suggest. Rarely are anthropologists prepared for the violent events that unfold around them, much less for the effects they have on them afterwards. While some anthropologists, when confronted with violence in the field, may fall mentally or physically ill, others may pursue intellectual paths that academic colleagues may find obscure. There are special difficulties in writing about violence, in objectifying that which has been consumed, harmed, or destroyed, that which is no longer there except in absences, traces, wounds, ruins (Borneman, this volume). Often there is a delay in writing up or a turn to activism. These "reaction formations" are not only traceable to the events experienced, nor should they be understood in a register of cause and effect. What is certain, however, is that after violent experiences there remains a residue that longs for expression. The symptoms of the ethnographer, and their effects on academic careers, often become the expression of this residue (Pandey, this volume). In this way these residues also constitute the discipline's inherent limits to produce insight and understanding, as they often cannot be overcome emotionally – or in writing.

The description of such symptoms poses many problems for the ethnographer, who on the one hand cannot ignore the connection between experience and its effects on body and mind, while on the other hand knows very well that subjective interpretation of one's own experience is but one part of a process of objectification that might lead to understanding of events in the field. Any act of direct association of symptom with violent experience, in the working-through process, is an act of interpretation *post facto*. If those interpretations find their way into our descriptive forms, they become communicable, open to the analytical gaze of the reader. In this way descriptive exposition is a necessary part of the ethnographic method, insisting on an opening to the reader. In the ideal case the reader can complete that which has escaped the author about her own text and, by extension, about her own experience.

Fourth, *violent experiences make for an interrupted reciprocity.* An encounter with violence establishes a specific kind of rapport between a researcher and a field site, and by extension, with academic institutions once the researcher returns home. To the degree that the event addresses the researcher existentially, there can hardly be any emotionally satisfactory response. After fieldwork, the ethnographer is left only with field notes, interview tapes, photos, memories. And, ultimately, one hopes, the material product of academic labor as answer for events experienced – usually a written text, possibly a film. The expectations and demands of perpetrators and victims can become a heavy burden for any such text; others have existential interests in what the ethnographer produces, or chooses not to. Equally, an experience with violence lacks closure; it leaves behind residues and can foster guilt for having witnessed without having intervened, doubts about whether more could have been done, an urge to share insights widely. The effects of experience are contradictory: material data that resists circulation while simultaneously compelling communication. These effects are capable of paralyzing the ethnographer or, on the contrary, jolting the ethnographer into a sort of cathartic babel – often derided as unintelligible by colleagues. The loss of control in the field is often replicated outside the field, and accompanied by a feeling of trepidation with language, about how what one brings back might be understood and read by others.

Sometimes colleagues are deeply suspicious of our attempt to make words fit and take the place of horrific experiences. They see researchers of violence as "obsessed" with violence, overidentified, a clear instance of contagious magic within the academy. Ethnographers report that initial interest in their insights and experiences metamorphoses into skepticism towards them and their work generally. The special authority established by the ethnographer of violence can unsettle a sensitive balance, a sound academic composure, an assumed distance to and disinterest in the object of study. Yet ethnographers caught by violence in the field must struggle to create this object. That struggle is ongoing and interested. Since "scientific objectivity" can no longer be asserted without entering into epistemological mud battles, the ethnographer of violence herself becomes suspect as a person, in extreme cases leading to alienation from colleagues who would otherwise be sympathetic.

The banal brutality of violence, whose experience most often escapes language, at times compels *poesis*, a form of academic infusion, where what cannot be rendered in normal ways becomes transposed into a highly complex language, which is often later critiqued and viewed by colleagues as a form of obfuscation. To be sure, assuming narrative control over an experience permeated by a feeling of helplessness is an arduous task and it can ultimately fail. The reader of narrative products of violent experiences, however, especially those that promise adequate "understanding" and "explanation," should remain aware of the fact that they can be subverted forms of denial, displacement and repression in themselves. Both transparent writing as much as obscure renderings can be forms of defense against the effects of experiences. Expository writing is thus also an attempt to speak the unspoken that lies behind every existential experience, where what one claims to know is also an instance of something that one does not want to acknowledge. Often, for example, writing conceals the fact that one was irretrievably harmed in the encounter, or that one's actions were in no way heroic, but self-interested, naïve, or ignorant. Most significantly, we in this volume seek to open a space that allows others access in the form of presentation of our essays, so that the reader can interrupt, add to, and interpret the discourse of the ethnographer.

Fifth, *the forms that violence takes in specific locations are not identical.* The residue of violent experiences can become productive for future work and can determine how violence will be theorized, how cause and effect will be established, what books will be read, what question will be asked. In other words, the theorizing about violence has much to do with how violence was initially perceived and experienced, as well as how it is represented locally – in short, how it entered the researcher's consciousness (Straight, this volume). It is these moments that we are trying to retrieve in order to introduce a reflexive moment into the analysis of violence, frequently lacking in work on violence, especially outside the discipline of anthropology. The way we as researchers understand violence is never completely separate from the way it is represented locally, its symbolic form (Ghassem-Fachandi, this volume).

One might caution that this sort of endeavor is only possible to the degree that the experiences in question were not so extreme as to splinter recollection and disable constructive memory work (as in trauma). If violence expresses itself differently in relation to diverse geographical, political, and cultural contexts – state terror, insurgency, revolution, war, raid, communal violence, class conflict, security measures, penitentiary violence, sexual violence – the fieldworker on whose experience it is based has an intimate knowledge of these forms only if she was able to establish some distance from her experiences in the process of writing.

Sixth, *due to the increasing corporate nature of academic anthropology, field experiences have become part of the professional armature of the academic persona in the symbolic economy of expertise.* In academic institutions, anthropologists relate to one another through competition (for jobs, postdocs, fellowships and grants) and unwieldy field experiences become micromanaged and deployed strategically. In this way they ultimately fail to provide the reflexive screen out of which long-term ethnographic maturity can grow. Although the contingency of fieldwork – rejection, ambiguous relationships, animosities, and unwanted encounters – are as vital for producing insight about a place as a well planned-out graduate education, these experiences are usually relegated to informal venues or disappear entirely. Eliding these experiences by not providing a stage to communicate them, however, risks making anthropology a dishonest and facile discipline.

To be sure, a certain degree of discreetness about personal experiences is certainly preferable to a sort of institutionalized confession, which could fast degenerate into new ways of exerting institutional power. An *experience,* however, is not something that one can succeed or fail in: one can only describe it. Narrative descriptions have the advantage – or: the nasty side effect – that they escape the intention of their authors. In this way they allow a careful reader to gaze into the scenes with a different sort of insight. A description of an experience with violence lays bare one's concrete actions and emotions in violent moments, as well as the fault lines of their erasure during the writing process. All of the authors of this volume are aware of this fact, which remains a valuable asset for the process of working through. Of course, many of the authors might act differently today and that with time they might write differently about their experiences as their understanding of the events will have transformed. Nonetheless, they have been willing to share. It is up to the reader to acknowledge this courage and show generosity in this respect. In the end, it is only through a reader that a genuine reflexivity can be accomplished.

Seventh, *in violent contexts female sexual subjugation seems to be the preferred mode of humiliation across cultures*. What becomes apparent in a majority of these narratives is the special position of gendered violence against women. For the editor of this volume this was unexpected and in no way foreseen. Most of the fieldworkers were women and their narratives depict attempts of sexual violation against them, at times successful, in diverse social and cultural contexts. The way in which female bodies become the instance of men's affirmation of masculinity (Straight), in honor killings (King), an opportunity for violent abuse (Pandey), the fantasy of it (Drybread), or the threat of it (Isbell), as preferred site for sacrificial consumption (Ghassem-Fachandi) and a possibility for subverting normative femininity (Maiale), shows how fieldwork vulnerability is structured by a clearly marked gender inequality and, at the risk of sounding old-fashioned, by patriarchy. If it is true that women often seem less of a danger for natives in local contexts, one should add cautiously that in violent contexts female bodies are entered into violent exchange much more readily and, it seems, almost automatically at times. In moments of violent transference, with which fieldworkers are confronted, female sexual subjugation seems to be the preferred mode of humiliation across cultures. A woman showing self-confidence and generosity towards local ways seems in no way safe from such forms of violent encounters.

Finally, eighth, this edited volume is also about those books that have not been written, especially in the case of older, more experienced ethnographers, or ethnographers who have chosen to leave the discipline because of their field experiences with violence. An inability to find proper expressive forms prevents these ethnographers from communicating what they have experienced. If this defines on the one hand the limits of anthropological writing about violence in field sites, it on the other hand also provides an opening beyond the disciplinary cannons of writing, the possibility of transposition into more creative and less circumscribed expressive forms. Notably, in the case of Billie Jean Isbell, the inability to write anthropologically about her experiences with Shining Path and military forces in Peru has given birth to a play, *Public Secrets from Peru,* and a novel, *Finding Cholita,* on which she worked for over 20 years, choosing artistic expression in lieu of what a more narrow scientific style could have achieved. It is to be expected that some of the other authors, too, most of whom are early in their respective careers, will find similar solutions to the impasses of academic writing about violent experiences.

What unites the ethnographic accounts of this volume is that the researchers provide access to the field by sharing an experience that is intrinsic and symptomatic for a particular place – violence that becomes inscribed onto the body (Isbell), that is denied while used as communication between individuals and groups (Maiale, Ghassem-Fachandi), that is openly celebrated (Straight), that spells fear (King), that becomes petrified into security measures (Zaretsky), that causes dreams of punishment and transference (Borneman), that engenders fantasies of stabbing and rape (Drybread), and is enacted physically (Pandey). These intimate experiences create a sort of humbling insight, which seldom lends itself to official representations and, at the same time, is not readily recouperable for projects of resistance to such authority.

Short Summary of Individual Chapters

In "Written on my Body," Billie Jean Isbell describes the long years of her relationship with Peru, her experiences with Shining Path and the Peruvian military's anti-insurgency campaigns, which have shaped her life for decades. The inability to ever publish her interview tapes, collected during the military's operation in the 1980s, was due to the fact that her material could be used as evidence of atrocities by security forces, as well as evidence of Shining Path's atrocities against rural peasants. Isbell was never able to resolve the impasse of knowing too much and yet never feeling able to communicate this knowledge without putting acquaintances at risk. The experience with the insensitivities of academic colleagues, the dangers of fieldwork in the shadow of a brutal regime and a violent revolutionary movement against it, and not least the fear of her own countries' security agencies with their geopolitical interest in the region, left her alternately speechless, paralyzed, and aching. It is these experiences that become inscribed into her body, inaugurating a series of organ failures, diseases and inabilities to assume an academic form of exposition for what transcends by far the disciplinary logic of academia.

Parvis Ghassem-Fachandi's "*Bandh* in Ahmedabad" tells the story of a 2002 anti-Muslim pogrom he witnessed in the city of Ahmedabad in the Indian province of Gujarat. His experience with this unexpected violence during fieldwork was in disturbing contradiction to official accounts of "Hindu anger" that media outlets used to frame the pogrom. The actual forms of violence on the streets of Ahmedabad, he found, took the form of a festival celebration, with joy and laughter. Moreover, phantasmagoric images of an intimate Muslim enemy were circulated and viewed with pleasure, collectively, and then shown to him. Although Hindu identity was infused with a rhetoric of nonviolence (*ahimsa*), the collective consumption of images of burned bodies suggested a simultaneous desire, not permitted expression in quotidian life, to eliminate – through cutting, butchering, and burning – that part of the Hindu nation that insisted on distinction: the Muslim. In refusing incorporation into Hindutva ideology, Muslims became the object for Hindu anger, something to get rid of by making them into one's own in sacrifice.

Diane E. King "Fieldwork and Fear in Iraqi Kurdistan," describes the author's riveting experiences in the Kurdish region of Iraq during the 1991 to 2003 interwar period. While the central government led by Saddam Hussein had effectively withdrawn and left the area under Kurdish control, the new administration's sovereignty went unrecognized by the outside world and uncertainty reigned. During this confusing time, a time of "competing sovereignties," Iraqi Kurds were forced to cope with real and imagined dangers. These included the threat of a reassertion of Saddam Hussein's reign of terror that had included attempted genocide, dangers posed by Turkey's interest in the region, conflict between the *peshmerga* fighters of the KDP (Kurdistan's Democratic Party) and PUK (Patriotic Union of Kurdistan), attacks by the PKK (Kurdish Worker's Party), tribal revenge killings, and Islamists who threatened to turn violent. The daily need to dodge risks of possible death meant constantly evaluating the interests and actions of other actors such as Turkey and the United States, international NGOs and the UN, as well as the machinations of the Iraqi secret police, the *mukhabarat*. Out of this barrage of risk, a detritus life is lived at the margins of the absurd. King shows how the omnipresent fear is answered by passing jokes about a tyrant and that its voicing can paradoxically produce relief as fear that is shared is purged – if only for a moment. When all that is left to exchange are anxious narratives, their exchange creates a community under the shadow of shared fear. The author's own practices of listening were altered as she came to understand the collection of ethnographic data and decisions as to whom to trust and whom to avoid as deeply bound up with her own physical safety.

Bilinda Straight's "The Sense of War Songs" reflects on many years of experience with Samburu pastoralists in Kenya. The Samburu not only boast of their violent accomplishments in war – they frequently also engage in interethnic cattle raids with their neighbors, the Pokot and the Turkana. In the 1960s the Samburu became victim of a deadly attack by Somalis and in 2005 a new round of violence erupted between the Samburu and the Pokot. The author describes how her eldest son, who accompanied her to the field, becomes gradually initiated into the warrior ethos of Samburu life, and subsequently considers joining the U.S. airforce in the war in Iraq, against his mother's wishes. Juxtaposing her own initial fascination with the celebration of bravery and romance in Samburu war song genres with the violent realities on the ground, she comes to inhabit a position in Samburu society that opposes the need for young men to prove themselves in battle: mothers who mourn their lost sons. Samburu mothers critique the need for bravery and the complicity of many Samburu girls, who encourage young men to become killers by anointing and honoring them.

Kristen Drybread's "Sleeping with One Eye Open," describes experiences inside a Brazilian youth detention center with the euphemistic name "Center for Resocialization of Minors" (CRM). After initial problems of access to inmates, a self-inflicted knife wound that lands her in a hospital establishes her credibility and legitimacy amongst inmates. Knife stabbings are crimes that many juvenile inmates are identified with – be it as victims or perpetrators. The accident, and its material proof in the form of a scar, morphs into rumors about the "knife attack" that she allegedly survived and inmates start to protect her from possible harm like theft, rape, or murder. Simultaneously, however, although her presence is acknowledged as calming tensions among inmates, the new trust she receives from inmates now renders her suspicious in the eyes of the institution. Increasingly she comes to be treated as a criminal, finally culminating in her exclusion and the premature termination of her ethnographic work. As becomes clear in her narration, the violence that detention is supposed to ward off continues within the institution, in which a brutal hierarchy is enforced by prison wards and inmates alike, recreating the violent order that the institution is supposed to remedy.

Brenda Maiale's "A Hell of a Party" speaks of the relationship with her first fieldwork assistant Francisco in Oaxaca, Mexico. Initially studying the role of women in local cheese making production she soon comes to realize that many cheesemakers are in fact not women, but *muxe* (pronounced *moo-shey*), a Zapotec category of transgendered people. *Muxe* inhabit an interstitial space channeling hyper-femininity through beauty, and hyper-masculinity through male machismo, in a context of poverty, violence, and heavy alcohol consumption. Francisco, who is *muxe*, encourages her to sponsor a major fiesta, which promises her integration into local circuits of reciprocity. Yet, unaware of the local dynamics of prestige and shame, Maiale's financial cosponsorship causes Francisco to be humiliated as sporting a "girlfriend" to finance the fiesta. The following cycle of resentment and violence spirals into a disaster. It is this ambivalent relationship that most effectively allowed her to understand the social nexus of poverty, violence, and social abjection that defines the life of many *muxe* in Oaxaca.

Natasha Zaretsky's "Arriving in Jewish Buenos Aires" follows the author's search for the Jewish community in Argentina's capital in the wake of deadly terrorist attacks in 1992 and 1994 respectively. Upon arrival the author is immediately confronted with an array of heightened security measures surrounding a vulnerable community that has lost its confidence in the local government's willingness or ability to protect them. The Jewish community often becomes visible in the city's landscap through measures that seek to ward off potential threat, yet these measures also carry consequences for their relationship to non-Jewish residents. In this cycle the author becomes initiated into what it means to be part of the Jewish community in Buenos Aires. In one particular instance she herself becomes implicated as posing a possible threat. Through this experience she came to understand security measures not only as means to ward off danger but as sites of memory in which fear is circulated and transmitted into the fissures of everyday life in the city.

John Borneman's "Dreamwork and Punishment in Lebanon" narrates an array of experiences with memories of war and collaboration after the sudden withdrawal of Israeli troops from southern Lebanon. Through dreams and encounters with residents in Lebanon and Syria in the year 2000, Borneman paints a psychic landscape ravaged by layers of violence: bombings, civil war, war, occupation, torture, retribution against collaborators and premonitions of the very real threat of renewed future conflict. The thickness of violence and the many registers of memory and trauma that define not only Lebanon but this politically intractable region is revealed in informal conversations and unplanned contexts, which in turn produce multiple discourses in which to think, and multiple, often impossible demands on him. Borneman begins his account with his own dreams of punishment, and then focuses on the processes of transference and countertransference – in shared words, dreams, confidences – integral to all ethnographic fieldwork that relies on personal encounters. In a former Israeli detention center used by Israel for interrogation and torture – now a memorial site run by Hezbollah – he gets caught in such a process: a young man appeals to him, the American visitor, for recognition of an Israeli massacre at Qana. Borneman acknowledges the wrong, but this does not satisfy the young man, who insists on an equivalence between the Qana massacre and the Holocaust. Borneman, in turn, interprets this claim as an inappropriate attempt to elevate the massacre to the crime of genocide. But what is inappropriate to the anthropologist carries urgency for the man who represents the victims of Israeli violence. If the Holocaust becomes frequently used as an apologetics for Israeli violence, then perhaps getting an American to admit historical equivalence would be the initial condition necessary to secure that desperately needed recognition. Caught in this impasse between what he perceives as a legitimate demand for empathy and an illegitimate demand for a recognition that entails equating incommensurable events of suffering, Borneman flees the encounter.

Annarose Pandey's "Unwelcomed and Unwelcoming Encounters" tells the author's personal experiences with abuse in Sidi Ifni, a culturally conservative town in Southern Morocco. After enthusiastically arriving in the small town to learn Arabic and begin fieldwork, Pandey is confronted with several forms of local rejection and harassment, first by state officials then by locals that she bravely tries to grapple with. After several attempts to stave off negative encounters including insinuations that she was a prostitute, her stay culminates in an instance of molestation and sexual assault. Consequently she left "the field," both Sidi Ifni and the discipline of anthropology. Her account casts doubt upon many unquestioned assumptions about fieldwork as a *rite de passage*, something that one is compelled to pass through and should force oneself to endure. Her account also criticizes a discipline that seems incapable and unwilling to genuinely address and discuss failed encounters. When do we know that we are not welcomed? And what do we do if we are not welcomed? And when do we acknowledge that an encounter has failed?

−1−

Written on My Body

Billie Jean Isbell

Cangallo, Peru, 1975

"Doctora, this way please, the investigator wishes to speak to you. He's waiting upstairs," and with these words it all began in May of 1975 as the mayor of Cangallo ushered me upstairs to a windowless room in the back of the second floor of the municipality where the Peruvian Investigatory Police (P.I.P.) official from Lima was waiting. We walked up the hand-hewn wooden stairs and down a dark hallway to a room in the adobe, colonial building. In the dim light, I could see a figure waiting and I felt nauseous as I approached. He flicked his tongue over his lips like a lizard catching a fly before welcoming me with: "*Doctora* we are honored to have such an esteemed researcher at our humble celebration." His eyes betrayed his real intent as they swept up and down my body slowly, undressing me, pausing at my breasts, crotch and then appraising my legs. I detected a sneer as he examined my heavy walking shoes. School teachers and wives of bureaucrats wore high heels even though they made walking hazardous on the stone paths. Instinctively I wanted to cover my body so I hurriedly pulled my poncho on over my sweater and culottes, a compromise between pants and a full skirt that gave me freedom to squat on the ground. He motioned for me to sit on a lone chair in the center of the windowless room. When he waved his hands toward the chair, I noticed that they were unusually small for a man, and extremely well manicured with polished nails. That struck me as humorous and I smiled nervously. He must have taken my smile as a signal of sexual attraction because he stretched to his full height of about five foot, five inches (six inches shorter than me). He ran his manicured hands over his slick hair. Prancing on his tiptoes over to where I was seated, he stood over me with his hands on his hips and his legs wide apart. Señor P.I.P. was about my age, in his late thirties, dressed in an ill-fitting dress jacket and pants that had been badly altered. He reminded me of Peru's national bird, the Cock of the Rock, Rupicola Peruviana. The males of this species fluff their bright red hoods and compete in a prancing bobbing dance to attract the drab brown females consigned to build the nests and raise the baby birds while the males are off to compete in their perpetual performance to attract more females. Women I know in Lima say the bird is an appropriate symbol for the machismo they have to endure.

On the evening before this eventful day in Cangallo, I had received a message from the Prefect of the Department of Ayacucho, the equivalent to the governor of a state, at the home in the capital city of one of my *mestizo compadres* who was a school teacher in Chuschi, the site of my fieldwork. The message "invited" me to attend the fiesta that the town of Cangallo was celebrating for its 100th anniversary as the seat of the provincial government. The message did not explain why my presence was required, only that I was the subject of an investigation. Under investigation? For what?

I slept fitfully in my rented room in the old hacienda house that night, tossing and turning, I spent the night watching the bright blinking eyes of the weasels that lived in the thatch roof sixteen feet above my bed. As I was throwing a few things into a backpack the next morning, my *comadre* slipped into the room and whispered: "*Comadre, dale bola al Prefecto y pides un puesto en Ayacucho para tu compadre.*" I had become a "co-mother" to her daughter by sponsoring a mass for the girl's health and *my comadre* felt that gave her the right to tell me to give the Prefect a little piece of ass and then ask him to transfer her husband to Ayacucho! I replied: "You are out of your mind." She only laughed and patted me on the back as I rushed past her and marched out of the room into the crumbling interior courtyard. The Prefect was waiting, leaning on the colonial fountain that no longer functioned, except to hang laundry on to dry. The entire extended family and several renters accompanied me through the small access door cut into the massive, double wooden portal that bore the remnants of sixteenth-century carvings and cheerfully waved goodbye as one of the national guardsmen politely opened the back door of the Prefect's ancient Ford and said: "At your service, *doctora*." My *comadre* grabbed my shoulder before I got in and whispered in my ear: "Don't forget."

What a disgusting woman, I thought. How did I get entangled in *compadrazgo* relationships with people that I detested? At that point I had ten godchildren and I liked the peasant Quechua-speaking families but the *mestizo* shopkeepers, teachers and bureaucrats, were grasping and greedy. Early in my fieldwork the school teacher and his wife had offered to rent me a room in the old hacienda house in the city of Ayacucho that was under the dominion of his mother, a powerful matriarch. Their family had a 350-year history in the district of Chuschi as descendants of the administrator of the first colonial salt mine located in the mountains above the community.

Once I was installed in the matriarch's house, the schoolteacher and his wife asked me to sponsor a mass for the health of their daughter in the hope of climbing a few rungs of the social ladder. I thereby became godmother to their daughter and *comadre* to her parents, which extended spiritual *compadrazgo* relationship to the entire family. I thought about these entanglements as they waved goodbye and said in unison: "May God be with you, *comadre;* we'll be waiting for your return."

In 1975 I had returned to the village of Chuschi with the intention of establishing a bilingual Spanish/Quechua program in the primary schools under the auspice of the ministry of education with funding from the Ford Foundation. I did not understand until later that many of the teachers had become supporters or members of Shining Path, the Maoist-inspired insurgency that waged a 20 year war to overthrow the Peruvian government to establish what they called the New Democracy of Peru. Rather than a New Democracy, the insurgency developed into a rigid, hierarchical death cult that worshiped its leader, Abimael Guzmán, who began his revolutionary career as a philosophy professor in the University of Huamanga in the capital city of Ayacucho and ended his 20 year reign of terror captured and jailed for life in 1992. Through the 1990s he was still revered by a few followers as *Presidente* Gonzalo, the father of Shining Path.

Guzmán was a stern disciplinarian who demanded total loyalty and obedience. In one of the pledges recorded in the book of *Presidente Gonzalo's Thought* that became a cadre bible along with the Little Red Book of Mao, members of the movement were required to swear that:

> We give our full and unconditional submission to the greatest living Marxist-Leninist-Maoist on earth: our beloved and respected *Presidente* Gonzalo, chief and guide of the Peruvian revolution and the world proletarian revolution, teacher of Communists and party unifier. We give full, unconditional submission to the scientific ideology, the infallible ideology that illuminates our path and arms our minds. We give our submission to the world proletarian revolution. We give our full and unconditional submission to the quota. We will cross the river of blood to victory.

Submission to the quota meant dying for the cause. The only way to leave the insurgency was feet first. According to the Peruvian Truth and Reconciliation Commission report published in 2003, the river of blood over which the insurgents had to cross to achieve the New Democracy, was made up of approximately 70,000 fatalities, of which 85 per cent were civilians. Most were from peasant Quechua-speaking communities like Chuschi in the department of Ayacucho. Shining Path officially declared its war against the state of Peru by burning the ballot boxes in the village of Chuschi on May of 1980 and celebrated that date as the I.L.A., *la inicia de la lucha armada*, the beginning of the armed struggle, even though shots were not fired on that day. The pronunciation of I.L.A. is the same as *Illa,* which means "messenger" in Quechua and refers to offerings made to the mountain deities and to *Pachamama*, Earth Mother. As a message to the state of Peru, the theft of ballots was a key symbolic act because it was the first time in Peruvian history that illiterates were allowed to vote and moreover, it was also the first democratic election in 17 years. At the time no one took the event very seriously and the ballots were replaced. I later learned that the theft of the ballots was carried out by teachers and students of the secondary school in Chuschi as the initiation of the long-term strategy for taking control of the region that began in 1975.

Five years later, when they burned the ballots in 1980, Shining Path already controlled the schools as bases of indoctrination and had instituted improvements in education. They increased their efforts to replace the bureaucratic officials in the towns of region with their own members without the knowledge of the departmental or state governments. In that year they began their campaign of punishment of thieves with public executions, which was initially supported by communities. However, when they began executing village officials and forbidding rituals and celebrations for patron Saints, opposition to the insurgency grew, especially when Shining Path attempted to shut down the regional market system with road blockades and instill communal production for the war. By 1983, villagers began to flee the region *en masse* because they found themselves "between the wall and the sword" – taking heavy casualties from both the armed forces and Shining Path.

When I arrived in 1975 to establish a bilingual Spanish/Quechua school sponsored by the state, the groundwork was being laid for the insurgency. At the time the teachers' opposition puzzled me because in previous years these same teachers had participated in my research with children. I remember crossing the stream that separated Chuschi from Quispillaqta, the neighboring village, and climbing the hill to the whitewashed, single-storied, five-room adobe school built with communal labor that was situated on the path that climbs out of the valley to the high flat plateau, the *puna*. This same exit route was used by Shining Path in 1983 when they fled to the *puna* after an armed encounter with the combined forces of the army, navy and police, leaving the civilian population to face severe repression: the heaviest casualties occurred in the years of 1983–5.

Piecing the history of the insurgency together, I learned that the Maoist faction in the University of Huamanga had won the debate over what type of revolution was necessary for Peru. The supporters of Cuban- or Russian-style uprisings lost the debate and Guzmán emerged as leader of Shining Path. While I was in Chuschi in the summer of 1975, Shining Path leaders were traveling to China for training in guerrilla tactics even though they did not initiate their "popular war" until five years later in 1980 with the burning of the ballots. Meanwhile in 1975, I was engaged in a battle of a different kind: a battle of telegrams to the Prefect of the department. The director of schools in Chuschi, who was also the municipal mayor, accused me in telegrams to the Prefect of being a spy for the C.I.A. I countered with telegrams accusing him of offenses with which he was later charged by Shining Path before he fled their wrath. But in 1975, his *palanca,* or "pull" with the Prefect, was stronger than mine which resulted in my polite "fiesta arrest" and command appearance in Cangallo.

Sitting in the back seat of the Ford with the Prefect, I felt claustrophobic and fought surges of panic by focusing on minutiae – for example, a bug was fighting against the wind on the outside of my window and I watched intently. When the bug lost the battle and was swept away, I identified with the creature and my panic rose and brought tears to my eyes. I wiped my eyes pretending that the dust was bothering me and the Prefect barked an order for the national guardsmen to roll up their windows. When I turned to thank him, my gaze fixated on the grease spot in the middle of his ridiculously short tie. As I stared at it with watering eyes, he pulled out a gray, dirty handkerchief from the breast pocket of his shabby suit and offered it to me. I dug quickly for a Kleenex and said: "No thank you," and dabbed at my eyes. He took his handkerchief and ran it across his balding head because he was sweating profusely even though the early morning air was cool. He wiped his face and hands with his grimy handkerchief and then returned it to his pocket and reached across and patted my arm, assuring me that everything would be "A O K," in his best American accent.

Eventually, I turned to the Prefect and asked if "my invitation" to the fiesta in Cangallo had anything to do with the telegrams that the mayor of Chuschi had sent him. He nervously said, "Perhaps, but the P.I.P. has been interested in you for some time." I imagined my name on some kind of list that would mean that I would be under surveillance forever. I countered with: "Well, Señor Prefect, I sent you telegrams informing you that the mayor has been accused of stealing municipal funds. He has also been charged with raping a student." "Yes, I know," said the Prefect, "We have someone watching him and when he steals more of the munic- ipal funds we'll arrest him."

I was dumbfounded and just sat in silence. He didn't even mention the rape. Gazing at the Prefect's profile with sidelong glances, I noticed that he reminded me of a fat version of one the masked figures that I had seen in indigenous dance performances of the conquest of the Incas. The dancers playing the role of *con- quistadores* wore wire fencing masks that had been painted with long pointed Spanish faces; black, pencil-thin mustaches that curled slightly at the ends; blue eyes; long, thin European noses and thin mouths. The masked dancers had made me think of *mestizaje*, the mixture of the races because I could still see the Indian features through the wire mask of the dancers. But looking again at the Prefect, the only feature that was "Spanish" was the pencil-thin mustache that was a definite statement of "Spanish blood" because indigenous men usually had very little facial or body hair. The Prefect had dozed off so I could inspect his features more closely: his cheek bones where high and broad, his lips thick and his face also broad, not long and thin. Moreover, his eyes were a dark brown and his hair was straight and jet black. In addition, he was long in the torso with short legs, another "Indian" feature. In fact, physically, he looked typically Indian, only his dress, fluency in Spanish and education placed him in the *mestizo* class that had enabled him to gain his political position. I decided to take a nap myself and as I fell asleep

I remembered that the conquest dance performance ended with the Inca regaining the throne and expelling the Spanish.

It took three hours for the old Ford to crawl up the rutted roads to Toccto, the highest pass, before descending in zigzag switchbacks to the Pampas River Valley. The Prefect suggested that we stop for a bite to eat before continuing and I wondered for the 100th time why would they put a restaurant at the highest point on a pass at 4,240 meters? I already had a headache that was either caused by altitude sickness, *sorroche*, or my nerves. I said I would enjoy a cup of coca tea, the customary prescription for *sorroche*. As I stepped out of the car, I noticed that the sun was up over the mountain ranges and the high treeless landscape was warming up but there were still frozen ice chunks here and there glistening like crystal from the nighttime frost. It was still cool so I kept my poncho on as we entered the rustic, cavernous restaurant, which had an open hearth with cooking pots balanced on stones and a bank of primus stoves with frying pans on them. The twenty or so tables were half full of market vendors, men and women making their way to numerous village markets whose trucks outside where piled high with pots, pans, and plastic containers, school supplies, as well as drums of cane alcohol and kerosene. Their trucks would return to the capital city filled with slaughtered beef, sheep, as well as live chickens, eggs, cheeses, vegetable produce and the occasional hand-woven article of clothing for the market in Ayacucho.

As we stepped across the threshold, the owner rushed forward and embraced the Prefect, addressing him as *Doctor.* Most likely he had a law degree. He turned to me and introduced me as *Doctora* Juana, the anthropologist in Chuschi who was the honored guest for the anniversary celebration in Cangallo. I thought, "honored guest my ass, I'm under investigation." The owner said that *cuy*, guinea pigs, had just been killed that morning and were ready for frying. "*Que bien*," replied the Prefect, "let's all have *cuy!*"

"Not for me," I responded, "I'll just have *mate de coca.*" Then I changed my mind and ordered soup remembering that upon our arrival in Cangallo, I would be plied for the rest of the day and evening with beers and glasses of 120 proof cane alcohol because fiestas always included obligatory, marathon drinking. When the owner brought my coca tea, he asked if I had a headache from the altitude and I shook my head affirmatively even though I had grown accustomed to the altitude and my headache was probably from tension. He smiled and clucked, "*Pobrecita gringa*, it must be difficult for you in our uncivilized land."

Three steaming guinea pigs arrived: The heads were intact with protruding rodent teeth, crisply fried ears, and sunken eyes. I remember the first time I saw guinea pig on a plate like this: The sight caused me to remove them from my list of cute pets. In fact, returning from Peru in 1976, my three-year-old daughter saw the pet guinea and brightly announced to her Montessori class: "Oh a *cuy*, let's cook it and eat it." We raised them as a food animal and prepared them in the traditional fashion – before frying the hair is singed, and they are slit down the belly.

Then when they are put into the frying pan, a large stone flattens them so that they are splayed flat and fried crisp.

The Prefect attacked his plate with gusto, breaking off a crispy ear and saying: "The head is the best part." He turned to me and asked if I had every tried *cuy* and I replied. "Certainly; it's delicious but it's a bit early for me. I prefer soup in the mornings." The greasy *cuy* and French fries made my stomach lurch upward and I fought nausea. I recounted that I had tasted *cuy* for the first time years before in this very restaurant. I didn't tell them that when they brought the plate I thought I had been served a giant rat with the tail cut off. I had asked what *cuy* meant and I was told rabbit, *conejo*. I remember staring at the critter on my plate and thinking "that's no rabbit." I learned to like the dish; it tastes like pork, but I could never eat the head.

The soup arrived: it was hot and delicious, containing *quinua* (goosefoot), potatoes, broad beans, carrots, onions, native greens and chunks of mutton. We finished our meals and the Prefect made a display of offering to pay for all of us, knowing that the owner would refuse, thus gaining "credit" in the game of exchanging favors between bureaucrats and merchants.

Cangallo, the provincial capital, was a town of about 10,000 inhabitants, twice the size of Chuschi, the capital of a district. The Spanish had laid out the towns to conform to a standardized plan with a square central plaza, locating the Catholic Church on one side and the government buildings on the other. Various stores and vendors occupied the remaining space on the plaza: it was definitely *mestizo* space with the peasant Quechua-speaking population living in the various named *barrios* beyond the plaza. The fiesta was in full swing with the town authorities gathered on the balcony of the two-storied town hall on the plaza and the peasant Quechua-speaking masses below watching a bull fight that was in progress – or rather a "cow" fight because cows raised in the high herding region, the *puna*, are far more ferocious than bulls. One drunken local contestant was in danger of being trampled by an especially determined cow but two *varayoq*, literally "owner of the staff of office," rushed into the fray and waved their ponchos in the cow's face while two others dragged the drunken man to the sidelines where his wife, a vendor of food in the plaza, proceeded to loudly berate and pound him with her fists for being such a drunken fool. The crowd cheered appreciatively and the upper class, the *mestizo* authorities high above the hubub of the plaza, applauded. This drama of class structure etched into social space has been played out in various forms for several centuries.

Standing over me, Señor P.I.P.'s body blocked out the light coming from the doorway of the room but, when he moved, his prancing antics look like a shadow puppet dancing in the dim light. The interrogation began. The Peruvian Police Investigator, Señor P.I.P., asked me if I was working with a Dutch anthropologist and students from the University of Huamanga in Ayacucho who were communist agitators. His agency, the P.I.P., had reports of these agitators operating in the River

Pampas valley. He was referring to T., who had been my thesis advisor at the University of Illinois two years earlier. I found it particularly funny that they thought T., a violin-playing structuralist, was a communist agitator. I tried not to laugh as I answered, yes, that I had worked with him and a team of anthropology students from Huamanga beginning in 1967 when we initiated research in seven communities in the River Pampas River basin. I told him that they were certainly not communist agitators. He then asked if there had been foreigners, in Chuschi or in the other communities that I visited. I answered that there were no strangers in Chuschi or the surrounding villages.

At the beginning of the war, Shining Path contingents that swept through villages were said to be *jala runa,* or foreigners – literally the "naked people," in Quechua referring to the fact that you could not "read" the style of dress of the combatants and determine their village of origin. Also, villagers said that no Peruvian would commit such atrocities on other Peruvians. Therefore, initially, government officials, the armed forces and Quechua-speaking villagers thought the violence originated with "foreign" intervention. Villagers soon learned differently and, as the war progressed, Shining Path combatants and military patrols that disguised themselves as insurgents, a common practice, were called *puriq runa.* "those who walk from place to place" because they were uprooted, lost; they had no place to call home. Many officials and the military retained the belief that Shining Path was a foreign-born movement even after the end of the war, which was not true.

Señor P.I.P. had put his finger on an important concept but what he evidently didn't realize (nor did I) was that Shining Path was a home-grown insurgency, influenced by the Chinese Revolution and Mao's teachings, which had found fertile ground in the University of Huamanga in the city of Ayacucho and was instilled in the schools of the Pampas River valley as early as 1975. The teachers in Chuschi, and other surrounding communities, were supporters of Shining Path, preparing the way for the war that was to last almost twenty-five years. After my preening, prancing interrogator was through questioning me, he took my arm and propelled me out onto a balcony that overlooked the plaza where the *mestizo* officials of the region were congregated. As I was seated next to the mayor, Señor P.I.P. leaned forward and whispered: "We will be watching you." His menacing smile gave me a foreboding chill.

The mayor of Cangallo greeted me affably and pointed to a brand new red dump truck that was parked in front of the municipal building. He handed me a silver bucket from the church that was filled with holy water and then gave me the silver sprinkling wand. I was instructed to step forward and baptize the truck with the holy water. I thought, good lord, now I'm godmother to the dump truck, along with soccer balls and team uniforms, a basket ball court and ten godchildren. The mayor could call me *comadre* and I was expected to reciprocate with *compadre.* I wondered what favors he would expect: The most common type of requests from *compadres* of godchildren was, "*Comadre*, please take your godchild to the U.S. to be educated." For the dump truck, it could be a request for new tires, or a battery. What was important was to establish a relationship of mutual obligation, which carries with it mutual respect, but not trust.

After the baptism I was led to the school where the traditional officials, the *varayoq* and their families, were preparing food for the *mestizo* celebration. *Varayoq* in Quechua refers to the hierarchical organization of staff bearers, who spend a lifetime serving their communities and who, in recent times, had become subordinated to the state-appointed *mestizo* bureaucrats. In this dual society, spatial separation by race and class was observed: the Quechua-speaking members of the community identifiable by their village-specific styles of dress, were excluded from sitting at the long tables set up in the school house for the festive meal even though they provided all the products and the labor; they were required to eat outside, squatting on the ground. As part of their ritual obligation, the families of the *varayoq* had to slaughter animals, make *chicha*, corn beer and prepare vast quantities of food from their own stored provisions for the festivities. The literate, educated bureaucrats reciprocated by keeping records of birth, deaths, and marriages and managing the town budget with funds allocated from the department capital. This reciprocal contract had been in place since the conquest. The scenario of the fiesta was running smoothly, except for me: I was out of place. I made a point to speak Quechua to the peasant women serving the food, withstanding frowns from the wives of the bureaucrats, but enjoying the furtive smiles of the Quechua-speaking women.

The afternoon wore on into evening with a lot of speech-making by the Prefect, mayor and other town officials accompanied by flowery toasts with case after case of beer purchased by individual bureaucrats as displays of liquid generosity. After sunset, a string band arrived, made up of two violinists, a blind harpist and a drummer who began to play *huaynos*, the typical songs of the Andes. The mayor instructed the indigenous authorities to move the tables to make room for a dance floor. The wives of the bureaucrats sat rigidly in chairs lined along the wall. When they rose to dance, they had to smooth down their short, straight-cut skirts. I caught a glimpse of the Quechua men and women dancing in the schoolyard. The women were whirling kaleidoscopes of color: bright satin blouses, beautiful hand-woven *lliqllas,* or shawls with designs specific to Cangallo that hung down their backs, and their four or five long, full, brightly colored shirts making dizzying circles of brilliant hues. Their hats, festooned with flowers, bobbed as their rubber-tire sandals stomped out the rhythm. Men, slightly bent at the waist, heads down and with their hands behind their poncho-clad backs, answered the rhythm. I admired the taut muscles working in the calves of the men who wore the traditional black, to the knee, home-spun *bayeta* pants. Inside the schoolhouse, the high-heeled women in tight skirts and sweaters and the men in suits seemed washed out and faded by comparison.

As the evening progressed inside the schoolhouse, the men congregated in small groups and continued to drink. Repeatedly, someone would stand in front of me and say: "Doctora, I salute you" and pour me a drink that I had to chug-a-lug. I was also required to dance every dance, the exhausting stomping dance of the *huayno*. When a slow waltz was played, Señor P.I.P. came forward for the first time and pulled me onto the dance floor. I resisted because he was drunk. He pulled me against his body, his head buried in my breast. He looked up at me and declared loudly: "Gringa, you are going to get to know a 'real man' tonight." The short, fat, Prefect stumbled drunkenly onto the dance floor and shoved Señor P.I.P. in the chest and shouted: "You son-of-a-bitch, the *gringa* is mine tonight! *I* brought her here." Señor P.I.P. responded: "*Carajo de mierda*, no she's mine!" The two men punched at each other and then the mayor stepped in and tried to grab my arm and pull me off the dance floor but the Prefect and Señor P.I.P. stopped scuffling long enough for each of them to grab one of my arms. The mayor stood by helplessly as the two men pulled at me. I shouted in Spanish: "Why don't you two bastards go fuck each other and leave me alone!" The women seated along the wall covered their mouths in shock as the men clung stubbornly onto my arms. I felt panic rise as I thought, Jesus, I going to be fucked by sleazy bureaucrats.

At that precise moment assistance arrived, as if in a western flick when the posse arrives to save the damsel in distress – except that this posse didn't thunder over a hill on horseback: they walked over the mountain from Chuschi. This posse was led by the *alcalde varayoq* of Chuschi, the highest indigenous *varayoq* in the community who was also my *compadre* as I had sponsored the baptism of his son, which is considered the highest degree of *compadrazgo*. Unlike the *mestizo compadres* I had, he was a man that I held in fond esteem: he was a respected ritual specialist, musician and curer who had taught me so much about his culture. When he heard that I had been driven by the Prefect to Cangallo to be interrogated by the Peruvian Secret Police, he had commanded four of his subordinates to accompany him to Cangallo. They had walked three hours over the mountain to come to my rescue. As social order collapsed when they crashed the *mestizo* festivities, stunned silence fell inside and outside of the schoolhouse. Holding their staffs of office outstretched vertically in their right hands to signify that they were on official business, they strode onto the dance floor and surrounded me to form a security guard in order to escort me out of the school. The Prefect and Señor P.I.P. were left standing open-mouthed in the middle of the room as the bureaucrats' wives whispered to each other behind their hands. The gathered Quechua-speaking throng buzzed as we passed them. The old social contract between indigenous subjects and the state had been broken.

We hurried away from the startled crowd and walked over the mountain to Chuschi in silence. The full moon lighted the path as though it were in the late afternoon. My knees were still shaking and we moved slowly up the mountain. Upon arriving, news of the events had already reached the community. My *compadre* took me to his house where his wife was waiting. She prepared a bed for me with animal skins on top of the potato storage bin. I slept fitfully and had nightmares in which I was torn apart by angry men with huge, erect dicks.

The indigenous officials gathered in the *alcalde varyoq's* house the next morning to discuss what to do next. They debated whether to bring charges against the two men, but as one of them, the Prefect, was the highest authority in the department of Ayacucho, that idea was abandoned. In the evening, a delegation of teachers, who had told me a few days before that they could not speak to me in public, came to talk to me about the events in Cangallo. If I had known what I know now I would have been able to interpret their words and actions more accurately. They talked about the corrupt Prefect and the P.I.P. official and how one day they would be brought to account. As the war developed, Shining Path brought many officials, some corrupt and some not, "to account" by holding public trials and executions. The director of schools, who also held the post of municipal mayor of the community with whom I had the long-running battle of telegrams was notably absent from the delegation of teachers.

In an act of vengeance for extricating me from Cangallo, my adversary, the municipal mayor of Chuschi, abused his power by destroying my *compadres'* birth and marriage documents as well as those of his family members, which rendered his entire family nonexistent in the eyes of the state. This meant they could not travel outside of Chuschi. I had to work very hard in Lima to get their records restored or they would have been in grave danger without the proper documents as the war developed. Identification papers, usually birth certificates, were regularly checked and anyone without them would have been held on suspicion of terrorism.

When Shining Path gained full control of the region after 1980, the municipal mayor fled to Lima where he could melt into the masses of refugees escaping the violence in the Department of Ayacucho. He had received formal notification from Shining Path that they were going to bring him to justice for stealing funds from the community and the schools and for raping the fifteen-year-old indigenous girl who had come to Chuschi to enroll in school. The community had supported Shining Path in this action.

Peru, 1986: Violence Becomes Inscribed on My Body

- Abstracted from the 2003 Truth and Reconciliation Report
- An estimated 69,280 deaths occurred between 1980 and 2000 (statistics put the death toll somewhere between 61,700 and 77,552).
- Thirty-two thousand victims are named and their cases detailed.
- Shining Path caused 54 per cent of all deaths.
- The armed forces caused 30 per cent.
- Tupac Amaru, an urban based revolutionary movement, caused 2 per cent

- The remaining 14 per cent were caused by government-backed peasant militia (*rondas campesinas*).
- Eighty-five per cent of the deaths occurred in the department of Ayacucho and four out of five of the victims were native speakers of Quechua.
- Four thousand mass graves have been recorded and the commission recommended exhumations.

Shining Path intensified the armed struggle in the initial years after announcing their war in 1980; *mestizo* shop keepers fled and teachers and bureaucrats were replaced by loyal Shining Path members. Insurgents controlled the River Pampas region and many other parts of the Department of Ayacucho. The Peruvian state declared martial law and intensified the war by bringing in forces from the army and navy that did not speak Quechua, fearing that Quechua-speaking troops would identify with the insurgency. Casualties, especially disappearances and massacres, were heaviest in the three years between 1983 and 1985 and I found myself struggling with the dilemma of what to report and publish. Would publishing victims' names render their families vulnerable to attacks from either side? What actions could I take to minimize the violence against the people I had worked with for nineteen years? By 1986 I couldn't enter the River Pampas Valley where Chuschi is located. Refugees were fleeing both the armed forces and the insurgents by droves and settling in camps in Lima. I interviewed refugees and documented massacres at the hands of the armed forces and reported on the events in academic settings.

During one such presentation at the American Anthropological Association meeting in 1986 in an enormous ballroom with crystal chandeliers twinkling above a couple of hundred people in the audience, I felt vertigo during my talk and had to hold onto the podium. After my presentation, one of my colleagues filled me with disgust when he asked: "Well, Billie Jean, how do you really know these things happened? You were not there so you didn't witness them. They are only reports by people in Lima." My answer was: "Aren't you taking ethnographic authority too far? 'Those people' in Lima are survivors of massacres and torture." My presentation had been based on clandestine interviews I had conducted with women in a Catholic safe house in Lima.

One of those women, Guadalupe, whom I had known since she was a child, became a leader of the organization that formed in the city of Ayacucho in the early 1980s called, The Families of the Disappeared, Detained and Kidnapped. They became the backbone of the peace movement in Ayacucho. Their work included legal petitioning and searching for the disappeared and detained but also relief work such as organizing soup kitchens for refugees from the countryside with funds from Catholic relief and maintaining a house that served as an orphanage for children whose parents had been detained or disappeared. They also worked with International Human Rights lawyers to demand evidence of the whereabouts of their missing relatives. They are still active in seeking justice and have testified before the Truth and Reconciliation Commission.

In 1986, Guadalupe went to the military garrison in Ayacucho to present a petition demanding a *writ of habeas corpus* for the cases of the disappearances of her brother and husband who were snatched in 1983 from their beds by hooded military Special Forces called *Sinchis*, a Quechua word meaning "fierce warriors." She was taken into custody in Ayacucho, tortured with the "water treatment" – a favorite form of interrogation that involves forcing the head of a victim under water repeatedly. It leaves no bodily trace afterward. From Ayacucho she was transferred to El Frontón prison in Lima and during her three months in prison, President Alan García, who was reelected in June of 2006 after sixteen years in exile, ordered the military to quell coordinated demonstrations in Lima's prisons. Over 300 prisoners were shot after they surrendered in El Frontón as they lay prone on the floor. Guadalupe survived and was transferred to Lurigancho Prison. Amnesty International gained her release and I interviewed her shortly thereafter in a Catholic safe house in Lima. She fled to Chile where the diocese of Santiago provided safe haven for Peruvians, but in 1990, against everyone's advice, she returned to Ayacucho to vote in the presidential election. Ten days after the election she was dragged from bed at night by hooded men and taken barefoot and in her nightgown to the P.I.P. headquarters for interrogation. Her children witnessed the abduction: she was never seen again.

Events became surreal in 1986, culminating with a memorable American Anthropological Association presentation after which I cancelled my membership and instead worked with Amnesty International and Peruvian human rights organizations to free peasant leaders from jail who were held without being formally charged for terrorism. If we were successful in negotiating their release, we had to pay for bullets expended in each person's capture. Another memorable event that stands out in my mind was when I interviewed members of the U.S. embassy in Lima that year. During one such interview, the U.S. information officer left me alone in a room with telegrams in front of me on a desk obviously wanting me to see them. They were intercepted messages to and from human rights organizations around the world to human rights organizations in Peru. When he returned after about ten minutes, I asked him about the telegrams and he replied: "We are just monitoring the situation. We believe that the main human rights organization in Peru has Shining Path connections." Horrified, I told him that making such accusations could get human rights people killed by death squads. He gave me an indifferent – "so what" look. Through those interviews I learned that there was disagreement about Shining Path among the embassy personnel. Some agreed with the Peruvian military that the insurgency was financed and led by foreigners; others believed that it was a home-grown movement that began in the university of the poorest department of Peru – in the city of Ayacucho. The latter turned out to be true. The official policy was to support the Peruvian government in its counter-terrorism efforts and a couple of the Embassy staff had counterterrorism experience in Afghanistan and in Honduras. The unspoken policy was to turn a blind eye to the mounting human rights abuses, which at least one official lamented.

After particularly stressful sessions of interviewing refugees of violence from Ayacucho, I decided to go to Cuzco with two friends, one from the U.S. and one from France. When they arrived in Lima, I took them to the central plaza of Lima to see the sights: the cathedral, historic buildings and governmental palace but the plaza was cordoned off by military personnel in storm trooper gear. I approached one of the guards and asked how long the plaza would be off limits but before he could answer, a plain-clothed policeman was beside me and told me he was in charge of security and that the plaza would be opened in about an hour. We began to chat and it turned out that he had been the body guard for the judge that had taken human rights complaints in Ayacucho. I was determined to interview him so we made arrangements to meet in a café on the corner of the plaza. I felt safe because I had my two companions with me. We met and sat in a booth: I was against the wall with the policeman next to me and my two non-Spanish-speaking companions across from us. I shuddered when the policeman, an attractive, tall man in his early forties, told me he was an officer with the P.I.P. At one point in our conversation after a couple of rounds of beers, he unexpectedly took my right hand and pulled it around his waist and placed it on the butt of his gun in a holster at the center of his back. Then he reached across my body and took my left hand and placed it in his crotch: I realized that he had a hard on!

I felt as though I had touched a hot stove and I immediately jerked my hands away. Finding my composure, I looked at my companions and said: "Well, I guess I could shoot his hard-on off, couldn't I?" They laughed nervously and one asked: "Are we doing anthropology now?" The tactile memory of the direct display of sex and power – his penis and his gun – overcomes me every time I think of how the Peruvian armed forces used rape as a display of power that left thousands of women in the highlands of Ayacucho with various forms of embodied trauma. My form of trauma is minor by comparison: I feel my left hand burning from touching his hard-on and my right hand tingling from touching the cold pistol. Their traumas are more serious: alcoholism, depression and spontaneous abortions relived over and over; the inability to nurse their children because they believe their memories can be carried to their babies in their milk, which would cause their babies to grow up with the images and flashbacks of their mothers' rapes.

It took us some effort to extricate ourselves from the café and we fled the plaza in a cab. What I didn't realize was that Señor Hard-On had a man follow us to where I had rented an apartment from a colleague. For the next week we were under P.I.P. surveillance. Somehow, he managed to get my colleague's phone number and called me daily. I had been conducting interviews with victims who had fled Ayacucho and with this added stress I developed bronchitis. Señor Hard-On gave me the address of his garrison and his phone number. I consulted with a

Peruvian male friend who advised me to write him a letter and tell him that a family member had died and that I had to rush to the U.S. but my friend also advised me to emphasize that I was going to return as soon as possible and that I would get in touch with him.

My friends and I rushed to Cuzco where I collapsed with pulmonary edema, *sorroche*, or high altitude sickness, which quickly developed into cerebral edema. Pulmonary edema is the condition when the lungs are filling with fluid causing difficulty in breathing, headaches and nosebleeds. As I worsened, I felt like I was drowning and I began to turn blue. Cerebral edema involves fluid in the brain causing hallucinations and can be fatal in seven or eight hours. My friends and I had stupidly helped push a taxi that had broken down on the way to the city of Cuzco from the airport and my weakened lung capacity with bronchitis kicked off the pulmonary edema. My friends were fine. Within hours I was close to death.

During my episode with cerebral edema, I experienced the most incredible hallucination in the *pension* we had checked into, which had been the House of the Chosen Women, the *Aclla Wasi*, under Inca rule who were priestesses of the Moon Goddess, the wife of the Sun God. The walls were enormous cut stones and when I passed out one of the stone blocks opened and I fell through a spiral passage into the underworld and landed at Pachamama's feet. Pachamama is the Earth Mother, the principal deity responsible for growth of crops and wellbeing of the earth. In my hallucination, she was huge with vegetable tubers, such as potatoes, *ulluco, mashua,* and other root crops growing out of her body. She turned and I could see that she had two faces, a benevolent one on the side where the root crops were located as well as a malevolent one with a skull, the fox, and the *amaru,* her underworld snake companion, on the other side. On the side of growth and sustenance, a baby llama nestled at her feet. She had on the most sumptuous *unku*, the ceremonial Inca garment, made of shimmering gold and silver threads. I shaded my eyes from the brilliance and saw that in the warp and weft of the garment fish and other aquatic life swam.

Suddenly, Pachamama looked at me and asked in Quechua: "What are you doing here? You don't belong here!" I meekly answered: "I know and I don't want to be here either." She took a deep breath and blew me up to the surface on a spiral of water. When I landed I gained consciousness and saw the faces of my two traveling companions who had returned with a graduate student of mine from a tour of the city. The student and her husband took one look at me and knew that I had a serious case of altitude sickness: my skin and lips were blue, my breathing was labored and I kept going in and out of consciousness. Thank god that the student and her husband knew enough to rush me to the airport and argue with Air Peru to transport me to Lima or I would have died. When we arrived at the airport, I collapsed again and went into convulsions. My companions acted quickly and had attendants give me oxygen. When I gained consciousness, I looked up to see a ring of *gringa* faces looking at me; they were students from a women's college on a study trip led by a former graduate student from Cornell. One of students pointed down at me and said: "You mean that's Billie Jean Isbell, the author of the ethnography that we are reading for this trip?" I was told later that I looked at her and said: "Holy shit! You could die and not even know it." When I arrived in Lima, I was hospitalized with pneumonia.

When I returned to the U.S. in 1986 I was very ill, discouraged and deeply shaken. Shortly after my return, I was hospitalized with a lesion in my throat. It was a lesion that would not heal and when a biopsy was performed, it turned out to be a benign growth. But the growth puzzled the doctors. Why didn't it heal? I was puzzled as well. Is it possible that the growth was a manifestation of my inability to deal with the research materials? I had returned with over one hundred hours of taped interviews with victims in Lima as well as tapes of interviews from the zones of violence in Ayacucho conducted by the Human Rights commission of the Peruvian Congress. Facilitating their work with my research funds, the commission, formed (but not funded) by the government could finally interview victims of violence in various zones of Ayacucho. They provided me with copies of the interviews and a friend from the American embassy allowed me to send the tapes in the U.S. embassy mail pouch. However, I was stymied by the dilemma over what could be revealed and what had to be kept secret. Nevertheless, I used the remainder of my grant to have the tapes translated and transcribed and wrote a proposal to the Woodrow Wilson Center for a residential fellowship in Washington, D.C., which I was awarded for six months in 1986 to work on the interview material.

At the Woodrow Wilson Center I participated in a panel discussion on the situation in Peru in May of 1986. The next day, on the 19 May, a newspaper article appeared in *Extra,* the populist paper in Lima, with headlines that read: "Abimael died at the beginning of the violence reveals North American anthropologist." The bulleted second headline declares "Billie Jean Isbell has contact with the leaders of Sendero Luminoso" (Shining Path). The piece states that I reported at the news conference at the Wilson Center that through interviews with the leaders of the Shining Path movement that "began the dirty war" I learned that Abimael Guzmán, their leader and philosopher-king, died early in the conflict. Moreover, the article goes on to say that I compared Shining Path to Pol Pot. I was stunned. I had not said anything that could have remotely been interpreted as such a statement. Richard M. Morse, the director of the Wilson Center and I both wrote to *Extra* and to *El Comercio* and demanded a retraction, which was printed on 30 May.

I later found out that the article had been planted as disinformation, probably by the C.I.A., by using a "stringer" – a reporter without a byline from Peru who was known to have worked for the C.I.A. This event further eroded my resolve to publish the interview material. How could I be sure they would not be misused? Instead, I started working on a novel, fictionalizing the interview material.

During the latter part of my fellowship, I received a visit from the newly appointed director of U.S. Information Services (U.S.I.S.) for the embassy in Lima. He was a stocky, muscular blond in his late thirties with a brush cut. As I was in my late forties and a professor, he treated me with deference and respect. We chatted for a while: He said he was trying to prepare himself for his new job and asked about conditions in Ayacucho and I said as little as possible, weighing every word and avoiding specific names, events and especially any references to human rights work. I was afraid that anything I said could be used again for disinformation or put people's lives in danger. I remembered interviewing his predecessor, the U.S.I.S. officer who left the telegrams out for me to see.

Perhaps frustrated by how our conversation was going, he pulled out a file and commented that I had been born in Utah. Then he said that he was from Utah as well. He asked if I was member of The Church of Latter Day Saints (Mormon) and I answered no. He then commented that he was a member. Finally, as I was getting tired of our cat and mouse game, I said that it was rumored that the director of U.S.I.S. was always the C.I.A. contact in the embassy and gave him a knowing smile. He remained absolutely calm and simply responded: "Well, it doesn't matter which position we play, we're all on the same team, aren't we?" He then asked me if I could write reports for him on the situation in Peru and I shook my head and declined, saying: "No, I don't play sports."

After the fellowship at the Wilson Center, I was invited to the École des Haute Étude in Paris for six months but I was worried because I had made so little progress on the interviews except to outline chapters of a novel. I was determined to work on them and when the executive secretary of the Wilson Center offered to pack up and ship my research materials, I, of course, accepted. She said it was a service they offered to all fellows. To my horror, when my boxes arrived in Paris, they had been rifled and the tapes had been garbled. My French colleagues were as alarmed as I was. Luckily, I had sent the master tapes to Cornell along with the master list identifying the individuals on the recordings. I gave numerous public lectures while I was in Europe and often Shining Path supporters would attend and heckle me. I remember one young man said that I didn't differentiate who caused the civilian casualties. He claimed that the armed forces had killed and disappeared civilians but Shining Path had not. Actually, I was of the same opinion but years later we would learn from the Truth Commission that Shining Path was responsible for 54 per cent of civilian casualties and the armed forces for 30 per cent.

During my one year of fellowships I wrote only one article and even then I could not bring myself to quote directly from the vast set of interviews I had collected from victims. They hung around my neck like a heavy evil amulet. In 1987 I returned to Cornell and developed a second mysterious lesion that would not heal; this time it was on the left side of my tongue and had to be excised. Again it was benign but puzzling: the surgery removed a large segment of my tongue and left me speechless for months. But nevertheless, I attempted to work with the corpus of interviews. I could not abandon those voices describing the violence in Peru. I had become obsessed with them. After many failures at academic writing, I finally shaped the interviews into a drama, *Public Secrets from Peru,* and I presented it at several universities around the country along with the *Quilt of the Disappeared from Peru*, a quilt made in Peru modeled after the AIDS quilt with names and dates of victims of massacres and disappearances. Each performance took a heavy toll on my health and emotional well being but I had finally found a path of expression through poesies, my play and an incomplete novel.

Still, I could not solve my dilemma of what was safe to reveal. This paralyzing fear that had been with me for almost ten years was confirmed in 1992 when four elected officials, mayors from Chuschi and three surrounding villages, were forcibly "disappeared" by a Peruvian National Guard officer who had recently taken command of the newly established post in Chuschi. The four village mayors had refused to form the government sanctioned civil patrols that were required by the armed forces to search for Shining Path. Later, we would learn that they were responsible for 14 per cent of the civilian fatalities according to the Truth and Reconciliation Commission. Witnesses told me that the National Guard commander screamed, "I will disappear the lot of you!" at the mayors in a reunion he called in the plaza of Chuschi: He kept his word. After the disappearances, a delegation from Chuschi traveled to Lima to the American Embassy and demanded to see the ambassador. They wanted to deliver a demand: stop all aid to Peru because the U.S. has a law that aid will be suspended to countries that abuse human rights. "Our rights have been abused," they said. Of course, they were not allowed to deliver their demand to the ambassador. I asked the ambassador later if he been informed of their visit and he said no that he had not. The commander of the National Guard Post in Chuschi was promoted and transferred but not charged with the disappearances.

In 1992 Guzmán was captured and the insurgency began to fall apart. I thought it was now safe to travel to the highlands of Ayacucho. I returned and collected protest songs and art that were visual representations of the horrors of the war depicted as three-dimensional scenes called *retablos* and *arpilleras*. The protest songs were ironic dialogs with the state. I worked on these materials and in 1997 submitted an article to the journal, *The American Anthropologist.* Another lesion on my tongue appeared that wouldn't heal – resulting in another surgery, another autopsy, another mystery. The article was published in 1998 after I recuperated from my surgery, which rendered me speechless for a time yet again. During the 1990s, as I traveled with my drama and the *Quilt of the Disappeared*, worked on the corpus of protest art and music, attempted to address the now translated and transcribed box of interviews, each presentation that I gave was accompanied by melancholia, crying and physical pain. My rheumatoid arthritis worsened causing a series of falls: I broke my leg, fractured the first lumbar vertebra and dislocated my shoulder. The two vertebrae below the fractured one twisted causing a curvature of the spine. I literally shrank four inches. These falls drove me finally to an orthopedic surgeon and I had two knee replacements. During that decade, as I spent more and more time with doctors, I started to realize that the lesions on my tongue, the rheumatoid pain in my joints, the falls that resulted in fractures, were embodied violence written on my body, which I could not find expression for on the written page.

In spite of this realization, I could not abandon the focus on violence in Peru that I had been obsessed with for so many years. I continued to search for a way to write about what I had seen and heard. Those traumatic events seem to have become part of my body. Perhaps the memories were inscribed on my bones and ligaments as arthritis deformed them. Perhaps they were trying to speak through my tongue that developed lesions. I continued to work sporadically on my novel and I developed courses on human rights that expanded my focus on violence around the world but I found that I still could not listen to the voices that I recorded in the mid 1980s. I could not represent them as testimonial literature, the genre that became so common in the 1990s. So, why did I persist? I could not abandon the focus on violence even though I could not write about it effectively. Perhaps I felt somehow guilty and responsible. Time and again I felt at an impasse. I could not move beyond the experiences, the memories, even though my body was complaining to me unambiguously and even though I was not writing about them. The memories and experiences were writing on me.

When I returned to Chuschi in 2002, my favorite *comadre*, the wife of the *alcalde varaoq*, who saved me from rape in Cangallo in 1975 asked: "Why did you abandon us?" During the 1980s, I had not written to them out of fear of putting them in danger, while at the same time, in all these years, I had felt guilty about it. Now, I realized that I had been accompanying the dead and not the living. My *compadres*, and many other survivors were moving on with their lives, perhaps with the exception of the victims of rape and the families of the disappeared who are searching for justice and closure. I also realized that just as I had embodied the experiences I had recorded that were written on my flesh and on my bones, Quechua-speaking women embodied their experiences and memories as liquids that circulate through their bodies. As I mentioned above, they believe that their traumatic memories of the war are transmitted to their infants in mother's milk. Therefore, they do not nurse them.

One of the treatments that I sought was cranial-sacral adjustments from a physical therapist involving massage and manipulation. After the treatments, or sometimes even during the treatments, I would experience memories of violence: voices of my ghost victims would return to me and I would cry helplessly. My dreams were also vivid after treatments. The therapist told me that the surfacing of memories was very common. My health slowly improved but I realized that I was suffering from compassion fatigue and I had to find closure on this chapter of my personal and professional life. With a grant from the Cornell Library, I was able to put my work in Chuschi online, including 1,500 photos and the play, *Public Secrets from Peru* (http://isbellandes.library.cornell.edu/). I have also donated my entire professional library to the Department of Anthropology of the University of Huamanga in Ayacucho, which was under the power and control of Abimael Guzmán during the war. Today, I have finally closed the chapter on violence and purged my emotions by writing a novel: *Finding Cholita,* University of Illinois Press. I worked most intensively on it during the cranial – sacral treatments. I am now working in the north of Peru on topics filled with hope for the future – biodiversity, conservation of seed, water management with the people of Vicos who participate in the global Slow Food Movement aimed at deindustralizing agriculture and food production. That work, along with the history of applied anthropology in Vicos, can be seen at http://instruct1.cit.cornell.edu/courses/vicosperu/vicos-site/, accessed 5 December 2008.

My work on violence is not actively being inscribed on my body any more but the scars and pain remain. Moreover, the boxes of interviews with the voices of victims of the war in Peru remain largely untouched after twenty-five years. I'll probably deposit them in Cornell's manuscript and archive library for future researchers to work on. Hopefully future researchers will have more emotional distance from the materials and more bodily stamina to focus on the voices of the dead.

−2−

Bandh in Ahmedabad

Parvis Ghassem-Fachandi

On the morning of 28 February 2002, B.[1] dropped me off in the middle of Shubash Chandra Bose bridge – a neutral space separating two halves of a city stretching over the dry Sabarmati river bed. We had just spent some time with his boss at Ambedkar University, drinking tea and discussing "riots" between Hindus and Muslims, which were expected that day. Initially, I had come to Ahmedabad to do fieldwork on the peculiarly Indian doctrine of *ahimsa*, non-violence, made famous by Mahatma Gandhi in his fight against British colonialism. But instead I was caught witnessing a pogrom: the type of violence that *ahimsa* is supposed to address. Determined to capture the moment that communal violence comes into its own, today I was to witness a city that was completely outside of itself.

B. did not want to accompany me any further. He turned around and drove home. I also initially turned around and went back onto the west shore walking carefully south to Mahatma Gandhi bridge – an area I was more familiar with. Gandhi made me feel safer than Bose. I walked alone over the bridge into the Shahpur district, what residents call a "sensitive area." Within a few city blocks, I was in the middle of peculiar scenes for which I was unprepared. I quickly passed one, then two, then three, then four cars upended, set on fire, vigorously burning. Shops were ransacked and the street was full of dust and smoke. On one corner, in the safety of the charred ruins of a white Ambassador car, two policemen sat on a metal case, probably a box for cold drinks. Facing the bridge with their backs to the rampage behind them, they were smoking in silence. About twenty-five cows, large for a cluster of cows, lingered around them and the policemen seemed intent on guarding them. They ignored me.

A day earlier, two bogies of an overcrowded train, the Sabarmati Express, full of Hindu pilgrims on their way back from the temple town of Ayodhya in Uttar Pradesh mysteriously caught fire after a skirmish between Hindu passengers and Muslim station vendors in the small town of Godhra in Gujarat. In the fire fifty-nine passengers were killed. For the following day, Hindu organizations declared a *bandh* (closure, standstill), which was seconded by the Gujarat government and supported by all relevant political parties and organizations, including the opposition party. Subsequently, the largely poor and embattled minority Muslim community became the object of collective ire in a statewide anti-Muslim pogrom. Politicians and some newspapers inflated the Godhra incident into a "collective act of terrorism," supposedly executed by local Gujarati Muslims in connivance with Pakistani intelligence and demanded immediate retaliation. The so-called "reaction" (*pratikriya*) to what is now termed the "Godhra massacre" (*Godhra hatyakand*) was enforced on the street by youths with orange headbands. The young men positioned themselves strategically all over the city on street corners preventing residents to go to work while schools and shops were coerced to close under the threat of violence. It was then that the city was to take its deep plunge.

Ahmedabad is the largest city in the state of Gujarat – a state associated with the birthplace of Gandhi in Porbandar. Areas and localities in which communal violence between Hindus and Muslims is likely to erupt receive designations such as "sensitive area." Every resident of the city carries in his head a precise geography of risk, knows about street corners and neighborhoods, the numerical relationship between minority and majority, as well as the resulting local modalities of their interaction. In times of tension and conflict it would be foolish to ignore the fault lines that structure the intimacy between communities. As a foreigner, I was relatively safe because I was not part of this intimacy and remained external to the conflict – a fact that I came to exploit unwittingly as an ethnographer. For most locals moving through these spaces, even if uninvolved ideologically, never cancels the risks of being classified as "Hindu" or "Muslim" respectively. Thus there always remains the danger of becoming the medium and object of communal communication, something to be consumed: smashed, killed, and destroyed. In times of communal effervescence the physical body becomes the site of a sacrificial possibility whose destruction communicates complete sovereignty over the victim community. Making the other the object of one's own enjoyment is desired while the reverse simultaneously feared. On the streets of Ahmedabad, young men were convinced that Muslims in Godhra had used Hindu girls for *enjoi*, a synonym for rape and mutilation (derived from the English word "enjoy"). At the same time, they took part in such acts as spectators and narrated what they had seen or heard with unselfconscious fascination participating in the spectacle of violence all over again.

Sensitive city spaces are of two kind: the so-called "mixed areas" where Hindus and Muslims actually share physical space, living intimately among one another, using the same shops, driving through the same lanes, and daily rubbing shoulders. The second kind of "sensitive areas" are those where a predominantly "Hindu area" is immediately adjacent to a predominantly "Muslim area," a segregation that is usually product of former bouts of violence. Here, one side of the street can spatially confront the other, a Hindu street corner a Muslim street corner, forming something like a tense nerve ending in a complex city body. All residents of the city know these "border areas," the nooks and seams of the city, quite well. Now, in anticipation of communal violence, a "mixed area" can easily transform into a "border area," as members of the respective residential minority choose to move temporarily to a safer location.

I walked further up the road. People were on a rampage against all cars and scooters. Men ran back and forth. I saw no Muslims, and in this sense I was reminded of the new city in the west, the better half of the city, where I had my residence. Muslims, who make up a large part of the population of the Eastern city, had disappeared out of sight, into areas where they were in the majority and thus safe. What was yesterday a "mixed area" had now become a "border area." A *mini-Pakistan* immediately adjacent to a *Hindustan*, as locals explained. The cows, too, had gathered, or were herded, into safe corners and were being guarded. Further ahead a crowd triumphantly attacked an unoccupied car. Another car had been successfully mastered, turned over, the tires brightly aflame in a jolly fire. Running feet, burning cars and scooters, jubilant noises. Smoke and dust engulfed me.

I passed a *paan* shop, supposedly closed but surrounded by many onlookers who watched the events in a seemingly relaxed manner. The shutters were down but the shop did offer *paan*, betel leaf rolls with areca nut, and cigarettes for a higher than usual price, a typical conduct during curfew in the city. The higher risk for the shop owner to sell goods despite the imposed *bandh* translates into higher prices for the customer. People gathered around chewing juicy *paan*, spat and watched. A man who seemed to be the shop owner waved at me and greeted me with a smile. As they looked at me people wiggled their heads in the typical affirmative unison. They talked about me but I did not understand what they were saying. I was afraid to draw too much attention but I wiggled back. I noticed to my right a group of about ten policemen with water jugs, their rifles leisurely leaning against a brick wall. Some stood, others sat on blue plastic garden chairs under an open tent that protects them from the blazing sun. They silently watched the "car-killers," about 50–100 youngsters acting out their infantile aggressions. I positioned myself next to the police, just to be safe. Children brought instruments – stones, bricks, plates and iron rods – for the adolescents who were rioting. One policeman looked intently at me but remained completely silent. Perhaps he felt ashamed. I am often addressed, but this time they said nothing to me.

The last car still alive was flipped over and set on fire, detonating a noiseless explosion and a short panic in the crowd. About twenty youths suddenly scurried away from the upended car and a burning liquid seeping from the car quickly followed them. The lower pants leg of one youth caught fire and he tried, first calmly but increasingly frantic, to put out the dancing flames while moving away from the car. People around him tried to help put out the fire, and ultimately succeeded, though I could see that his lower leg was badly burned. Large light red spots speckled the tan skin of his leg. He limped away, and some people went with him. The policemen began discussing what we had just seen. They commented on the fact that the car caught fire in an unexpectedly strong explosion. How foolish it was, they said, for untrained people to light the tank of a car without knowing how much fuel was in it.

In a building nearby, people, what seemed to be children, were throwing stones on another building. No one stopped them. I wanted to cross the street and move closer to the buildings from which stones were thrown, but people started shouting at me as soon as I approached the street. Their attention took me by surprise, as I thought I was successfully submerged into the other spectators in the crowd. One young man wearing a long red T-shirt with a metal rod in his hand immediately moved towards me. He said, almost politely, "You better go," gesticulating towards Gandhi Bridge. It was clear that he did not think I belonged here. I tried to rejoin the policemen, who still just stared in absolute silence. Strange policemen, I thought, as they did not even tell me to leave.

Finally a middle-aged, clean-shaven and well-dressed civilian man appeared, holding a cell phone. He acted with authority and, speaking only Hindi, unambiguously ordered me to leave. His demeanor and clothing made me think that he is definitely as out of place in this part of the city as I was. He shouted to the youngsters to lead me away but I indicated I'd rather leave alone. To my surprise, the rioting youths were more polite than he was, and they fortunately did not accompany me. I passed the people at the pan shop, who again smiled and wiggled their heads. *Saru chhe ne*? ("It's great, isn't it?") I circled back and turned around the left corner, passing the two smoking policemen again in order to reach a place from which better to see what the crowd was throwing stones at. I addressed them and they say, "All the city is like this now." They did not tell me to go home but instead offered me a *bidi* (Indian cigarette). They told me, "Inside there [*ander ma*], it is even worse," referring to the dense labyrinth of lanes in the old city center, the bowels of Ahmedabad.

I entered another square in front of Shahpur Darwaja on Ring Road where an even larger audience with no policemen observed the attacking mob. The ring road was once a fortified wall, protecting the old city from enemies. Today, the wall has been demolished allowing air ventilation into its dry lanes. The city is now divided by a complex array of invisible walls between residents and communities. Three shops were already burning and the immense fire could be felt from the other side of the street. Nearby a street temple had also caught fire, and the white paint slowly turned dark. No one paid attention. Sitting on scooters and bicycles on the road a silent audience of perhaps fifteen to twenty people stared at the rampaging crowd. Some sat on newspapers placed on the pavement, others on their *rumal* (scarves), protecting their pants from stains. One man tells us, "They are all insured." I asked if that is true and he said "Yes, of course, they will all get money. They all left."

From all sides people were throwing stones at a compound in front of us, from the roofs of adjacent houses, from the street, from behind a large tree decorated with hundreds of "Hindu" flags, which suggested there was another adjacent temple. I asked if there are any Muslims inside. Another man said "They already left last night." A man caught me by the arm telling me that "There that is a Muslim building." Those throwing stones were enthusiastic and excited, but there was no anger in the rioting crowd. I expected to see anger but I saw only fun.

A newspaper seller (*chappawalla*) arrived with his bicycle. I bought one, sat with the others and began skimming it. The thin Gujarati-language paper called the *Western Times* boldly announced the latest events: "In the city people are rioting." It carried the headline "Frightened, Burning Gujarat" (*Bhadake Baltu Gujarat*) and spelt out in great detail all the areas, districts, and subdistricts of the city as well as throughout central Gujarat where violence had broken out and curfews had been imposed. It said the entire Shahpur district, too, where we were sitting, was under curfew. But here we were sitting on the street and people were rioting right in front of us. Many people bought a paper (less than five cents a paper) and the seller made good business. Turning our faces away from the heat of the burning shops, we started to read. No one seemed to find this moment rather extraordinary.

The newsprint was hard to read in places because of its cheap quality. Words were smudged or parts were missing where the paper had been folded or crinkled. Almost half of the entire first page of the *Western Times* carried advertisements: a mouth freshener *Must Vahar* for "clean breath and lovely mood," miraculous Ayurvedic capsules called "Big Body" that promised more bodily strength with only one capsule a day by increasing appetite and weight while simultaneously lessening physical fatigue. An advertisement for "breast cream" and "Only-me Spray" by Synthico Exports for multiple erections depicted a rare erotic scene of a man on top of a women in a suggestive pose. There was even an advertisement for the "Gujarat Police and Military Store" on the paper's fourth and final page, framed by a gun and a rifle on each side. The guns were explicitly praised for "*svarakshan ane nishaan mate*" – for self-defense and as symbol (ensign). After a pious introduction, it advertised air-pistols and air-guns for 600 to 3400 Rupees. In brackets it said, "*license ni jarur nathi*" (no license required).

I asked a man sitting next to me to read the paper with me but he had just bought a paper himself. He points to the burning shops in front of us and told me in a flat tone: "This is what is happening." He meant that there was no need to read the newspaper because I could see in front of me what is happening. But then I wondered why he bought a newspaper. The paper showed black-and-white photos of the bizarrely charred bodies in the burned-out S6 coach of Sabarmati Express. The front page and the last page showed also riot scenes, policemen and burning houses. But there were no rioting people in the pictures. The streets were empty, as if no one was there, or everybody has already left the scene when the photographs were taken. Strange, I thought, as I watched the streets filled with rioters in front of me while the published pictures of those very streets omitted the people.

Beside me a young man wearing blue jeans and an American sweatshirt sat on his scooter and silently stared at the burning shops. Through a hand gesture he asked to see the paper I had just bought. We talked. R. speaks Gujarati mixed with some weak English. He is a college student at a university in the other side of the city. He talked of Ayodhya. They will build a temple there, he said, even though the Muslims are against it. I asked why the shops were attacked. "They are from the *musalmans*," he said. "Muslims have attacked Hindus in Godhra," he added dispassionately. "That's why these shops are being burnt. They have taken our women." His manner was detached, unemotional, and he seemed to be mouthing words rather than inhabiting the meanings of the words he was speaking. I asked him why shop owners in Ahmedabad are responsible for the attacks on Hindus in Godhra. In lieu of an answer, R. simply took my hand and said: "Come, you want to see? Come on, I'll show you."

Leading me by the hand, he briskly walked toward the burning shops where animated youths stood and threw stones. We passed the heat of two burned-out shops in a little alleyway. Standing between the shops, the heat from the still glowing fires was so great that I had to cover my eyes. R. joined the others and started throwing stones. Firing one after the other, he went on the assault. But the stones were not directed to what was left of the shops. They landed behind a high white wall along a small *chawl* (small road). I assumed there are people there but, if so, they made no noise, there was no response. I felt embarrassed and somewhat ashamed, standing amidst people attacking a Muslim structure of worship. R. wanted me to throw but I simply turned around and left. I did not know what to say.

I had unselfconsciously hesitated for a small instant, caught between wanting to please R.'s unexpected call to participate and my resistance against it. Something in me had been tempted – the seduction of the crowd? The power of contagion? In retrospect, it seemed as if R., after seeing the newspaper photos, put himself in the picture, the empty picture of the newspaper. He looked at the empty rioting scenes and then took my hand in order to put us both in the picture. The *Western Times* not only informed the reader of what was happening but it encouraged him to take part.

Confused, I walked back and positioned myself on a traffic island next to a blind and bearded old man who was squatting there silently, seemingly protected from view by another closed *paan* shop. It is not uncommon to see individuals like him sitting somewhat indiscernibly on a traffic divider or street corner as if merged with the city's hardware. These figures eat, sleep and die on this pavement. They are treated like a lamppost: they are invisible and escape the logic of the city. For a moment, I was tempted to ask him if he happened to be a Muslim but I abstained in order not to frighten him in case he was. Behind us lies Shahpur Darwaja (gate) and its mosque, guarded by two policemen, who had also bought a newspaper from the seller, again in order to read about what they were looking at. It made sense that the crowd would not attack this structure as behind the Shahpur gate began a Muslim majority residential area. And the Muslims of Shahpur would certainly try to retaliate if someone was to enter their safe area. I wondered a moment why the police guarded what was not being attacked.

The old man wore thick glasses and it appeared that he did not hear well. He was couched next to a huge block of ice covered with jute sheets, which provided some protection from the heat. In front of us we watched the breaking in and looting of three new shops on Ring Road at Maiya Fateh ni Chali. From the outside, there was nothing to suggest that these were Muslim shops. But in the crowd there were leaders, big men, or men of the moment, who rushed to specific shops and gave signs with their hands for the others to come. The young men were secure and self-confident. They wore neither masks nor helmets.

The crowd managed to break open a beverage shop. Happily shouting at their accomplishment, they drank the soft drinks as if they had earned them following a hard day's work. They smashed the empty bottles on the street. One boy opened a bottle with his teeth, knowing full well that we were all looking at him. He was on stage. In front of us was a garage shop called Nutan Tires. The men gesticulated and seemed to know the shop. They broke open the door with a loud bang and many "Arrrayyyss." They used stones and steel lances to smash the locks of the gutters. The old blind man asked me which shop it was. I told him "Nutan Tires." I had to shout several times "Nutan tires, Nuutaan Tiiires!" until he got it. He nodded mechanically. It was clear the shops were handpicked. The crowd selected only this shop, a Muslim shop and not the shop to the right or to the left. Again I was offered a *bidi* but, ironically, we had no match despite all the fire in front of us. The old man showed no emotion of discomfort, fear or anger toward the attacking youth or the targeted Muslim community. He simply seemed to want to wait it out until the storm had past.

The very first thing removed from Nutan Tires was a scooter, probably parked inside the shop as a precaution. It was dragged out and lit on fire with great ceremony. Then one young man brought out a small stereo, a kind of ghetto blaster. To my amazement they immediately smashed the machine on the pavement and kept slamming it down with large roundabout movements to make sure it was completely destroyed. Several parts were picked up and smashed again and again. Aside from vehicles, ghetto blasters were the most sought-after objects of the young and poor working class. Next, a big red phone was being brought out and joyfully demolished, repeatedly throwing it to the ground until unrecognizable. Another man brought out a large mirror and triumphantly smashed it on the pavement. He stepped on the glass shards with his thin sandals, startling me as I thought he might injure his feet. I saw no anger, just excitement. The idea seemed to be to make the items splatter in all directions. No one kept any item. It was about destruction in a dramatic fashion. But if this was merely a performance, then who was the audience? The answer might turn out to be uncomfortable for me. But the rioters did not only perform for us, the bystanders. Behind us lay a predominantly Muslim area on the other side of Shahpur Gate, which was not being attacked. The audience was also the Muslims, especially those who had left the previous day for safer grounds – neighbors who rubbed shoulders with the attackers on a daily basis. That's why the objects were not kept. To keep them would have meant that the Muslim neighbor would have recognized them later.

The small, violent crowd finally left and disappeared in an alley in the direction of Jayantilal Punjalal Marg. Its attention had gone elsewhere. A tribal woman, or perhaps a member of the Vagri community, stood in front of the ransacked Nutan Tires shop and watched in fascination the debris of things she could hardly ever afford. Suddenly a burning scooter made a loud bang. A policeman approached her and scolded her for standing so close to the burning vehicle. He told her to move on. I remember this little scene because the policeman was sincere about her safety, but the context of his care was so absurd. An armored police van appeared and we all had to run for cover as it shot water and tear gas chaotically in all directions. Still wondering why the police targeted us, the spectators, instead of the armed bands of rioting youth, I got tear gas in my eyes. I ended up in a Vagri *mohalla* with narrow lanes and masses of people pushing in.

We all rested there. Some women were closing their shutters and shops as we all moved away from the spreading tear gas. Men and women were distributing iced water in the heat. People stared at me. I felt that I was out of place. Without much ado they showed me the way out, roughly, and with hubris. I left the narrow lane in a hurry but outside of the lane three women approached me, stopped me and said, "Do not leave, why do you leave, fight for us!" The Vagri women smiled and had an interesting collection of dots on their faces and decorations on hands and feet. They addressed me jokingly, as if they were openly flirting with me. They asked where I was from and what I was doing here. I told them I was German but I lived in Naranpura. After some discussion, and with the usual amazement that I actually spoke Gujarati, they agreed that I should leave. They smiled mockingly, and before they let me go they made me say "Jai Sitaram."

I hurried back over Gandhi Bridge into west Ahmedabad, wary of the police van behind me. Two boys stopped me and introduced themselves. We had "lots of fun," they said, expecting I would agree. With watering and hurting eyes from the teargas, one told me that I should take him to "this Jarmany." He wanted to study German and live in Bangalore. Both showed no fear and I was amazed how aloof they were from all that is happening around us. I asked them why no one was afraid. Isn't this supposed to be a riot? Where are the Muslims?

They told me that Muslims were hopelessly outnumbered. There would be stabbings soon, they added, and the police will fire real bullets at some point in the future to stop the rioting. But today, there was no real danger. I asked why all this was necessary. The older of the two does not mention the Godhra incident of the previous day, nor the Ayodhya agitation but simply said, "This is what we do here once a year." Seeing my astonishment with the answer he told me that Muslims had abducted "pretty Hindu girls" in Godhra. He stressed that they were "very pretty girls," as if that would make the abduction worse.

In the first few days the epicenter of the Gujarat pogrom was not in the old city, where I had ventured expecting to witness "communal violence" at one of the traditional trouble spots, such as Shahpur Darwaja. What drew me onto the streets that day after a year of intensive language study had been frustration with my inability to converse with city residents in a satisfying manner about the cycle of violence in Ahmedabad – a city riveted with such experiences. Locals had a curious way of keeping an outsider from glimpsing the city's unwanted underbelly. Nothing palpable ever came of these discussions despite the fact that I had witnessed curfew and communal effervescence before. The most notorious and astonishing response to my queries had initially been flat denials that collective violence had ever occurred in the city – an assertion that is difficult for me to grasp even today.

It would be easy to see in such responses willful obfuscations, conscientious strategies of representation. But that would be to simplify what they performed. I know that many of my interlocutors believed their own words, while they were uttering them and that when they told me that Ahmedabad was the "safest city of India" they sincerely meant what they were saying. They were referring to the experience that one can walk through the city at night and not risk rape, robbery, or murder – or at least that the numbers for such crimes was much smaller compared to other cities. Communal violence, in turn, was something altogether different. It occurred *despite* the above and in excess of it.

If prompted Hindu and Muslim residents might utter the same immediate estimation: everyday decent people are not to blame for bouts of communal violence, but rather those in power, or "politics" (*raajkaran*), as the phrase goes. This automatic response was not merely a misconception or a simplification – although it was perhaps also that. More significantly, however, it was a sort of defense. It allows people to return to their lives (and their "enemy" neighbors) after the occurrence of cyclical violence. To talk about communal violence, then, risks to undo a silent consensus and risks making visible the sinews of the city by arousing uncontrollable emotions and apportioning blame, all of which are further instances of conflict. There is danger in talking about what one finds oneself caught in, about what one engages in despite of oneself. It was the form that violence took on the streets that day in relation to the silence that preceded it which made me understand that contemporary *ahimsa* was not simply about renunciation but about collective abreaction.

The scenes in Shahpur that I have described above were short of anything like a "riot," but rather were a strange festival of sorts of one community in the absence of the other, while the police guarded cows, smoked *bidis* and read in the newspapers. In other parts of the city, however, from the early morning hours to the late afternoon Muslim residential areas such as Gulbarg Society and Naroda Patia were literally pounded with waves of attacks by armed killers, while huge spectator crowds and sometimes even the police, participated or looked on. If mobs successfully entered Muslim compounds, they killed the men, raped the women before killing them and burned the residences to the ground. Surviving eyewitnesses have reported widely that Muslim victims were made to speak *Jai Shri Ram* ("Hail Lord Ram") and *Vande Mataram* ("Hail to the Mother") before being killed.

The massive killings were accompanied by false rumors of abduction of Hindu girls and of impending Muslim counter-attacks, which never occurred. In the early days of the pogrom, vernacular newspapers circulated gruesome images of burned victims, which were viewed in homes and roadside tea stands. Some imagery was also circulated through pirated DVDs. The terminologies in titles and captions of newspapers were suffused with sacrificial and culinary terms, such as "roasted bodies" (*bhujaai marya hata*), fire and blood offerings (*homaya, bali*) as well as ghosts and demons (*pishaachi, hevaaniyat, shaytano*). One particularly revolting image on the front page of *Sandesh* newspaper of 2 March 2002, depicted the burned corpse of a woman with several burned children strewn closely around her. The arrangement of the corpses was such that they seemed to form one single smelted body, flesh melted together by the heat of the fire that had destroyed them. In this newspaper, as is usually the case, the religious identities of the victims remain unstated, although totally self-evident to those people consuming the imagery. Diverse groups and communities appropriated this imagery, which they took as evidence of the unnatural and extraordinary cruelty of their respective opponents. Fact-finding reports have noted that some of these newspaper images were actually held up by murderous crowds and shown to Muslims on the streets in front of their homes, after which members of the crowd attacked and shouted "This is what we are going to do to you now." For most residents in Ahmedabad, this image became the trope of "mother brutally burned with children," viewed and consumed collectively with fascination and horror.

Besides government connivance and visible police passivity, there was also direct police participation in many locations of the city. Politicians and several members of parliament were seen on the street encouraging crowds of attackers to burn Muslims homes.[2] The widespread use of gas cylinders, kerosene, acid, sharp weapons and a white, chemical powder that burned, gives evidence to the coordinated, systematic and planned nature of the attacks. The advancing mobs used electoral rolls and tax records, instruments of the modern state machinery, to find victims in those cases where locals knowledgeable for the residential structures were not at hand. The most violent attacks occurred where Muslim residents were hopelessly outnumbered or where they consisted of Muslim migrant communities from outside Gujarat, not well connected to local Muslim networks. After the first few days of pogrom, an identifiable pattern developed in which killings were concentrated in areas far beyond the inner city wall at the fringes in the east part of Ahmedabad (in areas such as Meghani Nagar, Naroda, Odhav, Amraiwad, Bapunagar, and Gomptipur). Whereas the inner city had always been officially designated as "highly sensitive area," the largest and most pervasive attacks occurred elsewhere.

The carnevalesque quality of violence, a sort of communal Saturnalia, of the first three days of the pogrom would soon become rationalized retroactively in terms of a self-proclaimed "Hindu anger" (*hindu krodh*), the perceived energy behind a collective *pratikriya*, a "counter-action" or "reaction" to the Godhra train incident. *Pratikriya*, a word that derives from the domain of ritual, communicates a sense of immediate karmic retribution, a mechanism that works automatically and cannot be stopped. Where Muslims had personally fled their shops and residences, as in Shahpur area, gangs satisfied themselves with the goods in their shops. Where Muslims were physically present, however, especially if they were poor and had little property, their actual physical bodies became the object of play and violent consumption.

Fact-finding commissions consistently make disturbing references to the way in which the bodies of the victims were treated during and after the attacks. Men were not simply killed but preferably cut into pieces while still alive (in some cases in full view of family members) and then thrown into a prearranged fire. Women were not only raped and murdered but their orifices were penetrated with sharp weapons after killing and their genitals mutilated (preferably with *guptis*, a farmer's tool used as a weapon, and *trishuls*, Shiva's trident). Both, the treatment of goods from Muslims shops that I witnessed in Shahpur, and the murderous acts on live Muslim bodies elsewhere, give evidence to the performative quality of the violence. There is a homology here between people and things, where the attackers went out of their way to destroy the objects seized completely in a dramatic fashion, as if consumed by "Hindu anger," which curiously took the form of enjoyment and fun.

Within a few days, several hundred Muslims were killed, the number rising after several weeks to over a thousand; 150,000 refugees soon crowded countless relief camps throughout central Gujarat; large numbers of Muslim religious structures were desecrated or destroyed. In the city of Ahmedabad alone, fifty-five religious structures were attacked on this first day of violence. Even after the immediate pogrom violence abated, smaller attacks continued for many months. The city never returned to any form of normalcy until after my departure in April 2003. Several human-rights and nongovernmental organization (N.G.O.) activists, both Hindu and Muslim, as well as politically engaged intellectuals and academics, had to "disappear" and find refuge with close friends from the Hindu majority community during the pogrom. These were mostly people who in the past had been active in urban peace committees, had openly promoted secularism in their respective communities and tried to ensure communal harmony in the future. Many affluent Muslims simply left Gujarat and went to Bombay, London, or New York.

The discussions with members of Hindu middle classes in the following weeks stunned me by their complete unwillingness (or inability?) to distance themselves from the events surrounding the pogrom – the exact opposite of my prior attempts to discuss violence in Ahmedabad. Most Gujaratis I spoke to invoked idioms of diet and sexuality, often defensively, to describe the continuous everyday harassment they felt exposed to by Muslims. Whether Muslim colleagues at work, students at school, friends who had betrayed them, or neighbors who could no longer be trusted, the issues brought up repeatedly were variations on the theme of invasion by a phantasmagoric Muslim figure. These images of invasion were predominantly invoked in relation to ingestion (disgust for the meat eating of Muslims), penetration (fear of Muslim desire for Hindu girls) and dissection (resentment for the practice of cattle slaughter and partition of the mother country). Their symbolic consistency and pattern has remained with me since the events in 2002, subsequently reappearing in dreams, some of which were nightmares.

For example, in 2004, at a Meeting of the Association of Asian Studies (A.A.S.) in San Diego, I had explained to a colleague familiar with Gujarat why the fantasy of rape and the slaughter of cows were experienced as homologous. Then I had the following dream:

> I see a corpse but the corpse is a piece of meat too. It is a woman and a cow merged in one body. There is some Ur-ritual in which both have been merged. I have lost this part . . . There is some revelation why women and cows are the same vis-à-vis men, the masculine. The burned creature, neither cow nor woman, actually looks like a roasted pig. It seems to have an animal head. Perhaps a bull's head with long ears. Like the warrior monsters with bullheads in Mesopotamian mythology. And a large body of a gutted chicken spread out. It is spread out in the middle or sown together at each organ's end. It reminds me of cooking images and thus there is something chicken-like about it, because I cook so much chicken. It is burnt like a roasted piece of chicken. There is disgust and desire for this roasted meat.

This dream of 2004, one of a series of such dreams, indexes actual experiences of the violence of 2002, the extreme imagery in vernacular newspapers, the sacrificial and culinary terminology that accompanied this imagery, and utterances of participants on the street. But it also expresses another important insight about the deeper collective psychology of the pogrom, which seems contradictory at first. In the context of violence, when being Hindu or Muslim becomes a matter of life and death, religious identity is nevertheless superseded by gender: what becomes the preferred spectacle of sacrificial consumption is the *female* body. The same image can be used to express one's own community's legitimated anger for being wronged, while at the same time also showing the barbarity of the enemy community. The circularity is astounding. What becomes apparent here, in my opinion, is not at all a new insight, but nonetheless an important one: communal or pogrom violence is fundamentally structured by gender.

The walk back home through Naranpura in the late afternoon of that same first day of the pogrom, 28 February 2002, was deceptively idyllic. I noticed that I slowed down my walking pace, breathing in, letting the impressions do their work in me. Bereft of the usual noise and dust, one could actually enjoy these trees, the singing of these birds and the hot climate. I caught myself in the perversion of the situation. But to my surprise, I was not the only one. In parts of Naranpura and Ambawadi, I saw married couples sitting on their garden swings (*hitchko*), enjoying the calmness of the day. The unperturbed residents had no interest communicating with someone who has seen disturbing things across the bridge and the usual curiosity towards all foreigners seemed short-circuited. Members of families swing and want to be left alone. The *bandh,* which in the east city freed laborers from work to engage in violence, translated in the west into an atmosphere of bourgeois leisure, a cultivated ignorance, where one could enjoy a day off with the accomplishments of a middle-class life.

Ambawadi and Naranpura are posh districts considered "good areas." Residents appreciate that they are absolutely safe from Muslims as there are none around, while members of lower classes, who are able to live or work here, simply praise what they refer to as "full facility," that is, the availability of jobs, water, electricity and public services. This quality is made possible through the financial clout of the *savarna*, communities of the Gujarati middle class consisting mainly of upper castes, like Vaniya, Brahmin and Patidar. The typical "no Muslims around" means that the Muslim community *as community* is not present in any way, even if an occasional middle-class Muslim family finds its way into an apartment here and there. The consequence of this invisibility of the Muslim community is that there are no "mixed" or "border areas," making the area seem "safe." The relaxed atmosphere subsequently changed, however, when *agent provocateurs* started spreading false rumors of impending Muslim counter attacks. But for the time being the mood was calm indifference.

I might have ignored these curious garden swings had I not, on that first day of pogrom violence, passed a series of fancy homes where residents swayed back and forth under the afternoon sun. The swing is a symbol of royalty in Gujarat and also the pride of every middle-class apartment or house. It is the symbol of Krishna, the deity, who is ritually swung back and forth in worship during the festival of Janmashtami, which celebrates Bal Krishna, the God incarnated as an imaginative young child lying in a swinging cradle. In popular *bhajans* (devotional songs) of the immensely popular Goddess Amba Mata, she too is frequently depicted sitting on a swing. Swings are not only used in gardens but also in multi-story apartment houses. Each family has a swing in the stairways right behind the entrance door grills. I often see elderly married couples swinging in middle-class homes, enjoying the cool breeze in the late evening.

On this day, too, as if narcoticized by their own clueless-ness, or perhaps soothing some nervousness, the well-to-do residents swing indifferently back-and-forth to the repetitive squeaking sound of metal joints amidst an unusual silence. This picture has stuck with me.[3]

There are many fact-finding reports on the 2002 Gujarat violence, which are of diverse quality and depth. For a start, compare Human Rights Watch (H.R.W.), "We Have No Orders to Save You. State Participation and Complicity in Communal Violence in Gujarat," 14 (3) (C), April 2002; Concerned Citizens Tribunal (C.C.T.), "Crime Against Humanity. An Inquiry into the Carnage in Gujarat," Vol. I and II. Ahmedabad: Anil Dharkar for Citizens for Justice and Peace, 2002; Human Rights Watch (H.R.W.), "Compounding Injustice: The Government's Failures to Redress Massacres in Gujarat," 15 (3) (C.), July 2003; Communalism Combat (G.G.), "Genocide, Gujarat 2002." Javed Anand and Teesta Setalvad (ed.), Year 8, No. 77–78, 2002. Mumbai: Sabrang Communications; and Report by the International Initiative for Justice (IIJ), "Threatened Existence: A Feminist Analysis of the Genocide in Gujarat," December 2003.

Notes

1. Some names have been abbreviated.
2 For example, R. B. Sreekumar, Gujarat's additional Director-General of Police (Intelligence Bureau) testified before the Nanavati-Shah Commission about direct police collusion with those accused of rioting. Police Superintendent in Bhavnagar Rahul Sharma has also made depositions before the investigative commission, revealing that key accused had been in regular touch with the police in the first three days of violence. He gave evidence through records of mobile phone conversations. Both established also that Jaydeep Patel, a V.H.P. leader, and Maya Kodnani, a B.J.P. member and M.L.A. (Member of Legislative Assembly) were indeed present at the Naroda Patia massacre, as eyewitnesses and Muslim survivors had claimed all along (cf. Bunsha 2006, pp. 36, 57–9).
3. I want to thank the Social Science Research Council and the Wenner Gren Foundation for their generous financial support during preliminary language study and dissertation field research. I also want to thank Gujarat University and Gujarat Vidhyapit for support, accommodation, and training during language study and fieldwork between 1999–2005. Most importantly, however, I want to thank individuals in Gujarat for hospitality and encouragement, friendship and critique: Mr. Raymondbhai P., Mr. B., Ms. and Mr. Mehta, Mr. A.

Shah, Mr. Prakash and Mr. Prakash S., Mr. Pathak, Kapil D., Dasharath and Ramesh Y., Sukrat M., Rajkumar, Hydaid Ali Shah Bapu Pir and Swami Dearamdasji, Nandini and Johannes, Mahesh, Iftikhar, Prarag and Rituben K., Arvindbhai B., Yogendrabhai V., Rajaishreeben T., Harsha H., Firozbhai, Salimbhai Pathan and Manoj Goswami, Anand, Pinkyben and Irmalaben, Makrandbhai and Shivji, Nilotpalaben, Iqbalbhai, Rumanaben, Matuben Topliwalla, Dearambhai, Rakesh S., Akbarbhai, Gokalbhai Rabari, Jearambhai, Kamalbhai Qureshi, Jehangir M., Chandulal Maharaj Joshi, Sikanda Shah Fakir, Yusufbhai Pathan, Narayanbhai Rabari, Manvarkhan, Raju and Askok, Pinnakin, Shyamal, Vimlaben, Veena and Raveenaben, Trupti and Rohit, Jatin and Bhavinbhai.

–3–

Fieldwork and Fear in Iraqi Kurdistan

Diane E. King

"[T]he effective check on excesses in the use of power is the threat of murder . . . violence has become institutionalized as the only mechanism at hand."

Fredrik Barth

"The very words 'project,' 'informants,' 'information,' 'interview,' 'evidence,' 'description' took on new and terrifying meanings."

E. Valentine Daniel

Before the Iraqi Baath regime's ouster in 2003, I intermittently lived and carried out research in the Kurdish-controlled part of Iraq. I often commuted between the towns of Dohuk and Zakho by bus or a taxi shared with other passengers. Each time the bus or taxi passed the junction just north of Dohuk at which one of the roads led to the government-controlled city of Mosul, passengers typically tensed up. In the distance, but within view, lay the last Kurdish checkpoint. Beyond it was territory controlled by Saddam Hussein, who had declared himself the archenemy of both disloyal Iraqi Kurds and the United States, my country of citizenship. On more than one occasion, a taxi driver announced loudly to us passengers that he planned to take a quick detour to Mosul. He then turned his head towards us to see the looks on our faces. At this point, the taxi driver would throw his head back and laugh heartily, delighted at his ability to get a rise out of us, especially out of a visiting American. We all smiled as the tension drained from our bodies and we passed the junction, remaining en route to Dohuk.

One day in March 1998 the public bus I was traveling in came to an abrupt halt just before the junction. We passengers craned our necks to see what was going on and reacted with alarm when we saw what had prompted the bus to stop: the street ahead of us was filled with soldiers in Iraqi uniforms. The people around me gasped and murmured that we must have just been "invaded" by the Iraqi army arriving via the road from Mosul. Holding onto the seats in front of us, we stood to get a better view, aghast. I heard nervous exclamations of "*Bismallah!*" ("in the name of God," an Arabic expression often uttered by a person in fear) followed by questions and speculations as to the implications of what we were seeing. My thoughts raced. It seemed possible that I was living some of my last moments and, judging from the commentary of the other passengers, they thought so as well.

During the previous few weeks the political tension had been even higher than usual. President Clinton had threatened to order the U.S. military to bomb Iraq for failing to cooperate with U.N. weapons inspectors. For weeks people had speculated that if this happened the fallout might include a hostile incursion by the Iraqi army into the Kurdish areas. (When later the bombs did start dropping on specific military targets on the Baghdad-controlled side of the border, no incursion materialized and eventually people in the Kurdish area paid them little attention.)

In moments that seemed to last an eternity, the bus cautiously crept closer to the junction. Only then did we discern a strange but relieving detail: the soldiers were in fact Kurdish, not representing the Iraqi government. This was attested to by a yellow flag bearing the insignia of the Kurdistan Democratic Party and other subtle signs. Their Iraqi uniforms were a strategic display of the Kurdish regional government's decision to promote Iraqi federalism, a much-talked-about idea at the time but one that had lacked visible implementation. By publicly clothing its *peshmerga* (Kurdish fighters who had been a guerilla force) in the same uniform as the Iraqi national army near the road to Mosul, the Kurdish regional administration could placate Baghdad, Turkey and the U.S. all at once.

This strategy performed Iraqi-ness by downplaying separatism while simultaneously providing a show of strength of *peshmerga* fighters amassing with Saddam's forces just a few hundred meters away. It served the purpose of sending the message that the Kurds were militarily sovereign behind their lines of control, and it implicitly warned the Iraqi army not to advance. It took only a few seconds for us passengers to sort out the complex semiotics of the situation and come to an understanding of what we were observing. I remembered that I had heard that the *peshmerga* were in the process of adopting the features of a regular army. We breathed a collective sigh of relief as the bus waited and then slowly proceeded, inching through columns of soldiers and then on to its destination.

Fieldwork in Iraq(i Kurdistan)

I first went to Iraqi Kurdistan in 1995, and visited on three occasions during the 1991–2003 inter-war period, the subject of this chapter. During the 1990s Iraq was, as it indeed is presently, synonymous with violence. In a game of charades such words as "security," "crises" and "violence" might bring to mind "Iraq" before the name of any other state. The Iraq that was led by Saddam Hussein was called a "Republic of Fear" by the author Makiya (1998) and by many other observers.

Human Rights Watch began reports with lines such as "The Iraqi government continued to commit widespread and gross human rights violations, including arbitrary arrests of suspected political opponents, executions of prisoners, and forced expulsions . . ." (Human Rights Watch 2000). An accounting of the Baath regime's crimes would include many well-known atrocities, especially in the several years before 1991. For example, it used chemical weapons against Iranian troops and Kurdish rebels and villagers, killing perhaps 100,000. It "disappeared" 8,000 members of the Barzani tribe in 1983. Millions of people lived under the regime's tyranny, never knowing when it might strike them personally.

The regime of Saddam Hussein and those loyal to him relied on the constant threat and exertion of bodily harm and execution to exert sovereignty over the inhabitants of the state. To live in Iraq was to contend daily with governance backed up by force. Not only did thousands die in infamous mass attacks – the regime tortured and killed many other people one by one. Amnesty International asserted that in addition to the more known attacks, "hundreds of thousands of other people have been the victims of extrajudicial executions during the 1980s" (Randal 1999: 214).

In the anti-Saddam sanctuary of Iraqi Kurdistan, Saddam's genocidal rampage in the 1988 Anfal campaign stood as as much history as possibility – history that could be re-enacted at any moment, and with almost unimaginable consequences. French philosopher Michel Foucault (2000: 340) contrasts a "power relationship" with a "relationship of violence." The former "can only be articulated on the basis of two elements that are indispensable . . . the 'other' (the one over whom power is exercised) is recognized and maintained to the very end as a subject who acts . . ." The latter is more extreme: "A relationship of violence acts upon a body or upon things; it forces, it bends, it breaks, it destroys, or it closes off all possibilities. Its opposite pole can only be passivity, and if it comes up against any resistance it has no other option but to try to break it down." The relationship between the Iraqi government and the inhabitants of Iraq felt like one that had moved beyond a mere power relationship to a purifying, reducing relationship of violence. Saddam's 1988 attempt at genocide against the Kurds was not so much a fight against an "other" as an attempt to destroy the adversary once and for all. While talk was rife in the global media and among both local and global political commentators that "the Iraqi people" should eliminate Saddam and bring down his regime, no Iraqi managed to act accordingly. Saddam's internal adversaries were passive victims who did not manage to strike back at Saddam in any effective fashion, much as they told me they wanted to.

I deliberately refer to the "inhabitants" of Iraq rather than to its citizens to emphasize the collapsing of social categories rendered by the totalizing fear engendered by Saddam and representatives of his government. Did the poison gas dropped by helicopters in the Anfal campaign kill only Iraqi citizens? Were the tanks poised to take Dohuk mounted with special "citizen sensors"? Did citizens need more (or less) elaborate plans for escape than noncitizens? No – fearing Saddam was for everyone inhabiting a particular space, the space of Iraqi Kurdistan. Everyone within the Iraqi state's reach, citizen or noncitizen, Arab, Kurd, or American, had to live within this constant possibility of violence. By our very presence, we inhabitants faced the possibility that the state would reassert itself over Kurdistan as it continued to do in the rest of Iraq. We feared the arbitrariness of arrest, the state's lack of accountability and the fact that the Leviathan of the state not only arrested those that committed some "wrong" but was out of control, excessive, irrational, killing and torturing merely upon suspicion and without reason.

By entering the territorial domain of this specter of violence and remaining there to carry out my fieldwork, I, too, was subjected to fear and surveillance and lived with the dangers of bodily and mental harm. I had the desire to leave to preserve my safety several times. My longest stay, of eleven months in 1997–8, was to have been eighteen months but it had been delayed by an incursion the previous year by the Iraqi military into the Kurdish city of Erbil. At the time I was waiting in Turkey for border-crossing clearance. In this I was more fortunate than friends on the Iraqi side of the border who fled for their lives, although Diyarbakir and its surroundings was no haven either, since a war between the government and the P.K.K. (Partiya Karkere Kurdistan, or Kurdistan Worker's Party) was under way. After a year spent in Turkey's Kurdish region and the U.S., a wait that seemed like an eternity, I finally made it back to Iraqi Kurdistan, entering through the more hospitable Syrian border. Although the previous year's events had left me short on time and money, they had also lit a fire under me. I was determined that this time my plan to be the first cultural anthropologist in several decades to carry out research in Iraq lasting more than a few weeks would not be thwarted. "Staying" was as bound up with choice, or more specifically made up of small micro-choices made continuously in waking consciousness, as "going." But staying had, for me, a determined aspect as well. From the start, even before I went to the field, I had had a sense of calling. Once in the field, this was bolstered by daily reminders that my life was not merely my own. Local people's speech was peppered with *Enshallah* and *Heker Xwide has dikit* ("if it is God's will" in Arabic and Kurdish respectively). Under the constraints we all faced, there was no alternative life, no possibility of a Sartrean life of free acts of the will. Anthropologists are infrequently called upon to give a spiritual accounting of fieldwork experience. But in my case, much of the answer to the question of why I stayed and what allowed me to stay in a place tainted by a pall of fear would entail such an accounting.

I lived in host households and visited others on a regular basis, including several in remote villages. I also taught at the local university. In these settings I heard constant references to the impact of "Saddam" on everyday life. This ranged from the potential for tragedy to the quotidian. If making reference to the future, a person might add, ". . . If Saddam does not kill us first." If speaking of an everyday frustration that could be blamed on the failure of the state, such as the lack of electricity, someone might say, "Damn the father of Saddam."

But people also joked about Saddam. Their jokes were a kind of triumph, a last word to a tyrant who relished robbing his victims of their humanity. He could kill their relatives and make them live in constant fear but he could not steal their laughter. One joke, for example, offered an explanation for hand gestures. Saddam was well known for waving to crowds in a stiff motion, bending only his shoulder, with all five fingers pointed at the crowd. Members of the crowd would hold up two fingers in a victory sign in reply. According to the joke, what the crowd really meant by the two fingers was, "Your mother had two husbands." What Saddam was really saying back to them with his five outstretched fingers was, "No, she had five." In a culture in which hardly a greater insult existed than to question the sexual fidelity of one's mother or the certainty of one's paternity, tellers and hearers alike found this joke delightfully subversive. I heard many other jokes as well. People seemed to laugh a lot.

When listening to locals I always heard in two modes. In one mode, I was a fieldworker listening ethnographically to the other in the same manner as any ethnographer. But I was also at the mercy of my cultural consultants for my very life and this made for an additional kind of listening that was self-focused rather than other-focused.

I listened to the people around me – especially during occasions of heightened fear – for whatever their reported facts, rumors, strategies, justifications, opinions, advice, and experience might contribute to my own safety. I listened not merely to document, collate, or archive their words for later analysis after "the field," although I did this too. My career depended on the former kind of listening, and my life depended on the latter. My listening fit neatly within the cultural motif of "visiting" between kin, neighbors and friends, which took place in nearly every household nearly every evening. During these visits people recounted painful episodes in the past, mourned those lost to violence, and speculated about present political machinations. Talking about their fears seemed to have a purging effect. It seemed to make everything all right for the brief moment during which a room full of hearers clicked their tongues in empathy and nodded in solidarity.

On my trips to Iraqi Kurdistan between 1995 and 2003, multiple sovereignties were operative in Iraq. The U.S., Britain and Turkey controlled the skies. Rival Kurdish leaders Mes'ud Barzani and Jalal Talabani and their *peshmerga* fighters militarily and administratively controlled their respective territories within Kurdistan and, from 1995 to 1998, engaged in a civil war. The U.N. had a limited security force on the ground and an ever-growing number of programs being implemented by its various agencies. Independent Western nongovernmental organizations (N.G.O.s) as well as agencies sponsored by Western governments carried out relief and development. The Iraqi government in Baghdad retained some of its old infrastructural roles, such as supplying some of the electricity (if "supplying" is the word, since electricity remained scarce in the Kurdish region; on my first trip in 1995, the electricity was simply off and later it came on for only two hours a day). The P.K.K. made incursions from the across the Turkish border to the north. In reply, a Turkish military presence inside Iraqi Kurdistan fluctuated, at minimum being represented by several tanks and sometimes many more. The U.S. also had a small military ground force until it departed suddenly in 1996. The governments of Iraq, Turkey, Iran and the U.S. each had, people told me, powerful covert security apparatuses at work. Various actors, especially Turkey and Iran, were involved economically. Saudi Arabia funded and built thousands of prayer houses and mosques and reportedly funded Islamic political parties. With so many actors bringing their presence to bear on everyday experience, rumors constantly flew as to what the future would entail and which actor was actually in control of a given location and/or situation.

But to many analysts in the West, and to me as I was preparing to carry out my research, the Kurdish part of Iraq seemed sufficiently distant from the reach of the greatest threat, Saddam and his agents, as to be deemed relatively "safe." I reasoned that the Western air cover would ward off any attempts by the Iraqi government to drop chemical weapons as it had in 1988. Iraqi Kurds governed themselves behind an internal border erected, mainly in the form of checkpoints along the roads and military face-off lines, during the heady days of their 1991 uprising as Iraqi government troops retreated to the south and east. Although many local people had endured unspeakable acts of genocidal violence, from the outset my experience was almost a ridiculous antithesis of the gratuitous violence that had gone before: I was warmly welcomed by virtually everyone I met, from my host families to the top echelons of government. For example, when on my first trip in 1995, I inquired as to how to go about obtaining official research permission, I was ushered into a formal meeting with the governor, who had invited a television crew. There, under the glare of cameras beaming the event to potentially millions of viewers, the governor vigorously declared that I was not only welcome to carry out my research, but that his government would make sure that I was safe and that I had total freedom to talk to anyone and travel anywhere. He, and other officials of a government unrecognized as "legitimate" by the community of "legitimate" world states, seemed to regard my presence as an American anthropologist carrying out a "scientific" research project as a contribution to their quest for recognition by the outside world and its major powers, especially the U.S.

In my research I was initially interested in local people's interpretation of the Western presence in their midst in the form of relief and development agencies. This later evolved into an interest in outmigration to the West, which was taking place on a major scale. The desire on the part of local people to "flee" to the West, which was much in evidence as people were acting on it in their thousands, seemed paradoxical. Kurdish migrants were leaving *en masse* for the West, and once there, were seeking asylum, claiming their home was unsafe. But for the first time in decades, their part of Iraq was enjoying the protection of 24-hour Western air cover and relative political stability.

Upon further exploration, I began to understand the role of fear in people's lives, just as it came to be a major factor in my own daily existence among them. Fear was people's rumination on the *possibility* of violence. It mattered little if the violence did not materialize because violence *had* materialized within the recent past. Fear of violence, then, took its place along other motivators for outmigration such as the pursuit of greater economic security, flight from actual violence and other factors.

So although Iraqi Kurdistan was considered relatively "safe," fear hung like a cloud in the air, stealing sleep, robbing its victims of a sense of ordinariness. Local people spoke frequently of the possibility of succumbing to violence. I did *not* observe a high level of violence around me in the sense of actually witnessing violent acts myself. While I did experience several episodes of hostile gunfire and even larger weaponry, the only corpse I saw was in a mangled vehicle shortly after a traffic accident. Indeed, the streets of the towns of Dohuk and Zakho, where I spent most of my time, seemed safer than most American streets. But they were ripe with fear. Virtually everyone I listened to portrayed their fears as palpable and ongoing as opposed to something in the past, when the Iraqi government had had active control over the Kurdish area.

Fear of "Saddam"

When Iraqi Kurds used the word "Saddam" in a phrase or sentence, they meant more than just the dictator and leader of the Baath party. Saddam was rendered in everyday conversation as a grossly exaggerated figure represented by any agent of the Baathist Iraqi government. Boundaries between Saddam as an individual and those who did his bidding were often so blurred as to be irrelevant. The expression "Saddam" in everyday parlance of Kurds did not simply denote the totalitarian leader but was an idiom standing metonymically for all members of the government and the atrocities committed in its name. Saddam's agents rendered him as having thousands of bodies whose eyes, ears and arms were imagined to reach anywhere at any time and were ready to act on his behalf at any moment. The fear of Saddam was necessarily a paranoid fear as his *mukhabarat*, the secret police, had been responsible for numerous forced disappearances and acts of horrific violence that often came out of the blue.

Moreover, Saddam's troops were poised along the internal border and appeared ready to take Kurdish territory at any time. I lived in relative denial about that possibility until Easter morning 1998, when I joined other Christians in a trip to the top of the bluff adjacent to Dohuk to celebrate Easter at sunrise. The setting was beautiful. A carpet of new grass interspersed with wildflowers covered the ground.

The sun was beginning to rise in a clear sky to the east. The city was barely rousing below. As the light increased, someone in the traveling party motioned for me to come and look in the opposite direction. I turned around and, to my horror, I saw that on a knoll in the distance, barely visible with the naked eye, Iraqi tanks were dug into the slope, parked in a row and pointing in our direction as though poised to take Dohuk on a moment's notice. Despite all territorial and political uncertainties, here was the Iraqi army dug in and assuming a posture as though it were ready to face the army of another country, the nation of Kurdistan, as if it already existed. Images and interviews with survivors of the Iraqi army's last charge on Dohuk in 1991, when more than 1 million people fled for their lives, flashed through my head. To our dawn celebration of life was added a sober reminder of death's constant and imminent possibility.

While Iraqi tanks were parked on the opposite side of the internal border, a different kind of threat from Saddam's secret police, the *mukhabarat*, was ostensibly operative inside Iraqi Kurdistan. Fear of the *mukhabarat* was rampant and pervasive. The logic of suspicion that somehow the *mukhabarat* was listening, whether through surreptitious electronic listening devices or in the form of an undercover agent who might be one's friend or relative, pervaded everything. It was normal for people to wonder constantly who in their social circles might be an agent. I heard references to this frequently and friends warned me about several of my acquaintances whom they thought might be agents. International observers concurred that Saddam's agents were active in the Kurdish area. A 1994 report by the U.S. Department of State (1994) warned: "For 3 years there has been a clear pattern of criminal acts linking the Government of Iraq to a series of assassinations and attacks in northern Iraq on relief workers, U.N. guards, and foreign journalists, including a German journalist murdered in northern Iraq last spring."

February 1998 was a particularly tense period. Washington and Baghdad were verbally sparring, and U.S. President Clinton was threatening to bomb Iraq if it did not allow UN weapons inspectors to carry out their work. People in the Kurdish area speculated that if the bombs dropped, Saddam might attack the Kurdish area. In my Zakho and Dohuk host households, we stocked up on food. I wore all of my money, passport and credit cards in a money belt around my waist 24 hours a day, prepared to flee on a moment's notice.

(Five years later, I went to the U.S. embassy in Lebanon to request more pages in my passport, which had become warped and nearly completely delaminated during its time around my waist. The officer behind the window looked at me strangely. "What happened to this?" she said. Should I tell an officer of the US government, which had expended great energy trying to prevent Americans like myself from going to Iraq, that my passport had become delaminated by sweat, mobility, secrecy and fear in an Iraq under threat of American bombs? I resisted the urge to share. I mumbled something about carrying it a lot and returned a bureaucratic stare. The inquisitiveness left her face and she mirrored this, sliding the form for a new passport through the security slot.)

At the university, most of my colleagues were Kurdish, but one was Arab. I learned that he had previously taught in the government-controlled part of the country and that he still lived there, making the commute of one hour each way several times a week. A colleague pulled me aside during my first week and warned me about him:

> There is a very good chance he is an Iraqi agent. When you talk to him, say only things that are very general. Do not let him know where you live, with whom you associate, and other details . . . We only hired him because we were short of people with his qualifications. Otherwise we would never have hired someone from that side, because of the connection to Saddam.

As I got to know him, he told me that he had been lured to teach in the Kurdish area because the pay was significantly higher. He also told me of facing suspicion at the checkpoints that he had to navigate every day he came to work. Several times he had been denied entry and thus been unable to reach work. In contrast, Kurdish colleagues reversed this logic and claimed that the fact that he managed to reach the Kurdish area freely at all suggested that he must be an agent. "If he were not working for the government, he would not be able to come and go like this," one of them told me. Such was the catch-22 of commuting to work between enemy territories. Paranoia ran so deep that the same set of facts could lead to diametrically opposed interpretations.

On another occasion I was a guest at a wedding in Zakho when another guest, who had traveled from the government-controlled city of Mosul to attend the wedding, approached me and asked pointed questions about what I was doing in Iraq. A friend discreetly intervened and warned me to speak with her only in a very limited way, saying that she was probably a government agent and that I should provide only vague information about my movements and activities – again insinuating that I faced the risk of assassination. The next afternoon, I was surprised to find her sitting as a guest in the home of the H.[1] family, with whom I was staying at the time. Upon seeing me, she urged me to sit and talk with her. Although pressed for time, I did so briefly, sticking to only general information as I had been advised. When I got up to leave, she said, "But I have many more questions for you. Political questions!" We spoke briefly before I excused myself, never learning the full extent of what she intended to ask me.

After she left, there was much speculation as to her motives for being there. Sure, she was an old classmate of someone in the H. household but was this her *real* reason for visiting? Or was she gathering information about me that she would then pass on to the government? I learned that she had asked a number of pointed questions about me. The most alarming one was "Where does she keep her back-up field notes?" One woman present volunteered: "She keeps the disks in a safe in the office of an NGO or UN agency." Afterward her sister had chastised her for giving away such sensitive information. Information was rumored to be for sale; a person who knew something that the government wanted to know and who passed that on could not only make a little money but was able to increase her or his standing with the government. Had the guest been on a mission to find out how the government could obtain my field notes?

After Saddam was deposed in 2003, I recalled this incident with one of the H. household members who had been there and who had been one of the people to warn me. She at first said she barely remembered it, and then brushed it off. "I am sure she wasn't an agent," she said with confidence. "She is my friend." The threat of government surveillance that once hanged heavy in the air had lifted with the change of regime. Other threats, such as from violent Islamists, remained, but they did not emanate from the same people and thus rendered this friend "innocent" – apparently even retroactively.

Specific Fears, Ambient Fears

The Iraqi government did not have a monopoly on the generation of fear. Other sources of fear were abundant. Some had a specificity to them; for those outside the relevant social category, a particular source of fear could have little bearing but, for those inside, it might be the worst fear they faced. Domestic violence, to which I heard frequent references and which I occasionally witnessed, was one such fear. Fear by girls and women of childbearing age of being victimized in an "honor killing" was another (King 2008). Feuds between lineages and/or tribes rendered some people, members of the group that had last perpetrated a feud-related attack, on their guard against the inevitable revenge. I once ran into a Western friend just after he had witnessed a feud killing in the market. What amazed him, he said, was the way a crowd had drawn immediately; bystanders did not seem to have any fear of being hit by the still-in-progress shooting. He reasoned that this was because of their confidence that the bullets were meant for a specific person and not for random people who happened to be in the vicinity.

Other fears represented more ambient danger, but with a personalized component. One such source of fear was from violent Islamists. An Islamist family lived across the street from the G. family, my Dohuk host household. The matriarch of the family would visit us now and then, vigorously drinking her tea and talking in an opinionated, heated fashion. She often chastised the G.s for not being religious enough and after she left they wondered aloud if she represented a violent threat. Then on one memorable occasion she screamed and ranted at me, calling me an infidel and telling me that I was going to hell and that she should send her son to kill me because I was a non-Muslim living among Muslims.

Another Islamist threat came less directly but carried with it great foreshadowing. On 30 August 1998 a local Christian leader warned me that he had heard from "very high P.U.K. sources" that a splinter group of about fifteen fighters from within the Islamic Party of Kurdistan (I.M.K.) had just declared their loyalty to Osama bin Laden and that, as an American, I should be especially careful because they had vowed to kill Americans.

The Turkish military represented a very different but no less pervasive threat. The Turkish government periodically sent in ominous-looking columns of men and military hardware, which were stationed near mountain villages frequented by the P.K.K., Kurdish guerillas fighting a separatist war against it. Local people feared that Turkey would one day lose its restraint and carry out an all-out invasion. I knew of two young men who had allegedly spent time fighting with the P.K.K., although their families were extremely secretive about this because of the P.K.K.'s archenemy status with the ruling K.D.P. One of the men had died after being tortured in one of the K.D.P.'s prisons, his distraught mother told me. From this family, I heard strident anti-K.D.P. talk, and it was clear that for them that the K.D.P. was a source of great fear in addition to the fear of Turkey that they faced by default because of their member's involvement with the P.K.K.

The P.K.K. often retreated into Iraq and clashed with Iraqi Kurds. One night while in the H.'s village house, which we visited periodically, the family and I were on our rooftop sleeping cushions preparing to sleep when dogs in our village and the surrounding area began barking excitedly. "It's probably the P.K.K.," someone said. "If they come we will hide you in the house," said another to me. But I did not like the idea of being singled out and I thought this would increase the risk of me being caught, so I suggested that we simply remain calm and that I not speak a word of English or do anything else that might give away my identity as a non-local.

None of us were sure what my foreignness would mean to the P.K.K., nor were we eager to find out. Previously I had met an Australian woman who had been briefly kidnapped by the P.K.K. She told me that they had marched her at gunpoint to a mountain hideaway and then made her sit next to a campfire all night listening to one of their members lecture, in English, about their ideology, history and struggle against the Turkish government. When they were satisfied that she had received a sufficient education, they urged her to become their advocate and let her go unharmed. But then again, the P.K.K. was responsible for numerous brutal killings, which I had heard about on many occasions and which had affected a number of people I knew.

Everyone seemed to agree to the plan that we would avoid singling me out. Just then, a tracer bullet arced across the sky. Someone had shot it from what appeared to be within the village lands. Then came a reply in the form of a few short bursts by Kalashnikov fire from the mountain behind us. We lay perfectly still.

My thoughts raced to the stories I had heard in which the P.K.K. were painted as the ultimate bogeymen: "Four girls have gotten into taxis in Dohuk and never been heard from again!!" "A sheepherder narrowly escaped death when the P.K.K. fired on him from the ridge behind the village! Several of his sheep were killed, and he is trying to get them to reimburse him. Damn the P.K.K.!" And then there was the time I was invited to pay my respects at the home of a young widow whose husband and six others had been killed the day before by P.K.K. members who had burst through the door of their village house and opened fire without cause. Unlike the typical *tazi* (an event similar to a wake) in which most attendees were visibly grief-stricken, at this one everyone sat stone-faced, as though too stunned to begin visibly grieving. The bursts of automatic weapon fire were the last event of the evening. Eventually our anticipation surrendered to sleep. The morning light revealed nothing out of the ordinary.

Another source of fear besides the P.K.K. came from the P.U.K. (Patriotic Union of Kurdistan), the rival Kurdish group to the south with whom K.D.P. forces sparred in the mid-to-late 1990s. For example, during my first month in the region, in 1995, I hitched a ride in an N.G.O. vehicle to Erbil, a strategic, centrally situated city. At the time, Erbil was controlled by the P.U.K., but K.D.P. fighters were trying to capture it (which they succeeded in doing a year later through a shocking act of treachery: a brief alliance with the Iraqi military). On our return trip, we were traversing the no-man's-land separating K.D.P.-P.U.K. lines of control when a voice came over the U.N.-administered two-way radio warning us of a battle up ahead. We were ordered to take an alternate route, which we did at breakneck speed as an American N.G.O. staff member in the front passenger seat received battle updates on the radio. My heart raced as we sped along. Eventually we made our way around the conflict, the journey narrated throughout by the animated radio exchange. Suddenly Iraq's violence seemed less theoretical than it had to that point.

In 1998, this experience repeated itself with much greater intensity. I went along on a field visit by the United Nations High Commissioner for Refugees (U.N.H.C.R.) staff to a refugee camp. Along the way, we encountered a battle between the K.D.P. and P.K.K. that was in full swing. The P.K.K. was on the mountainside, raining its ammunition down below. On and adjacent to the road was a contingent of K.D.P. fighters fully engaged in a standoff with the P.K.K.. Rasheed, the senior U.N.H.C.R. staff professional in the group, was driving. We had come upon the battle too fast to make a u-turn without putting ourselves in further danger, so he decided to charge ahead, passing K.D.P. fighters running in retreat along the road and past a battle outpost beside a roadside house from which the K.D.P. was launching rocket-propelled grenades at the P.K.K. above. We could see the smoke rising from the impact points. I managed to snap a picture out the window. As we came out the other side, I asked Rasheed, "I am afraid. But should I be? How dangerous is this?" He shot back with an incredulous tone, "Dangerous? It's very dangerous! I have been in many situations but this may be the worst! The P.K.K. is known to fire on the UN!" We were riding in a vehicle that had large "UN" letters on both sides and the top. If we had tried harder to be a conspicuous target, we could not have been. But somehow, we slipped through unscathed, with only pounding hearts, sweaty palms and a story to be recounted to others.

During the following months, Rasheed was transferred to Amman, Jordan, where I learned that he died, reportedly in an automobile accident. I and others, who knew Rasheed have wondered since whether or not the accident was staged. The Iraqi government was known to dislike U.N.H.C.R. and had on multiple occasions accused its employees of spying. Iraqi *mukhabarat* operatives were known to be in Jordan, and they were also known to use staged auto accidents as a method of assassination. But the answer will never come. Speculation in the face of such potent fear and its possible justification can continue endlessly.

Stories: Violence as both Engendering and Collapsing of Social Distance

E. Valentine Daniel (1996: 4) opens his "anthropography" of violence by exclaiming, "Stories, stories, stories!" and argues that it is stories, the telling of which constitutes part of the process of "the giving, the receiving, the transforming, and the disseminating of signs" (p. 121) that make humans human. He writes of a woman whose father had been brutally killed by being dragged by an army jeep, and who wanted her "'story' to be told to 'the world.'" Victims' experiences are validated when witness is borne by imagined people in an "outside world" where existence is imagined to be ordered by peaceful means.

Many of my experiences in Iraqi Kurdistan paralleled Daniel's. People seemed almost desperate to tell their stories to me. I listened to what sometimes seemed like endless stories of suffering. People would recount difficulties small and catastrophic, recent and in the distant past, often justifying the telling of their story to me in particular with the same logic, that I, as an American, somehow represented "the world," as though to have told me was to have rendered the recounted events as legitimate and worthy of more attention, horror, pity, or outrage than if they had gone untold to an outsider. I often felt like a counselor of sorts, whose job it was to listen to people recounting their problems. The litany of problems was frequently accompanied by an injunction. "Tell your government," I was often told.

Oftentimes the stories people told me were tragic but local and specific and not the kind of details that would be of interest to a distant power. Someone's relative had been the victim of a tribal feud and I was urged to tell my government so that it could mediate. Someone had been displaced by the Iraqi government's "Arabization" program and I was urged to take down the names and details of the specific case. But occasionally the subject matter was more grandiose. Once when

I was about to enter the U.N. building in Dohuk, a man approached me and called out to me. Though wary, I asked him what he wanted. He was visibly nervous. "I have a secret that I must tell the West," he said. I immediately objected, telling him there was nothing I could do. He asked if I was an American. While I wanted desperately to deny it, I divulged anyway that I was, and then began to turn away from him. But he continued to talk, drawing me into his story: "I live in the government-controlled area," he said

> and I traveled here to Kurdistan just so I could tell the United States or United Nations about something I have seen. I live beside a school for small children. For some time I have seen people coming and going from the school at night, moving quickly and in a secretive fashion as though they are intent on hiding what they are doing. Most recently, I saw people carrying heavy items inside. It looked like containers of chemicals. While I had had my suspicions beforehand, after I saw this, I was sure that these are the Iraqi government's chemical weapons. I think they are being hidden in or under the school because this is a place where the United States would not find them, or if they did, they would never bomb the site because they would not want to kill children.

As the man spoke, I felt an intense fear that this was all a ruse and that I was seconds away from being shot or kidnapped. Time seemed to stand still as the man's voice droned on under the hot sun. But when he reached the point of the inevitable appeal, my mind raced as I weighed what to say next. "Please tell your government," he begged. "I must get word to them. I have risked my life to come here and tell you this." The man's story seemed genuine. That he seemed frightened out of his wits seemed to lend it credibility; although I myself was afraid, I was not shaking and sweating like he was. "Here is what I will do," I told him. "I can go inside the U.N. building, and tell the people on duty in the U.N.G.C.I. office about you. You can tell them your story, and perhaps they can help." I thought this was a good compromise. He was not able to enter the building himself without an N.G.O. or U.N.-issued identity card. I could do him this small favor and be on my way.

Though it seemed clear that this was not his ideal, I managed to persuade the man that this was all I could offer and he agreed. I went inside and gave a quick synopsis to the U.N. staff member on duty in the radio room, who was my acquaintance from previous visits. "The story seems genuine. I think you should hear it," I urged him. But he refused. "We do not get involved with such matters," he said flatly. This seemed terribly at odds with what I knew: that another U.N. agency, United Nations Special Commission on Iraq (U.N.S.C.O.M.), constituted a major inspection apparatus that was charged by the Security Council with finding and keeping track of the Iraqi government's chemical and biological weapons. When I mentioned this, he smiled. "Yes, U.N.S.C.O.M. is looking for things like this. But U.N.G.C.I. is not, and we have no connection to each other so I would not even know how to get this information to them. Please tell the man outside to go away and forget about this." Despite pleading with him to reconsider, I got no further. I suspected that Hans too felt fear. After all, how could he convey this information in a safe fashion to the correct people, even if he wanted to? The *mukhabarat* was rumored to have a method of clandestinely opening and closing the sealed diplomatic pouches that were used to send ostensibly confidential information between U.N. offices in Iraq. The two-way radio was out for obvious reasons. A hand-carried note was too dangerous because it could be snatched and read. Even email was too risky because it traveled across phone lines, and email messages were rumored to be accessible to those with the knowhow. I thought about all this and wondered if it was in his mind as well, but concealed by the easy answer he offered, that the bureaucratic means of access did not exist.

Once outside, I found the man waiting and told him the bad news. There was more pleading on his part. "Tell the US government, tell President Clinton. He must know about this. Thousands of people may be killed by these weapons Saddam is hiding."

"I cannot, I have nothing to do with the government," I repeated. Finally we parted. As we did, the man had a dejected, hopeless look on his face.

Only after leaving the scene in a taxi did I let the thought of assassination or kidnapping leave my mind. And while normally I would have jotted down the details of an interesting encounter like this in my notebook, I refrained out of fear. As I write this, I am operating from memory because I did not record it in my field notes. What if the *mukhabarat* had stolen my notes? Although they were stored on a laptop computer protected by a security program as common sense and my universities' human subjects review committees had required, in certain instances such as this one, fear still prevented me from recounting an interesting event. This information, if read by the wrong party, would surely have marked me as a spy, and could well have been my coup de grace. (Not all of the story survived my efforts to remember it: While the man had told me the names of his city and neighborhood, I have no clear memory of either, only a hazy memory that the city in question was Kirkuk.)

Stories, stories, stories! Whether or not it was true, by telling his story to me, the man outside the U.N. building was attempting to insert himself into a drama of global proportions, the years-long standoff between the Iraqi government and the U.N. Whatever his motive, it seemed clear that he wanted his voice heard. It was his good fortune to encounter by chance (or had he waited for a long time?) one of the handful of Americans in Iraqi Kurdistan. He was an Iraqi victim, living across the street from innocent children who were potential human shields, and he was telling his story to the world.

In 2002 a Kurdish friend, a local U.N. employee in Dohuk, was abducted by Saddam's agents, transported to Baghdad, and imprisoned for two weeks in a filthy cell. Sounds of torture and execution wafted from other cells. She was beaten, threatened with death, and frightened out of her wits. While they were beating her they told her they wanted to do the same to me – "Diane, the American" – if they could only manage to capture her. I happened to be out of the country by then, or I might well have gone through the same experience that she did. Afterward my friend wrote a letter to President Bush, which she sent to the White House email address, explaining what had happened to her. That is how public she wanted her story to be. Such was the height to which she would seek to have her story told, the magnitude on which she felt the need to be heard. But she sent the email on her own and told me after the fact rather than pleading with me to help her gain access to President Bush, as would have better fit the pattern I had experienced with others. Perhaps my taking on, albeit unknowingly at the time, the role of potential torture victim in a cell in Baghdad meant to her that I no longer qualified as a conduit to "the world." Some of the social distance between us was collapsed by a beating and a wish to capture an American expressed in one of Saddam's torture chambers.

Paradoxically, ubiquitous violence and danger in the field has significant effect on anthropological practice and method in gathering just such stories. I did not use the voice recorder I brought to my main fieldwork stint in 1997, because I sensed that it might mark me as an agent of my own government (a possibility and/or actuality faced by other anthropologists as well – for example, Jennings 1998: 58, Shryock 1997: 4). In 1998 members of the H. household noticed the recorder for the first time as I packed my belongings in preparation to leave the country. One confirmed my concerns by shrieking, "I didn't know you had that!" Although it was low-tech and probably would have been unable to record anything surreptitiously, the look on her face suggested that she feared I might have used it covertly. The fear that some thought, some statement, some sentence might escape the intimacy of our conversations and reach the ears of "Saddam" was ripe. By then I too had learned to fear in this way, so their fear did not surprise me, but the moment felt awkward and unjust – as though a force outside of ourselves had introduced mistrust into a relationship we were about to affirm with a fond goodbye. But the externality of the source and the lack of control that any of us had over it, I think, rendered the situation easier to rectify: I spread my collection of blank cassette tapes out on the carpet and invited those watching to play them. Sheepishly, they tried several, verifying that the cassettes were indeed blank. I left with trust restored but without any recorded audio data from that eleven-month period of fieldwork. Stories. The full detailed telling of them, which the tape recorder would have facilitated, was curtailed by the threat of violence.

In his introduction to the edited volume *Death Squad: the Anthropology of State Terror*, Jeffrey Sluka (2000) writes about anthropologist Ricardo Falla, who lived in and wrote about Guatemala in the violence-wracked 1970s and 1980s. He describes how Falla placed himself in danger in order to document injustice committed against the Maya population. But the wording of his description places distance between Falla and the Mayas. For example: ". . . three Mayan communities where Falla worked were destroyed . . . He fled with them" (Sluka 2000: 19).

The violent political order under which I worked was a collapser of social distance. In light of this I would like to rephrase this description to mention not only Falla's *vocation* as someone who "worked" in the three communities but also the fact that he *lived* there. Rather than "he fled with them," I would note that "everyone fled." It is doubtful that during flight Falla felt different from anyone else in his company. His "possibilities," the kind Foucault reminds us are cut off by violence, were the same as the Mayans: either flee or succumb.

I end with a flashback to the frightening days of February 1998 when the United States was threatening to attack Iraq. In anticipation, a few people fled; one man from Zakho drowned while trying to swim across the Tigris River to Syria, and a friend from Dohuk fled to Turkey. The U.N. was rumored to be setting up hundreds of tents in Turkey in preparation for mass refugee flows.

During these days I was often in conversations with residents of Zakho and Dohuk as to what might happen. We speculated as to whether or not the U.S. would attack, what the consequences would be where we were, and under what circumstances we would flee. Members of my Dohuk host household, the G. family, discussed how their method of escape would simply involve taking a taxi to the border. Someone asked me, "How will *you* escape?" "I will take the taxi with you," I answered. Laughter broke out in the room. The G.'s looked at me to see if I was serious. "Surely a helicopter will come for you because you are an American." I insisted that no such thing would happen. There was more laughter, and I insisted further.

This conversation was a turning point in our relationship after which the G.'s treated me as one of their own. They had laughed because they found it absurd that I, a U.S. citizen from what they regarded as the safest place in the world, would have to flee with them, Iraqi Kurds whose lives were regularly punctuated by flight and refuge-seeking from collective violence. Before this conversation, the G.'s had regarded my identity/citizenship category as carrying with it great privileges, such as helicopter rides, and their own category as rendering them impotent in the face of danger. As the laughter died down and they realized I was serious, the conversation turned again to the practical. Where would we ask the taxi driver to go? How much would we pay him? Where was everyone else likely to head, so that we could go in a different direction? Under the pall of Saddam's threat, other possibilities and subjectivities were closed off and we shared a hypothetical taxi.

Acknowledgements

For their feedback, I thank Parvis Ghassem-Fachandi, Natasha Zaretsky and Christophe Robert, as well as the anonymous reviewers. I am grateful for financial support for research and writing from Washington State University, Wenner-Gren Foundation for Anthropological Research, American University of Beirut, the University of Kentucky, and the George A. and Eliza Gardner Howard Foundation. For research permission and access granted to Iraqi Kurdistan, I thank Kurdistan Regional Government officials in Dohuk Governorate. Working with research assistants Zhiyan Rozh and Nazira Mehsin Shamdeen enriched my experience immeasurably. My deepest gratitude is to the people among whom I lived and gathered ethnographic information.

Note

1. Some names have been abbreviated.

References

Barth, F. (1953), *Principles of Social Organization in South Kurdistan*, New York: AMS Press.

Daniel, E. V. (1996), *Charred Lullabies: Chapters in an Anthropography of Violence*, Princeton: Princeton University Press.

Fischer, M. M. J. (1986), "Ethnicity and the Post-Modern Arts of Memory," in J. Clifford and G. E. Marcus (eds), *Writing Culture: The Poetics and Politics of Ethnography*, Berkeley: University of California Press, pp. 194–233.

Foucault , M. (2000 [1981]), "The Subject and Power," in J. D. Faubion (ed.) R. Hurley (trans.) *Power: Essential Works of Foucault 1954–1984*, vol. 3, New York: New Press, pp. 326–48.

Human Rights Watch (2000), *World Report 2000: Human Rights Developments, Iraq and Iraqi Kurdistan*. See http://www.hrw.org/wr2k1/mideast/iraq.html, accessed 3 December 2008.

Jennings, A. M. (1998), "Nubian Women and the Shadow Economy," in R. A. Lobban, Jr. (ed.) *Middle Eastern Women and the Invisible Economy*, Gainesville, FL: University Press of Florida, pp. 45–59.

King, D. E. (2008), "The Personal is Patrilineal: Names as Sovereignty." *Identities: Global Studies in Culture and Power* 15(3): 317–42.

Makiya, K. (1998), *Republic of Fear: The Politics of Modern Iraq*, updated edition, Berkeley: University of California Press.

Randal, J. C. (1999) *After Such Knowledge, What Forgiveness? My Encounters with Kurdistan*, Boulder: Westview Press.

Shryock, A. (1997), *Nationalism and Genealogical Imagination: Oral History and Textual Authority in Tribal Jordan*, Berkeley: University of California Press.

Sluka, J. (ed.) (2000), "Introduction: State Terror and Anthropology," in *Death*

Squad: The Anthropology of State Terror, Philadelphia: University of Pennsylvania Press.

U.S. Department of State, Bureau of Public Affairs (1994) Dispatch 5:45. See, http://dosfan.lib.uic.edu/ERC/briefing/dispatch/1994/html/Dispatchv5no45.htm, accessed 6 December 2008.

—4—

The Sense of War Songs

Bilinda Straight

"Look how heroes are made.
Look how heroes are made."
> Samburu circumcision song, performed in the film *Bosnia Hotel*

Since 1992, I have personally heard, recorded, and studied hundreds of Samburu songs and narratives boasting of bravery and military victory. Thus, of course, I have long understood that the words celebrate violent deeds. Nevertheless, I have benignly ignored it on a regular basis and I want to take you through that process of de-emphasis, obliqueness, and sometimes spirited forgetting on the way to remembering violence in my own way, and in a way that respects the heterogeneity of Samburu values.

Samburu are typically described as pastoralists who raise cattle, camels, goats and sheep, although in the twenty-first century they engage in pastoralism in combination with a variety of means of generating cash income. Thus, to an outsider stepping into a town in Samburu district, the sight of young Samburu men and women continues to evoke postcard and coffee-table book images, as they walk through shops dressed in colorful cloth wraps and decorated with lavish beaded ornaments and red ochre pigment. Nevertheless, as I learned myself soon enough, Samburu have long been creating their own version of a globalizing modernity – one that blends evolving technologies and Western forms of education with pastoral practices which include livestock herding, elaborate ornamentation, lively song performances and an emphasis on young men's bravery.

In 1992, I was twenty-eight and a single mother of two young sons, aged six and eight, whom I took with me to Kenya to do doctoral fieldwork. I did not witness or experience violence in those two years. Instead, I stayed awake on moonlit nights listening to my Samburu friends singing about it – boasting and joyous:

Ooh Listen how we went about the safari so that you will know
And it is not a safari to feed ourselves
It is not a safari to feed ourselves
We prepared in bushy places where raiders would not be seen
In that place you can hardly find feathers . . . [high winds blow them away]
We slept where colorful birds sleep
Then our raiders' goal was a mountain called Lekimani where everything is available
Then we rested at a place called Ngaashar – a good shade tree
We gathered [literally, dug] excellent herbs where the white colobus monkey stays
That is where my beloved raiders take the best herbs
That is where my beloved raiders take the best herbs
Those herbs will make those lmurran [warriors] so hot-tempered they will never feel
the cold

I arrived in the field in late summer, 1992, and by early 1993 my eldest son was
fluent in Samburu and regularly participated in late night songfests – even when
"grounded," which was amusing even then because hearing his voice in the distance was a hint that he had snuck out of his room. My eldest son, like so many
women's sons, already had the "*lmurran*-bug,"[1] and he had the advantage over his
young Samburu peers that the combination of his whiteness, his fluency in
Samburu and his heart like a wild animal (in the view of my Samburu friends)
meant that *lmurran* were willing to let him tag along when they were at the river
putting on their finest. (Oil and red ochre do not readily wash out of blond hair but
he didn't care.) I learned what it means to be hot-tempered through this child of
mine who feared nothing and soon shared his friends' delight in killing birds,
gazelles, and other small creatures.

Samburu boys dream of being brave *lmurran* some day and, in preparation, they
mercilessly hunt and kill. Still the child of their mothers, eating the food their
mothers prepare, herding animals close to home, they are, nevertheless, in training
to become wild things of the bush who will leave their mothers to roam in pairs
and packs, feasting outdoors well beyond the confines of domesticity. The experience of seeing my son kneel with his friends to drink the blood pooling in the skin
of a freshly slaughtered goat (and throwing it up on my doorstep afterwards the
first time he did it) gave me a visceral understanding of this readily encultured
killing passion. At the same time, I shared with other mothers the occasional
humor of it all – the puffed up posture of *lmurran* as they walk into a settlement
and plant their spears near the house door. They might impress their girlfriends but
we mothers smile at each other because we have breastfed them and cleaned up
their infant urine and feces.

It was, of course, other mother's sons who were going off to raid in 1994 when
I first heard of Samburu entanglements with the neighboring Pokot. And though I
was a mother, on the eve of turning thirty I was somehow young enough to distance myself from it, hearing the songs in my ears, feeling the pleasure of dancing

with girls and with *lmurran* who wooed me like any other young woman. Sure, let them bring back cows. They are more beautiful than the Turkana, the Pokot, or anyone else they are raiding. The idea of actual killing seemed abstract, as far away as the places they ventured to on foot so that they could bring back tales of difference that disgusted their Samburu hearers.

> At the mountain of Kapisae where cattle have bright colors
> The owners enjoy eating green vegetables
> At that moment we did not catch wildebeest or rhino young
> We knew where our enemies were
> Those enemies bead their girlfriends with beads made from vultures' eggshells
> And the hair of their elders resembles modeling clay

Could girls really wear beads made from vultures' eggshells? That sounds interesting (and potentially beautiful) to me, but for those *lmurran*'s Samburu hearers its foreignness was absolute. Some women might travel great distances, but not in the same way or as intimately close to their non-Samburu "others" as *lmurran*. Instead, they relied upon the boasting songs *lmurran* tell when they return – songs that describe places and people in exquisite detail, giving a vicarious experience that is bloodless and safe. And in songs meant to goad and shame, girls are often blamed for sending *lmurran* careening into bravery:

> Give me two warlike lmurran ("warriors") there with me, in front during war.
> Now listen to what we did on our way
> We went to a place where girls incite men to kill and bring back a lot of livestock
> And with that, every warrior set off to kill and bring back a lot of livestock

And those experiences of girlfriends shaming, then praising and physically loving them, is one that men will continue to sing about as they play "Ntotoi," a mancala-like man's game, and "dodder" in the cool shade, as Samburu say of old age:

> Spoiled girls, our Nkasilei of Waso, which has spoiled girls, which has spoiled girls
> So that they put marks [keloidal scars] on their stomachs
> To be cut on their stomachs, our Nkasilei of Waso,
> Which girls talked about, then went off to have marks put on their stomachs
> [so that lmurran grab them sensuously].

Perhaps it is not so difficult to understand how songs of bravery can feel exciting and far away – exotic to Samburu feminine ears – nor very surprising that young women might feel empowered in the act of speaking their boyfriends into courage and action, particularly when life-sustaining cows might be had in the bargain.

Nevertheless, while this view is recognizable to Samburu and accurate in some respects, there is a great deal more at stake here. Like Renato Rosaldo, whose understanding of Ilongot headhunting deepened with the rage he felt at his wife's accidental and tragic death, my own understanding of Samburu violence has grown with maturity and the passing of young lives (though not of those as close as a spouse). My task has not been to develop an enculturated understanding of another society's culturally acceptable forms of violence however. Rather, my own passing through the life course has brought me closer to appreciating the breadth of the impact of violence.

Sometimes, it is important to listen in the silence.

So let us say that it is the 1960s. It is not the Lmooli generation who are Samburu *lmurran* as it will be when I arrive in the 1990s, but rather a generation the Samburu refer to as Lkishili. And they are being attacked by the Somali. Death is everywhere. It is actually 2003, and I am listening to a very old friend of mine tell me what she witnessed as a younger woman. But the story is so riveting, the experience so fresh for her, that I feel as if I have gone back in time and am standing transfixed in a war that took place long ago but is happening over and over again in the telling. And having given birth, having raised children and having lived so closely with Samburu while raising my children I can almost taste the entire thing. I am engaged in a new collaborative project about Samburu raiding, with questions that typically elicit the kinds of joys and boasting I have heard so many times before. But my friend does not tell me of joy. Instead, she tells me of the raid of another ethnic group against her own settlement.

> And they shot one woman, shooting her in the thigh with a pistol. Dawn had just broken and it happened that a child ran, some little girl like this one, while they were just sitting together. The child ran and left her mother, and then she [her mother] went running to look for her, to look, and people are shooting, and she came back, and just stayed for awhile, and then she ran again. Where could she go and look for her? And then she was shot – she was shot with a pistol.

Her narrative went on, of a woman whose hand was severed completely, of a child who sat motionless on a hide all day next to a dead old man, of houses set on fire with people burning inside of them. And of silence. Of silence, as Samburu *lmurran* came back from their counter-attack to find death everywhere and women standing, too stunned to speak much less sing. They wandered wordlessly among the bodies of those who had been their kin, friends, and neighbors.

> When these people came back, returning the cows, we were just standing there like this. And the majority of the people had gone. I don't know if we were how many, five? Or six? And as we went towards a woman who lay [dead] over there, this elder now returned to us before we reached [the dead woman]. He told us to go, go. "Why do you keep looking at these people who are finished? Go." And we went. We had been living side by side [with the dead people], having been how many large settlements? Three.

In that instant of hearing her, with all the emotion of the telling, I felt as if my collaborator and I should be asking instead what violence feels like at home.

Songs of bravery are sung when *lmurran* have gone off in the heat of their wildness to attack the settlements of their ethnic Others and have brought back the spoils of victory – especially cows for their mothers and sisters to milk.

> Even from a distance people will hear that the *lmurran* of those settlements have returned from a raid, and that all of them have come back. They are all fine. They will be happy when they hear singing because they know that no one has been killed.

When instead *lmurran* come limping back with dead comrades left behind and not a single animal for their trouble, they come in silence and are greeted with silence: "If anyone was killed, there will be nothing [no sounds of joy]." And when the news travels to the settlements where mothers and sisters wait for sons and brothers who aren't returning, uncontrollable shrieks and moaning break out everywhere.

In 2007 it is impossible to ignore the sounds and sights associated with grief, as the death toll in Iraq climbs daily and the media coverage increases apace. For those of us who have young adult sons, the reality is all the more horrifying. Soon after the U.S. attacked Iraq, my brother's eldest son joined the Air Force and I felt like screaming or sobbing or both. Later, a close friend's son was called to a tour of duty in Iraq and I could imagine her absolute fear. Then, last year, my twenty-two year old fearless son with the heart of a wild thing decided to enlist in the Army. (I thank the universe that he relented.) I am a pacifist and Quaker but who fully controls their children?

> No one encourages *lmurran* to go to war. There is no one to encourage them. They just go on their own. There is no one who wants them to go but they just go on their own. They sneak . . . And it is just thought that they went to visit some neighboring settlements but they have gone on that raid.

And here I remember the debate that ensued at the 2006 American Anthropological Association Meetings during discussion following the session ("Ethnographies of Violence") for which I presented a paper. The paper that provoked debate described the honor families felt for their sons who died as suicide bombers. A member of the audience felt that the paper's focus on honor glorified the violence. The session participant's response was that families would not wish their children to kill themselves and others in this way but that they needed to make sense of their deaths. In the U.S. as well, there is an urgency to forge heroes in the midst of acts and forms of violence that are beyond any single family's control.

Samburu mothers often ask their sons not to go to war. Fathers too, counsel their sons concerning war. If the need is clear because the community has been attacked for example, elders will give *lmurran* their collective blessing. At other times elders are reluctant. However, even if elders agree in some cases or can sometimes be induced to bless *lmurran* to go to war, mothers are less equivocal.

> As for us who are old, like me now, don't I have *lmurran* [sons]? When I hear about a girl who praises the lmurran I really hate that. I say, "Aish! She has sent them." This girl, this bloody one, when I find her somewhere I will tell her not to say that again when she sings to lmurran because I fear she will send them to raid.

> Can anyone tell them to go? Can you tell your own child [to go]? He can be killed. It is only arranged by children. Because *lmurran* are children.

They are children. They are the children of their mothers and fathers, raised in a context in which interethnic violence can occur at any time, and in which livestock must also be defended against natural predators like lions, leopards, and hyenas. Thus, even in peacetime, bravery is essential. And it is moving.

In the summer of 2006, my eldest son's closest Samburu friend was initiated into *lmurran*-hood. Since my son could not be there, a proxy fulfilled the important commitment of holding my son's friend's back as he was circumcised while my videotape rolled at the family's request. They wanted my son to see everything and in that way, to be present to this singularly important event. Having known this young man since 1992 when my son routinely went off to herd with him, I was already emotionally involved. But when he and his brother sang throughout their circumcisions and then got up immediately following, wandering around or being violent because of the heat of their hearts, I cried. My dear friend, the boys' father had fallen into trance and like his sons, could not be controlled. The occasion was intense, powerful, and surreal. I had already attended other circumcisions, but this was the clearest display of bravery I had seen. Some boys were silent throughout; some sang but then allowed themselves to be carried quietly into the house for healing. Yet here I was seeing before my eyes the making of heroes. These were the kinds of young men who would rush into the front of battle and bring back many cows. These would not be the ones who run back at the halfway point when their more experienced comrades tease them that those vultures over there are waiting for the meat you will become. Nor would they be the ones who grabbed the cows and ran while their comrades fought the "enemy" valiantly. These young men were the ones who would stay until the end, and bring back every animal, fighting with such fearless bravery that no one would dare leave them.

I felt all of these things as I stood there, proud of these young men I had known so long, proud as a mother could be proud. And yet I am a pacifist. I do not want a single young man to kill and my terror at the thought of my own son going to Iraq was not only at the thought that he might be killed but that he would become a killer. *What sense might I be forced to make of it?*

Yes, [girls] praise them because they [*lmurran*] come singing. They come. Because they have gone and done their work there, because when they kill someone, that one who has killed a person, people come and sing a song for him and some small copper wires are put on his wrist, just like you have done a very big job, putting copper wires to anoint him. They are anointing him.

Girls can anoint their brave boyfriends because they think of killing in positive terms rather than imagining the implications of those actions. "Yes, girls want. Are they not children? They are like the *lmurran*." Yet wives, sisters, and mothers do not want to think about it. Feeling as if it is beyond their control, they simply pray to Divinity over and over again and they feel anguish for those who die, whether their own or "enemy" children.

The cultural value placed on bravery does not cause violence in any simple, linear sense. Rather, the causes of violence are multiple and complex, particularly in a globalizing world in which local, national, and transnational political realities converge and in which poverty can become an effective political weapon for mobilizing people who would otherwise choose peace. When long-term tensions between the Pokot and Samburu erupted into violence in 2005, the war that ensued exemplified this increasingly prevalent low-intensity chronic warfare that brings together small arms (which have all but replaced spears in the past decade), local and national political rivalries, land disputes, and local desires. My story here evokes those local desires. Nevertheless, in most instances in the twenty-first century local desires are never caused in any simple sense but are, rather, crucial mechanisms, particularly as poverty pushes many destitute pastoralist young men to steal cattle with automatic weapons on behalf of Mafia-style bosses. These are what Carolyn Nordstrom calls "shadow wars," a clandestine economy masquerading in this case as "tribal" warfare. Yet if the result is that cattle can be added to a desperate family's herd then heroes may still be made. Short-term needs are traded for peace and the poverty-war cycle continues.

Girls mark the secret path along which stolen cattle will pass – unseen, hidden for a time, until they can be safely brought into the family herds. When all is well and no *lmurran* are killed, relieved mothers and young wives will thank Divinity and count the new livestock that will provide milk for hungry children. With the joy of safe return, and the welcoming in of livestock that are, after all, desperately needed in this place of chronic drought, songs of boasting and victory can be good to hear.

Hoi! That *lmurrani* was named after a tall cow
of the *lmurran* we conquered that time.
And we filled the homestead with cows.
Oh that tall cow (that warrior's name),

he filled the homestead with cows.
(Samburu praise song)

Heroes. Necessary sense-making.

Acknowledgements

This paper and the ethnographic field notes it contains are based on my doctoral work funded by Fulbright I.I.E. and the University of Michigan, individual research projects funded by Western Michigan University, and my interviews conducted during collaborative research with Jon Holtzman generously funded by Western Michigan University Faculty Research and Creative Activities Award and National Science Foundation Senior Research Grant #0413431.

Note

1. *Lmurran* is the Samburu plural for what can be roughly translated as "warrior." Samburu initiate young men into this status with public circumcision ceremonies, typically when they are in their teens or twenties. Once initiated, *lmurran* are collectively responsible for dangerous long-distance herding and protecting the communities people and herds. For Samburu, belonging to the *lmurran* is a glamorous status.

–5–

Sleeping with One Eye Open

Kristen Drybread

The Center for Resocialization of Minors (C.R.M.) is an all-male juvenile detention facility in one of the smallest states of northeastern Brazil. From the highway connecting the local airport to the city center, the facility looks innocuous – it could pass for a clinic, an accounting firm, or a real estate office. Most passers by have no idea that the complex immediately behind the nondescript office building they see from the road houses males aged 12–20 who have been judged guilty of committing violent acts against human life. I first visited the institution one morning in August of 2000, on a private tour arranged by a sociology professor from a nearby university.

On the day of my tour, everyone at the C.R.M. was on his best behavior. In fact, the inmates made such a good impression that after spending three hours inside of the facility, I ended my visit with the feeling that a stay at the C.R.M. was comparable to a summer away at camp – sometimes annoying or sad, other times grueling or lonely, but mostly rather pleasant. Only the behavior of my tour guide suggested that the C.R.M. might be something other than the utopia it seemed.

The tour was led by a brusque and patronizing psychologist whose behavior towards me – and towards the inmates she allowed me to meet – suggested that the adults involved in the administration of the C.R.M. were fearsome and unscrupulous and not particularly concerned with the wellbeing of their charges. I will call her M.[1] A short bulldog of a woman with fierce hazel eyes, she introduced some of the important lessons I would learn about violence inside of the institution. But, I only realized this years later – and after more than nine months of continuous fieldwork inside the C.R.M.

A Glimpse of Evil

"We need to start here," M. told me as she led me from the waiting room into her dimly lit and sparsely furnished office. "Everything you need to know about the minors and the C.R.M. is in our paperwork." I looked at her skeptically – a look that she interpreted as disappointment. "Don't worry," she told me with a chuckle, "I'll show you the inside where we keep the minors, but this," she pointed to her office, "this is where all of the work is." A haphazard stack of mildewing, hand-written folders covered the psychologist's enormous desk. It was the twenty-first century and she worked in a state-run institution, yet all of M.'s paperwork – and all of the institution's documents – were handwritten on a motley assortment of paper staff members had been able to find and secure for use. Resources in the C.R.M. were scarce and paper, like all other materials necessary for the proper functioning of the detention facility, was hard to come by. Yet, M. did not spare its use on my account. Throughout my tour she had a small pile of assorted gray, white, and yellowed sheets in her hand on which she wrote for me an outline of the institution's procedures: research notes, she called them. They were to prevent me from leaving the institution with misinformation. "It is very important to docu-ment things correctly." M. insisted, against my suggestion that she not waste valu-able paper on my account. "Documentation is the most important thing we have in this place; it helps you see the history and the facts of each case. And it is the prin-cipal point of access we have to the minors."

At the C.R.M., relationships between prisoners and the staff members charged with their reformation and evaluation were mediated by the information contained in case files. Most of the men and women hired to "accompany the progress" of C.R.M. inmates rarely made face-to-face contact with the teens. Other than quar-terly interviews conducted in the presence of security guards and special inquests called when breaches in security arose, the "technical team" (the staff of psychol-ogists, social workers, security guards, nurses, teachers and administrators) of the institution did not come into direct contact with the inmates; they got to know the interned through the information contained in individual case files. M. had selected the most logical place to begin a staff-led tour of the facility by intro-ducing me first to this documentation. At the time, I did not know this and thought it rather strange – and annoying – that M. and I spent nearly half of my brief tour looking through the documentation of a few select inmates. She was introducing me to the institution as she would any person with academic credentials; I thought she was wasting my time – or, worse, trying to deliberately intimidate me by showing me folder after folder with the word HOMICIDIO printed boldly on its cover.

In M.'s office, I read about the infractions inmates had committed, the injuries they had suffered and the diseases they had contracted. I read about their family relation-ships and almost non-existent academic histories. And I read the conclusions that the "technical team" of the C.R.M. had drawn about the potential of each inmate for "resocialization." Not one of the inmates I read about that day was considered to have any potential at all.

"This is how you should get to know the boys," M. instructed, waving a handful of files over her head. "One of these files will tell you the minor's past, present, and probably his future. It's all in here," she said, thrusting a file at me. "Here. Everything you need to know about this one is right here in your hands." As I looked through the mildewing gray folder with a name, file number, and infraction (armed robbery) written on the front in blood-red ink, M. decided I should take the file home with me. "You take it to show everyone in your country how we take care of our kids." She insisted, "If it stays here, it will just be thrown in the archives. The minor is already dead. Take his file. It will help me show the world all of the work we do here."

I looked at the grim pile of papers in my hands and thought of telling M. that it would be better if I left them behind; no one in the U.S. (or in Brazil, for that matter) would be impressed by a stack of mildewing, handwritten notes. However, I kept my mouth shut and obediently took hold of the papers. I did not want to do anything that could be read as disparaging of her work – especially since I had just met her and sensed that her impression of me would determine how much of the institution she was willing to let me see.

M. seemed satisfied with my response. "Let's go inside before it gets to be lunch time," she barked, signaling for me to follow her out of the room. I obeyed. I put the file in my bag, along with the "research notes" she had prepared for me and trailed her though the thick blue iron door a beefy young man wearing an incredibly wrinkled cotton shirt, at least two sizes too small for his unnaturally muscular frame opened for us. (This young man, G., stood – actually, leaned – apathetically against the hallway wall unlocking, opening, closing, and relocking the door all day long in response to entreaties of staff members on either side to open the only passageway leading from the yard into the administration building. He constituted the institution's maximum-security measures, since he was much more difficult to get by than the twenty-foot retaining wall surrounding the inner complex.) I thanked the gatekeeper as we walked past, feeling slightly intimidated by his sheer bulk. He shook his head in bored amusement and bolted the door behind M. and me.

My "tour" of the inside of the facility did not extend 100 feet beyond the *portão*, the blue iron door. When we entered, M. walked me straight to the large mango tree just inside the gate. It was surrounded by a circle of concrete that served as a cool bench for the handful of adolescents and Monitors (security guards), willing to endure biting fire ants for the institution's only public seat in the shade. A small crowd drew around us. Other than the four who came from "watching" a broken television under the pavilion in front of the dining hall, the teens came from inside the 14 small houses arranged in a circle around the perimeter of the yard. "This is an American visitor," M. announced. "She has come to study how lucky you are. In her country adolescents like you all are given the death penalty." She turned to me with a look that was, I was sure, intended to elicit my coerced confirmation. "Isn't that right? Haven't they given the death penalty to kids as young as ten in the U.S.?" I didn't have time to respond to her questions. "You all don't know how lucky you are," she told the guys gathered around us. "In her country you would be treated like adults and would be in prison for life. Or you would get the death penalty – talk to her. She will tell you how lucky you are. She is here to see how good you have it so that she can go back to her country and tell them all about the work we do for you here."

The guys were curious. They wanted to know if M. was telling them the truth. They also wanted to verify the myths they had heard about conditions in the U.S. and to learn more about the lives of North Americans – particularly mine. Questions flew at me from all sides:

"They really have the death penalty in your country?"

"Do they give the death penalty to adolescents?"

"Do all people in your country have blue eyes, like you?"

"Does every one in the U.S. eat hamburgers and McDonald's all the time?"

"Do you have a boyfriend?"

"Do they give little kids the death penalty for stealing food?"

"Do you live where all the movie stars do?"

"Have you ever made love to a Brazilian?"

"Kids don't go hungry in your country, do they?"

"Have you ever seen Michael Jackson?"

"Do they have *favelas* where you live?"

Each one of the guys wanted to know something. I was bewildered by the onslaught of questions and by all of the hands wanting to touch the two roller ball pens I held along with my notebook (which M. forbid me to write in – she wanted to compose my research notes herself). I was speechless.

"Yes," M. answered for me. "It's all true. And don't let them touch your pens or you will never get them back," she snapped at me. "They use them to draw on each other." I think I nodded. I know that I clutched my notebook to my chest and just stared. I felt like I had suddenly become a curiosity on display at some sort of human exhibition and I didn't know who or what to focus on to settle the swirl of attention. M. chuckled at my discomposure, reading it as nervousness. "They don't see many women here," she whispered menacingly. "Be careful. Some of them are rapists. Most are killers. You wouldn't want any of them to get too close." She repeated with dramatic emphasis, "Be careful. Be very careful."

Lightening her tone and raising her voice she added, "But don't be afraid. Don't worry; they won't do anything to you while I'm here. They all like me. Isn't that right?" M. demanded of the boys surrounding us. Predictably, they nodded.

I wasn't convinced: I did not find her a likeable person and thought that the gruffness with which she treated the guys probably did not win her their endearment either. And I wasn't worried. Blinded by my assumptions that juvenile detention centers were, the world over, full of kids who had committed minor infractions like shoplifting or excessive truancy and convinced that the personable young men in front of me could not be the evil monsters M. suggested they were, I did not feel fear. What I felt during my tour with M. was awkward: overwhelmed by all of the attention I was receiving, and uncomfortable with the psychologist's unmistakable efforts to manipulate and to intimidate me.

The inmates did not scare or even disconcert me. Unlike M., they were not openly rude or threatening; their inquiries were rife with curiosity, not danger. Even the questions put to me anonymously from the crowd about my sexual availability struck me as benign: "Do you have a boyfriend?" "Have you ever made love to a Brazilian?" These were among the first questions asked by every Brazilian man or woman I met. Hearing them posed within the context of the C.R.M. did not alter their meaning – to me at least. The discomfort M. detected had less to do with the questions I was being asked than with the uses she was making of my presence at the C.R.M. Against my will, she was using me to cajole and to frighten inmates. I did not like this. Nor did I like M. I did not trust her while in her presence I felt a nasty foreboding that put me on constant edge.

The end of my tour brought with it a sensation of enormous relief. Freedom from M.'s coercion and pushiness made me feel like I had narrowly escaped danger. I wondered if everyone who worked at the C.R.M. was as menacing, manipulative and arrogant as she? I hoped, for the sake of the inmates, they were not.

The following day, I spoke to the sociology professor who had arranged the visit and told her that even though I was grateful for the tour, I hoped I would never encounter M. again.

Not Quite Welcome

Despite my misgivings about M. (or perhaps because of them), I returned to the C.R.M. eighteen months later to study daily life in the institution. I had not planned to conduct extensive ethnographic research inside the facility but on the second day of my second trip to northeastern Brazil, I serendipitously accompanied a friend to the office of the State Secretary of Justice, the man in charge of administrating all the penal facilities in the state – including the C.R.M. Curious, he asked me what I was doing in Brazil. I explained that I was conducting research on the discourses and practices of adults who have selected to work with Brazilian "children at risk." He suggested an alternative project: that I study the workings of the C.R.M. and the lives of its inmates. To launch this suggested project, he gave me a *carte blanche* to the detention center.

The following day, after reading the Secretary's letter, E., the director of the C.R.M., simply told the beefy man in charge of unlocking, opening, and (re)locking the *portão* that he was to let me pass whenever I wanted to, from that moment forward. The director set no parameters to my movements or activities within the prison yard; he simply suggested that I speak with R., the staff social worker who occasionally directed research for the senior thesis projects of sociology students from the local university. To my great relief, M. had been dismissed from the C.R.M. for striking an inmate only a few days after taking me on a tour of the facility and no one took it upon himself or herself to replace her as my guide.

Part of me wanted to take advantage of the fact that not a single staff member had demonstrated interest in me or my work; I wanted to enter the yard immediately to see if I could negotiate research inside without the assistance of the institution's authorities. But, I didn't want to alienate adults whom I might have wanted to call on later for information or support, so I followed E.'s advice: before I entered the C.R.M. yard for the second time, I sought out R. After meeting me and hearing me explain how and why I was embarking upon research inside the C.R.M., he offered me full access to the institution's archives, suggesting that the "truth" about each inmate could be found in his case file. Echoing M. he told me, "It's not necessary to expose yourself to the dangers of the yard, especially since most of the inmates are manipulative and dishonest. If you want to know the truth about them you need to read their evaluations. These represent the truth – the professional assessment of the technical team."

I thanked R. for his offer and agreed that it would be interesting to later explore the inmates' case files. However, I insisted that I would like to become familiar with the stories of the various inmates by talking to the inmates themselves. "You won't learn anything of value from them," R. warned. I told him I was willing to take that risk. Realizing that I was set upon dialog with the inmates, he next suggested that I administer my surveys from inside the Room of Reflection, the former punishment cell that had recently been converted into a storage closet. Having only dealt with sociologists and social workers conducting quantitative research, he assumed that my investigation would involve the speedy administration of surveys or questionnaires.

I was given two days two draft a list of questions that I would like to ask of inmates. With so little experience inside of penal institutions in general and inside of the C.R.M. in particular, I struggled to compile a generic list of queries. R. did not hide his amusement when he read my list. " You sure you don't want to begin with the files?" he asked.

Again I refused. So, R. took me and my questions to the Room of Reflection and gave an announcement to those in earshot, "Kris is an American. She will be inside of the Room of Reflection to ask those of you who want to talk to her some questions. It's an interview." With that, he left me alone.

In the course of the next nine days, only four inmates approached me. I was later told that this was because the rest generally suspected I was somehow affiliated with M.

"When she came back the first time," N., a short and stocky 17-year-old with 10 tattoos and 4 murder convictions, told L. and the group he had called them together to introduce them to the tiny 14-year-old from his neighborhood who had just been sentenced to detention for armed robbery, "I thought she was going to take that crazy psychologist's place. I thought they were like this." He raised his right hand, holding his stubby index and middle fingers tightly together. The group laughed – my negative opinion of M. was by then well known.

"But it wasn't just that," J., his equally imposing friend, added. "It was also because she used to call us into The Room of Reflection for interviews – just like the psychologists and social workers inside the administration [building]."

"Yeah, we all thought you were one of them," Wilson agreed. "That's why we never went. They suck. It's not that all of them are bad, but you can't get near them. You can't talk about just anything, what's on your mind. If you talk too much they'll use what you say against you."

N. agreed. "The subjects we touch on with you, we couldn't touch with them."

"That's because I am here to learn about your lives, not to evaluate you, " I said. "It's a different thing."

"Now. But it didn't seem that way when you started," Wilson responded. The group laughed. With a bit of effort, so did I.

I wanted to forget the two weeks I had spent in The Room of Reflection at the beginning of my research inside of the C.R.M. – in part because it was such an enormous waste of my time, but also because it reminded me of the only time I had felt real fear while inside of the institution. (I will return to this fear later.)

Thankfully, this uncomfortable stage of my research was short lived. A new and much more rewarding phase began shortly after, when I returned from an unplanned, extended hiatus: I spent two weeks in the hospital. After my release, I came back to the institution with concrete questions about the place of violence in the everyday lives of inmates and their families, a reinvigorated resolve to learn about the inmates' lives, a reputation among them for integrity, and a mark that earned me status among – and a measure of solidarity with – them: the scar from a nearly-fatal knife wound.

A Stab of Insight

While hospitalized I learned that confinement in a "high-security" penal institution does not mean isolation from external networks of information. Sometimes inmates know more about the sagas unfolding outside of their prison house than they know of the conflicts brewing within. And, conversely, mothers, lovers and friends of prisoners oftentimes know more about the dramas inside of penal institutions than do the inmates themselves. Words move with relative freedom through prison walls – including those of the C.R.M. So, before I had a chance to tell them about it myself, the institution's inmates knew that I had been knifed. And, as they told the story among themselves, they supplied me with the reputation of a badass.

My wounding was not nearly as glamorous as the stories that were invented by the boys about it. On the Sunday prior to what was to be my third week of research at the institution, I suffered a knife wound while buying groceries at the supermarket. Passing by the supermarket's display of knives, I remembered that I had been intending to buy one I could reserve for cutting non-meat items (I am a vegetarian and was living with a carnivore). Single serrated kitchen knives are commonly sold without packaging in Brazil; if a customer wants to buy a prepackaged knife she must by a set of three. Since I only needed one knife for vegetables, I included a single one to my basket without reflecting too much on the potential hazards it posed. I assumed that the store would not sell unpackaged knives if they presented a significant danger to customers. The supermarket checker presumably did not consider the knife a particularly threatening object either, because he put it in a white plastic sack without covering the blade – as store policy requires he should. He treated it as any other innocuous item for sale at the grocery.

I only began to realize how dangerous a table knife is when I suddenly felt a warm, wet sensation in the region of my appendix as I picked up my bags and began to exit the supermarket. I looked down to see that the simple act of walking had set my grocery bags in motion, and that with the momentum created by one or two steps, the bags had swung against my stomach, providing the knife blade with enough force to pass through the layers of skin and muscle that make up my abdomen. The handle of the knife was sticking out of my midsection, but the blade was nowhere to be seen. Blood and blubbery white tissue – intestines? – were sneaking out of the sides of the wound, pooling around the handle of the knife. I pulled the weapon out in a panic, sure that I was soon to die.

Fortunately, I survived – but with no thanks to the supermarket which refused to assist me, or the private hospitals, which refused to accept my medical insurance. I was saved by an emergency operation performed at the State-funded hospital, generally reserved for the indigent. Following surgery, I was held in the hospital for several days of monitored recovery. The hospital was unbearably hot, dangerously overcrowded and in a dubious state of hygiene. It rang with the cries of relatives whose loved ones had recently departed. Its corridors were filled with patients forced to lie on the hallway floors because no spaces remained in the bedrooms and the hospital did not have enough mattresses to go around. I was lucky: my condition was sufficiently dire to qualify me for a mattress. It was not, however, severe enough to earn me a permanent bed inside a recovery room. I was placed on a rolling cot in the hallway of a female ward, where fresh air and hospital visitors were able to circulate freely around me.

I was not the victim of a teenaged mugger or a potential rapist but the hospital records hanging above my bed did not say this. They told the story of the wound itself, not of its cause. So, the visitors who read about the treatment of the knife wound in my hospital charts all drew their own conclusions – or, rather, causes; they invented the story of the wounding for themselves. Female strangers who dared to speak to me about the wound assumed that it was the outcome of a domestic skirmish and urged me to forgive the boyfriend or husband they imagined to have inflicted the wound. Most men assumed that I was the hapless victim of a purse snatching and urged me to use more caution. Though none of them ever spoke to me in the hospital, the relatives of the inmates of the C.R.M. must have imagined that my wound was the outcome of a run in with outlaws in which I was strong and savvy enough to have escaped, but tough enough to have confronted danger. This is the story that arrived at the C.R.M. In the eyes of its inmates, the three-inch scar on my abdomen was a mark of confrontation – of fearlessness and attempted self-defense. No matter how many times I told them about the events that actually led to my scar they refused to believe my story. They insisted that the stories they – or their family members – had concocted possessed greater truth-value.

Having survived a knife wound and experienced the pain, fear, and adrenaline rush of a confrontation with death gave me status among the inmates. It also gave us an impetus to talk about danger, suffering and survival; for the first few days following my return to the institution to continue research, we all sat around the prison yard telling each other the stories of our scars.

Going Inside

When I resumed my daily visits to the institution, both R. and E. had been released from their positions. Under the new director, B., my place within the C.R.M. was tacitly, yet resolutely, (re)defined. For reasons that were never made explicit to me, I was told that I was now to stay inside the prison yard with the inmates, and out of the Administrative building. No longer was I allowed to take my lunch with the "technical team," eating a well-seasoned meal from glass plates and using silverware. Instead, I was told to eat with the boys, in the yard, using whatever plastic or paper container I could find to hold my food (usually something well used and borrowed from one of the inmates). As it was located inside of the administrative building, I was forbidden to use the institution's only female restroom and had to either go home or crouch above the filthy toilet in the Security office whenever I had to pee. Even though it was accessible from the yard, I was forbidden to enter the Room of Reflection, a place now reserved for those with "technical" qualifications.

The more time I spent inside of the C.R.M., the more I seemed to be identified as one of the inmates. When I walked through the administrative building on my way to or from the yard, conversation stopped – as though staff conversations were unfit for my ears. At holiday parties and presentations, I was made to sit with the inmates. My American money trumped my outsider status in that I was still asked to contribute to purchasing party snacks and favors; nevertheless, I was now also included on the list of incarcerated recipients "deserving" of holiday treats. With increasing frequency, I was lectured and punished as if I were one of the boys every time a minor disciplinary infraction occurred, or was rumored to be in the works inside of the institution. Every day I spent at the C.R.M., I was treated more and more like a criminal.

And, every day I spent at the C.R.M., I became less and less innocent. Although I never participated in a criminal act while conducting research at the institution, I became increasingly aware of – and enmeshed in – the illicit activities that structure relations within the prison yard. In order to establish my own place as an independent and trustworthy observer within the C.R.M., I was required to make a decision: I had to choose whether or not to report the minor crimes I witnessed inside of the compound to the institution's authorities. I decided to keep my mouth shut. I silently witnessed activities like drug deals, prostitution and the hatching of escape plots, all the while struggling with my conscience and with my desire to question the inmates as to the wisdom, safety and ethics of their actions.

The boys very purposefully put on displays of rule breaking and criminality in front of me to test my ability to keep my mouth shut. The infractions I was made to witness were relatively minor and would not have led to excessive punishments had I squealed, precisely because the boys did not know whether I would nark on them or not. By silently witnessing minor crimes, I established myself as a *chegada*, a woman who could be reasonably trusted.

Cabuetagem, or narking, is an offense punishable by death inside of the C.R.M. During the period of my research, inmates staged upwards of six rebellions and put to death seven of their peers for disrespecting the unwritten code of silence that permits them to establish and enforce their own hierarchies, codes of conduct, disciplinary procedures, and economic relations within the institution. Stepping inside the yard of C.R.M. is a bit like visiting the island in *Lord of the Flies*. The boys are in a constant struggle for power and they fight according to their own rules; dominant society's normative expectations and regulations do not govern conduct within the institution – unless someone squeals, thereby inviting adult authority to assume control in a particular situation. In order to gain the confidence of the inmates, I had to demonstrate that I respected *their* rules and would not seek the intervention of adult authorities if they broke institutional regulations. Hence, I was put through a series of minor trials in order to prove that I could keep my mouth shut. As I passed each test, I was made aware that I was being assessed and that, through my behavior, I was gaining their confidence and respect. I used these moments of spoken evaluation to communicate to the boys that I would not release information that joints were being sold clandestinely throughout the institution and would not reveal to authorities that guards regularly arranged girls to make "intimate" visits with inmates in exchange for a fee – authorities suspected that both activities were occurring but had no concrete proof. I assured the inmates that I would not turn my observations or their words over to authorities as evidence to be used against them – even if I did not personally condone their actions. I also assured inmates that I would not pass on the rumors I heard brewing in the institution about possible escape attempts and fights – guards were paid to collect and disseminate such information. However, I also told the inmates that could not lie about observed acts of physical violence; if someone was attacked in my presence, I would have to bear witness. Hence, I only ever saw one inmate get hit by his peers during the entire time I was in the institution and his beating was a disciplinary measure taken by inmates who (wrongly) accused him of stealing from me.

I always brought my bag with me into the yard of the C.R.M. At first, this was because I wanted to have my notebook and sound recording device with me in case I needed either one of them for my research. In time, the practice took on an additional purpose. Staff members lock their belongings away before entering the yard because they consider the boys to be inveterate criminals; they are certain that to enter the yard with a bag is to invite theft. After receiving several suggestions from staff members to guard my belongings in the administrative building, I realized that I was the only adult who brought anything with her into the prison yard. From that moment of epiphany on, I began deliberately to carry my bag in the yard with me as a display of trust. By entering the yard with my bag, I hoped to demonstrate to the boys that I did not presume their criminality. It was my way of allowing our encounter to begin with the presumed trust that underlies – and perhaps makes possible – friendly relationships between equals.

My bag became an incredibly important symbol in the institution. Each day inmates would ritually take their turn looking through its contents, commenting upon the items that had been included or excluded from one day to the next. Some of the boys told me that they felt proud when they were looking though my bag; it was the only experience they had ever had of feeling trusted. One day I entered the institution with R$25. A few hours later I was called into the administrative building and asked to make a contribution to a party that was being planned for the inmates; I gave R$5. When I returned to the yard with my bag, the absence of R$5 was noticed. Without consulting me, the boys decided that the money had been stolen and that the thief had to be punished. While I was sitting on the porch of one of the dorms talking to a new inmate, a group of boys brought the individual they decided was the culprit over and put on a visible demonstration of punishing him in front of me. As soon as I was able to understand what was going on I put a stop to the beating and explained the reason for the missing money. With my prompting, the aggressors apologized to their victim. However, they insisted that, as far as they were concerned the beating had been necessary. "Now everyone knows what will happen if they disrespect you," J., one of the punishers, explained.

I wish that the beating had never happened. However, it would be dishonest to – by omission – pretend that it never took place. It did. And it was a meaningful event – principally because it was both so common and, yet, so extraordinary.

Perceived Dangers

Official records show that fights and beatings take place daily within the C.R.M. The institution's incident log reads like a detailed description of a street brawl: beatings, broken bones, severed limbs – blood, anger, revenge. Despite all of the reported violence inside of the C.R.M., during the nine months I was allowed to freely enter the yard, I only witnessed this one act of physical aggression. Several rebellions – a few of which were fatal – occurred while I was conducting field-work, but I was not present at a single one; they always took place on the days I was working at one of my secondary research sites (the juvenile court, for example). Hence, it was difficult for me to reconcile the violence I heard about with my experiences in the institution. Perhaps this explains why the one beating I witnessed became so significant to me: it proved to me that the violence I had always heard about inside of the institution was real and that the fact that it never occurred when I was in the institution was remarkable.

The fight also confirmed what the guards who policed the interior of the C.R.M. had been telling me since a few weeks after my return from the hospital: without deliberately setting out to alter the institution, I somehow intervened to make it less violent – at least temporarily.

"Our job has been a whole lot easier since you came," P., the head monitor was fond of telling me. He and his team of ten men were responsible for preventing escapes, controlling violence between inmates and maintaining order within the yard of the C.R.M. Unlike administrators, they were in constant daily contact with the institution's inmates. And, unlike administrators, they seemed to genuinely appreciate my presence inside of the C.R.M. Between his questions about women and beer in the United States, P. repeatedly marveled at the calming effect my presence seemed to have on life inside of the C.R.M. "None of them would dream of doing something while you're in here. They wouldn't want to do something that would hurt you or get you kicked out; the others would kill anyone who did."

P. was in his early thirties and had been a guard at the C.R.M. for nearly 10 years. He had been the most senior monitor on duty the night the first inmate was murdered inside of the C.R.M. and he had witnessed the vast majority of the rebellions and murders that subsequently took place inside the facility. When I first began my research, P. had treated me with cold reservation; he flatly told me that he feared my presence would be the catalyst for jealous rivalries between sex-starved young inmates, vying for my attention. "But," he later admitted, "once I realized you weren't responding to their songs [their advances] and weren't letting them intimidate you, I started to see that they liked having you in here because you treat them like normal people. You talk to them like they are humans. When you're around, when you're here, they're not just criminals. It's good for them. And it's much easier for us too. When you're here we can relax – a bit. The place just feels safer."

Administrators, who rarely – if ever – entered the yard, did not share P.'s point of view. Nine months into my research at the institution, they suddenly decided to block my access to the yard of the C.R.M., claiming that it was a measure taken for my own protection. "Those kids are dangerous," the woman who informed me that my access was being terminated explained. "You think you are safe but you never know when they are going to turn on you. They could take you hostage. They could rape you. We can't let that happen. It would be an international scandal. So, we can't allow you unlimited access any longer. Your research is over."

She politely told me that I could return to ask administrators questions and to interview them – at their convenience (a polite way of warning me that I would be turned away if I showed up at the door of the C.R.M. again). When I asked her how she and the other administrators suddenly came to the conclusion that I was in personal danger after having passed nine months inside of the institution, in close contact with the inmates and without ever having been publicly threatened or endangered, she simply replied, "You have been here long enough. You have seen all you need to see. Your presence inside is dangerous." After a brief pause she added – in what seemed to me to be an afterthought, "There's always the threat of rape."

Threats

Anyone who knows *anything* about life inside of Brazilian prisons would know that rape is one of the least possible dangers faced by a woman inside of a male penal institution. One of the key tenants of the unwritten code of conduct among Brazilian convicts is that rape (of a woman) is an unpardonable offense, punishable by sodomy and summary execution. In most Brazilian correctional facilities, administrators have taken to secluding convicted rapists in special, secure wings, in order to prevent other convicts from enforcing the extrajudicial punishments demanded by their own codes of honor. The C.R.M. is no exception. Imagining themselves as hardened criminals and the C.R.M. as a prison, the inmates have internalized the rules of conduct within adult prisons and unanimously maintain that, "The destiny of a rapist is to get fucked and dance" – the latter a polite way of saying "to die." Boys sentenced to confinement in the C.R.M. for having committed acts of rape are either secluded from other prisoners, or strict secrecy and

silence are maintained about their actual infractions by juvenile justice profes-
sionals who encourage teens convicted of rape to manufacture alternate explanations when telling peers about the acts which lead to their internment. Word of a
rape conviction would mean death.

Being taken hostage, suffering injury in a rebellion, falling victim to theft: all of
these were possible, but unlikely, hazards I admittedly faced each time I entered
the C.R.M. Rape, however, was not a danger. Despite the fact that I periodically
received love notes and invitations to "feel what it's like to *trepar com um
bandido*" (fuck a gangster), I was always able to deflect such overtures with candor
or laughter – as the situation required. The boys outwardly respected my "no." It
was quite likely that several inmates *thought* about having sex with me, but I firmly
believed that that there was not a single one who would have actually raped me.
And even *if* an inmate had entertained the thought of rape, I was certain that he
would not have hazarded it inside the C.R.M.; to rape a woman in the institution
would have meant death – and all of the inmates knew it.

I learned this crucial bit of information for myself in the middle of my second
week of research at the C.R.M. (only days before the knife incident). L., one of the
four inmates who agreed to speak with me in the Room of Reflection, interrupted
our interview in order to make a sexual proposal. His first proposition was verbal,
direct and not overtly offensive. I politely said, "no." A second proposition immediately followed; it was more brazen in every way. Again, I refused. With his third
proposition, the physically intimidating seventeen year-old began to use his size as
a means of influence: he rose from his chair and began to round the desk that separated us. I, too, stood and repositioned myself so that the table was again between
us. I also made my way towards the door of the Room of Reflection, knowing that
his advances would be checked by the presence of other inmates – and of course
– the guards. As soon as I came within reach of the door, I pushed the table towards
L., hoping to pin him against the opposing wall as I lunged for the doorknob.
Unfortunately, the door was locked from the outside.

A small garden separated the door into the Room of Reflection from the gate
leading into the prison yard. R. had directed a guard to remain in the garden,
outside the unlocked (in theory) door, in case an inmate who had come into the
Room of Reflection for an interview threatened me. Feeling threatened by L., and
realizing that I was unable to open the door myself, I called for the guard. He did
not respond.

L. seemed unconcerned by my cries to the guard for help. It was as if he were
confident that no one would answer my request. He made his fourth proposition,
this time attempting to sweeten it with a caress. I slapped his hand away from my
face with my left hand and gave him a hard smack on the cheek with my right.
"Stay away from me," I warned, not quite sure that my voice was unwavering
enough to demonstrate the courage and resolve I wanted it to. Grabbing my shoulders and shoving me against the wall, L. made his fifth proposition, ending it with

a kiss on my cheek. I responded with a fist to his solar plexus and a knee to his groin. Lying on the floor, gasping for breath and clasping his pain, L. yelled, "Open the door for this bitch." A key immediately turned in the lock. I left the Room of Reflection in a hurry. I did, however, notice the guard who was supposed to be on duty standing in the garden, with his arms crossed over his chest and a big smile on his face.

Months later I learned that the guard had been paid to lock L. and I inside the Room of Reflection. L. himself confessed that he had given the guard R$20 (about $7) in the hopes that I would agree to giving him sexual gratification in lieu of his granting me an interview. (Allegedly, one or two of the female members of the C.R.M.'s "technical team" had been known to accept similar offers from L. and other inmates.) In the midst of a lengthy apology for the incident L. said, "I want you to know that, in no way, would I have raped you. I know that I touched you and that I probably scared you, but you have to believe that I wouldn't have raped you."

If L. had told me this at the moment of the incident, there is no way I would have believed him. I had felt like I was about to be violated. I had been afraid. However, by the time L. worked up the courage to apologize, I had spent enough time in the C.R.M. to know that he was not likely to have raped me. Not only would he have been afraid of the punishments his fellow prisoners would have piled upon him – he would have also know that (unbeknownst to me at the time) I was under the protection of the most feared group of inmates inside of the C.R.M. They were five young men who saw in my project to collect their stories the promise of immortality – they would have, one of them assured me, killed L. if he had driven me away. Thankfully, L. was aware of this on the day he paid to be locked inside the Room of Reflection with me.

Given this experience, the administration's sudden concern that I was, after nine months of research, suddenly in danger of rape seemed to me nothing more than an excuse fabricated to remove me from the C.R.M. They wanted me to stop "snooping around," but they were not willing to say this outright. So, they invented a convenient excuse: rape.

Penetration and Prophylactics

Rape is about sex, but it is mostly about power. This case is no exception. When my permission to enter the C.R.M. was suspended by the administration, I went over their heads and obtained judicial authorization to continue my work, since the Judge of the local juvenile court had ultimate legal control over the facility and its inmates. He was responsible for the welfare of the inmates and the execution of their sentences, while the administration of the C.R.M. facilitated the execution of these sentences and maintained responsibility for inmate security (mainly for keeping inmates under lock and key). In cases of conflict between the two branches of power – the Judicial and Security – the Judge always had the last word. After listening to me explaining my research, its methods, progress, and goals, the Judge ordered the administrators of the C.R.M. to allow me to resume fieldwork at the institution.

In order to soften the blow to the authority of the institution's administrators that consent for my research constituted, the Judge allowed them to impose "necessary" security measures to protect the inmates and me during my research, without interfering in the research itself. The measure that the administration implemented was that of the "intimate search." The director of the institution rationalized the procedure as follows:

> To make sure you are not bringing in substances that are dangerous to your own safety or the safety of the institution, we have to do an intimate search. If you bring something illicit in it increases your danger of rape. We have to search you completely. The boys we have here – I don't know if you know what they've been involved in: rape, homicide, rape [*sic*], assault – everything that is evil. There are rapists being held here and we can't guarantee your safety. It would be an international scandal if you got raped in here and we said that we gave you permission to be alone with these boys when we already know what they're capable of. It would be better if you did not continue your research here. But, since you insist, we have to search you. The search is necessary for your own protection.

Even after a great deal of reflection I was unable to understand how someone searching the cavities of my body would protect me from (an imagined) rape. In my way of thinking, the procedure itself could be construed as an act of rape, since it was a forcible violation of (the "intimate" regions of) my body. As a security measure, it was completely absurd. As a technique of intimidation, however, it bordered on brilliance. Undoubtedly, it would have been highly effective if I considered a violation of my bodily integrity to be the most degrading insult I could possibly suffer; the proposed search would have led me to "voluntarily" terminate my study. However, the offense to my intelligence and to my work that the administration's hostile practices constituted was much more insulting to me than a latex-covered finger probing my vagina. I reasoned: this was the price I had to pay for penetrating too deeply into the inner life of the C.R.M.

The "security measures" implemented to control my visits to the C.R.M. were not about sex at all; they had to do with access to intimate information and the violation of privacy. My exclusion from the C.R.M. came directly after I refused to allow the C.R.M.'s "technical team" (its staff of psychologists and social workers) to listen to personal interviews I taped with some of the boys. The inmates granted me permission to tape life-history interviews because I promised that I would not let anyone else in the institution hear what they had allowed me to record. To surrender the recordings would have been a violation of their trust, and of their privacy – not to mention a violation of professional ethics. When the technical team called me in to demand to hear the recordings, I refused; I was punished. I was banned. When the judge overturned the ban, the intimate search was implemented, I presume to teach me that it is much less inconvenient to disrespect the privacy of the less powerful than to have the more powerful invade my own.

Research Motives

I frustrated and amazed C.R.M. administrators by braving five months of regular intimate searches (some more probing than others) in order to finish collecting the life histories of the inmates who had figured in my research within the prison yard. During this time I was repeatedly asked why I was willing to suffer the indignity and discomfort of the searches, when I could have easily fleshed-out the stories of individual inmates using information contained in their case files at the C.R.M. and at the juvenile court house. (My access to documents had never been restricted.) My immediate answer to this question was to insist that I needed to return to the C.R.M. to let inmates know that I had not forsaken them; I did not want people who had grown to trust me to think I had used them for information and discarded them as soon as I had gotten what I wanted for my research. I reasoned that it was necessary to return to the C.R.M. several times to make this message clear, since I was only allowed to speak to one inmate at a time, and many of the individuals I spoke with were unwilling to share such information with all of their peers.

My continued visits to the C.R.M. were also motivated by my readings of the legal and institutional case files of inmates I had not yet had a chance to formally interview. I found so many inconsistencies, omissions and blatant inaccuracies in official documents that I was unwilling to accept the files as my sole source of information. (For instance, one inmate was repeatedly cited as a participant in a murder that occurred inside of the C.R.M. on the second day of his third successful escape from the institution – an escape that lasted two weeks. If any member of the technical team had bothered to read the adolescent's entire case file, she would not have cited his participation in the murder as evidence of his inveterate criminality. But, since each evaluation relied upon the one immediately proceeding it to supply the personal and criminal history upon which the professional assessment of the adolescent's potential for reform was based, once written, the false charge attained the status of truth through its repetition.) Even if the inmates were fabricating or intentionally distorting events in their own life histories, as the staff of the C.R.M. alleged, their accounts had at least as much truth value as official records. Therefore, I considered interviews with individual inmates to be an important supplement to the latter.

Preserving what I considered to be the integrity of my research was not, however, my only reason for repeatedly returning to the detention center to speak with inmates. My primary motive was, I must admit, rather base: I was angry and wanted revenge. In the act of banning me from the C.R.M., administrators had turned the methods they used to maintain precarious control of the institution on me: they publicly silenced, ridiculed and disempowered me, while disseminating their fabricated narrative of my character and my actions as if it were an authoritative truth. Having become caught up in the routines, rituals and relationships that structure the institution, I fought back – unwittingly (perhaps) following the example of the inmates C.R.M. administrators seemed to identify me with.

In this way, my research itself became an act of deliberate aggression. Although I could try to cast myself as the hapless victim of a violently authoritarian institution, who was simply trying to maintain her own integrity and to do right by the subjects of her research by submitting to the imposed searches, I know that this is not how I saw myself at the time. I did not repeatedly return to the C.R.M. simply because I was a dutiful ethnographer. I returned because of my own desire to somehow fuck over those who would insist on penetrating me. Whatever contribution my research – the words you have just read included – might someday make to the field of anthropology, it will always also be act of revenge.

Note

1. Some names have been abbreviated.

–6–

A Hell of a Party

Brenda Maiale

When I awoke to a ringing phone close to noon that 15 February, I could not imagine standing ever again. I had had nights in Oaxaca in which I danced too much or drank too much and woke weary to face the ever-sunny day and vibrant good cheer of most Oaxaqueños. But that morning, even before my memory kicked in, my body remembered that the previous night had been unusual. Without rising I found the phone under a heap of beer-laden fiesta clothes. It was C.[1] I slowed his emphatic rapid-fire Spanish to hear, "Brenda, you are the host of the party. Send money for the *mayordomía* but don't come. F. says he will kill you on sight!" Yes, I recollected, it was actually the case that my field assistant had thrown a beer bottle at my head as a parting shot the night before.

Earlier the night before many questions raced through my mind as I scurried about looking for means to carry 150 sombreros, 300 plastic bowls, a stack of paper and plastic serving ware, and the bag of 200 hard rolls that I had spent the afternoon halving with a small serrated knife. I was dressed head-to-toe in the florally embroidered plush velvet dress of the Tehuana and was already drenched in sweat, although the temperature, like on most Oaxacan evenings, was in the cool lower 70s. I needed to make my way from my newly rented apartment on the second floor of an ancient house in the center of the *Mercado 20 de noviembre* in downtown Oaxaca City to the *Salón Abdiel* just three blocks away on Zaragoza street. The *Salón* was not far but it had not occurred to me that I might be making the trip alone. Why did it seem like such a good idea to host a party?

Cuéntame

F., who is a Zapotec from the Isthmus region of the state, had been my Spanish teacher years earlier and had become my research assistant and close friend during the first months of my fieldwork in Oaxaca beginning January 2002. I was originally researching cheesemakers in the region, who at the onset of my field-work I had believed were all women. However, the first cheesemakers F. brought me to interview were *muxe*. F. is *muxe,* as were many of F.'s friends. *Muxe* is a term among Zapotecs that describes men who define themselves as between traditional masculine and feminine gender and sexual roles. They are male bodied but exhibit dressing practices and behavioral characteristics of both genders: some dress entirely like women, some use only certain items of adornment that are considered locally to be feminine, some are quite feminine in comportment and some, like F., look quite masculine excepting certain gestural traits that are read as effeminate in Oaxaca. When I realized that *muxe* fulfilled not only work-related feminine roles, such as cheese-making, embroidering, and market-selling, but also feminine social and sexual roles, I became intrigued that the acceptance of *muxe*, effeminate men who have homosexual relations, was quite different from what I had expected in Mexico, a country that is reputed for its machismo.

I had thought F. had introduced me to the world of *muxe* coincidentally via his cheesemaking friends whom he initially brought me to interview. Over time, however, it became clear that he thought my project would do better to focus on *muxe* and better still to focus on him. As I accompanied F. during his drinking binges at the local cantinas midweek and fiestas come weekend, I began, subtly and informally, to align myself with his project. I had already aligned myself with F. in profound ways as he was one of the few Oaxaqueños who understood my then rudimentary Spanish. Although he taught me Spanish and Zapotec culture in the way a mother passes such to her child, with his shock of black curly hair and dark sense of humor, he reminded me of my father, and I was deeply attached to the familial structure of our relation. By summer I had switched topics formally to focus on *muxe* fiestas and gender transformations in the region more generally and planned a second year of fieldwork. In reorienting my project, F. was crucial in helping me to formulate questions. And, as he served as the president of *Vinnii Gaxheé*, a Zapotec organization of *muxe* in Oaxaca City that was established in 1999 to host fiestas and other social events, he would be my key informant.

For me that summer marked a transition from simply observing F.'s life to par-ticipating more fully in it. Although we had spent much time together, I had always excused myself when the evening wore into morning, when he sought men for sexual company and when his drunkenness turned aggressive. I realized, however, that *muxe* fiestas were part of a complex system of sociality formed largely through late-night conversations, sexual relationships and the exchange and shared consumption of beer. F.'s behavior provided key insights into the circuit of *muxe* social interaction, which had now become the focus of my research project. Therefore, in those moments I previously felt revealed too intimate arenas of F.'s life, I no longer excused myself to go home. I stayed late, I asked questions and, on occasion, out of concern for his wellbeing after so much beer, I intervened. I had a long-running joke with F. about his clumsiness, as he had frequently met me for language class sporting a black eye, bruised lip, sprained ankle and once a full-arm cast, which he had explained away as a result of poor coordination. I suspected that alcohol induced his tendency to accidents but I was later surprised to observe how often he was involved in physical altercations. I was especially disturbed when I began to participate in them. I thought I was a bystander, perhaps not innocent but at least rational.

F. too, on the surface, was rational, a charismatic and articulate person who like many Oaxaqueños relished double entendre and mastered the joking Spanish and Zapotec that marks a gifted orator. Talk then, which was cheap, could be turned into other things for someone as clever as F. On numerous occasions I saw him secure beer, sexual partners and fiesta sponsors by the insightful turn of a phrase. I also saw him use language as a weapon. The often initially oblivious targets of his vituperative attacks would smolder, unable to respond in kind. When they did respond, there was nothing kind about it. They often struck physically when they realized they were the butt of F.'s biting wit. For example, late one night at a taco stand on the corner near *La Chinampa* (one of Oaxaca's three gay bars), a man he had insulted earlier in the evening confronted us. F. wobbled off his stool and I stepped in front, hoping my presence and apology would calm matters. I missed most of the exchange but F.'s mention of the man's mother in such a setting was likely what prompted him to swing at me, landing a fist to my left cheek. When my vision cleared I spotted F. perched again on his red metal stool, adding salsa to his order. I returned to the stand and the taco vendor passed me a piece of ice for my eye. When I asked F. why he caused such trouble, his only reply, considering my plate, was, "If you're not going to eat those, pass them here." Clearly his life was such that a physical assault was no reason to let one's tacos get cold.

Two weeks later, however, we had to abandon a perfectly good platter of *barbacoa de borrego* when fleeing the ire of a local soccer club team. I had accompanied F. and his friend N. to a neighborhood restaurant on a Sunday noon after they arrived at my house that morning still out from the night before. I thought the meal would be restorative and always enjoyed a visit to Doña A.'s where the owner and waiting staff were friends of F. We were seated near a table of a dozen men in their soccer uniforms of bright yellow shirts and long socks. They had won an important early dawn game and had been celebrating for hours, drinking beer and mescal. They sent a round of mescal to our table, which F. insisted I consume, although for me it seemed too early morning. Drinking etiquette in Oaxaca was "either join in or leave." I was still unenthusiastically sipping the fiery pale yellow liquid when F. ordered me to sit with the soccer players who had invited me to join them. I protested but he insisted that my hesitance would be read as rudeness, so I took a seat at the end of their long table. They regaled me with the tale of that morning's victory, acting out the goals as each scorer in turn removed his jersey and did a triumphant circuit of the table. Their teammates applauded, but F. and N., who had continued to consume mescal and beer, made deriding comments about the physique of each shirtless player, humorously encouraging them to cover themselves so Doña A.'s patrons not lose their appetites.

The mood then noticeably worsened when F. called me back to the table for my meal. Some members of the soccer team said "no," that I was not yet going to return. They had had enough of F.'s bad manners. I stood and they stood blocking my passage. "Sit down" they encouraged; "relax, have another mescal." But I had lost my appetite – for mescal, for food, for all of it – as I dreaded a repeat of the taco-stand scene. Doña A. entered and suggested that I return to where my food was getting cold, deftly redirecting conversation to concerns about the men's wives and children. I quickly returned to F.'s side and encouraged a speedy departure. "Nonsense," he said, waving his hand across the table's bounty of roasted lamb, tortillas, and rice. In the meantime, Doña A. had retreated to her kitchen and the team again turned their attention to us. My name was yelled out and I looked up to see a yellow-shirted man fold the aluminum chair I had occupied and throw it into the cement wall aside the table. A momentary total silence was ended by the hurried goodbyes of all but three of the team members. I called N. aside and pleaded with him that we get F. and get out. But too late, I turned back to the table to see F. covered in blood; one of the soccer players who had approached in my absence had a fork sticking out from his shoulder. F. was then ready to leave and rushed by us to the door yelling "hurry, hurry." Thankfully the waiter, F.'s friend J., was observing the scene, and as we passed the inner iron door he closed and locked it behind us, securing the soccer players inside. He pushed us out into the street as I appealed that he return for my wallet and keys. In half a minute J. shoved my bag through the barred window and we fled into a nearby taxi. F. turned to me and jovially asked, "Where to?" Eyeing his blood-splattered shirt, I burst into tears. "Don't worry," he replied, "The stains will come out."

For me the stains never did come out but, remarkably, F. claimed to not remember these incidents. When I questioned his motives, his judgments, the ordinariness of these violent episodes, he claimed ignorance. He appealed to me as the anthropologist and storyteller. "*Cuénta me,*" he would plea, "You tell me." I spent hours trying to make sense of his story, the death of his mother when he was one month old, his complex sexuality, his addictions. My role in his life became one of biographer, as a receptacle of stories and memories of which he need not burden himself. But I was indeed burdened and began to advise that he drink less, choose safer sex partners and not mouth off to large drunken men. During the day he took my suggestions as the affection and concern I intended; late at night, he claimed I was interfering with his good times and that he did not need my intrusive surveillance. More and more he began to demand that I go home, get lost, leave him in peace. With just a few weeks of summer left till my return to the U.S., I began to rethink my plan to return in January for another year of fieldwork. Would F. as research assistant be any assistance at all?

Reciprocal Concerns

Before I reached any decision on the future of my fieldwork, J. called to tell me that F.'s father died suddenly of a heart attack. I immediately went to the language school where F. worked and the staff told me that he had departed already for his family home in the Isthmus. He phoned me later that afternoon and I asked what could I do. Please come, he replied, so I took a late night bus and some Dramamine to make the seven-hour winding journey though the Sierra Madre del Sur to the coastal plain. I had previously met several members of his family in Oaxaca City and we had developed a warm relationship. Most of F.'s family had no prior contact with foreigners, thus my presence in the compound served as an odd but pleasant distraction to their shocked grief. I spent nearly a month with the family per-forming the mandatory funerary rites and rituals. I helped prepare and serve food to the numerous guests who arrived during the first days, attended evening prayer vigils, and made frequent morning trips to the cemetery to bring flowers and care for the gravesite. Though F. had returned to work in Oaxaca City, I stayed on and was incorporated into the family as F.'s *marida* (spouse) and affectionately referred to as *nuera* or *cuñada* (daughter or sister-in-law).

At the time I thought my integration into a Zapotec family was a critical move in my fieldwork from outsider to insider that I could then participate and observe from an embedded subject position. Perhaps this was true, but F. was not nearly as pleased with my role as his fictive spouse – that I was a well-educated American who was his faithful companion was on the one hand a source of pride for him; that I was a woman was an increasingly disturbing source of ambivalence and repressed anger. His mother's early death and his father's remarriage made him feel already like fictive kin in his own family, an insecurity I shared as an adoptee. Moreover, although his sexual preference was clear, custom in his home required that he present his lovers as "nephews" (*sobrinos*). His family clearly understood these men were neither affinal nor blood relatives but the terminology elided the sexual nature of the relations. The story became even murkier when I, as a female consort, threatened to mark him as heterosexual. As his family began to confide in me their concern for F.'s emotional instability and anxiety about his recklessness when drunk, he began to intervene in my relationships with the intention of alien-ating me from his family.

I returned to Oaxaca City just days before my return to the U.S. and was quite surprised that F. wanted to meet to discuss my future plans. I thought he was going to tell me that I should find another field assistant but he had a different proposi-tion. He was asked to serve as *mayordomo* (host) of one of the largest *muxe* fiestas held each year in February. Did I want to cosponsor the event? He suggested that by serving as *co-mayordoma* I would have first-hand access to the planning and preparation of the fiesta, as well as entry to the circle of reciprocity that the cycle of these events entails: participation observation at its finest. Thinking of the tension in our personal relationship I hesitated momentarily. As F.'s friend I thought the sponsorship would divert some energy from mourning his father's death. As an ethnographer I decided that the benefits of collecting such detailed information and securing contacts with more members of the *muxe* community would outweigh the risks. I agreed. I would return to Oaxaca in January prepared to cohost the event. As a last act before my departure, we attended Oaxaca's first Gay Pride March.

Guelaguetza

I returned to Oaxaca that January, just three weeks before the *Vela de Vinnii Gaxheé*,[2] but in the intervening months I had spoken to F. weekly and just as frequently wired him money for some fiesta expense. As joint hosts (*mayordomos)* we were responsible for securing a permit, renting a salon, hiring two musical groups, paying security guards, ordering 600 cases of beer and as many plastic chairs, and providing food and gifts for our guests. I solely was responsible for paying for it. I invested over $1,200 of my own research monies to sponsor this event. Based on F.'s advice and my previous experience attending fiestas in Oaxaca, I believed that those who attended and received my hospitality would be obligated to invite me to their events for the duration of my fieldwork stay.

Unfortunately, I had misapprehended the complexity of the situation on several levels. First, F.'s emotional state had further deteriorated in my absence and was not purely coincidental. Although F. asked me to sponsor the event with him, as he had the social prestige to serve as host but not the funds, even before I returned to Oaxaca, he began to resent the power dynamic of the financial hierarchy. His fellow *Vinnii Gaxheé* members knew that I was the source of the funding and used this information to embarrass and shame him on several occasions. His fragile pride was repeatedly tested, although I continually told him that his assistance and my participation in the event were invaluable to my project. Second, I was a woman and, as I learned in the months that followed, far from the ideal partner for a *muxe*, even as a fiesta cosponsor. My Spanish, which F. had taught me, was replete with the idiomatic expressions he frequently used and drew attention to the close contact we had developed. Our similarity in speech and constant companionship had become an accepted target of joking among F.'s friends, and he was frequently subject to the horrifying schoolyard taunt, "F. has a girlfriend!" A more stable individual might have shrugged it off but F. found it insupportably discomforting. That the previous August we appeared together in the local newspaper arm-in-arm leading Oaxaca's Gay Pride March was an additional source of jest.

The weekend before the *Vinnii Gaxheé* fiesta, I accompanied F. to his Isthmus home. I was sensitive to his insecurities and hoped this time together with his family would help ameliorate the stress the fiesta preparations had wrought on our relationship. But, again I was wrong. On this return trip I was affectionately received by F.'s stepmother, M., brother O. (who is also *muxe*) and his sister R., as well as his numerous aunts and cousins who lived in the same compound. They fondly remembered my stay with them and resumed kin-like relations with me. F., who in my absence had become sexually and emotionally involved with a young man in Oaxaca, viewed as farce the kin terms that his family used to refer to me. He drank heavily and became verbally abusive, claiming that I meant nothing to him. However, these attempts to denigrate me in his family's eyes had the unintended counter-effect of garnering their support on my side. He irrationally concluded that they preferred my presence to his, which further worsened our tenuous relationship.

Everyone in the compound seemed sadly aware that F.'s once neurotic behavior was becoming increasingly pathological and ever more dangerous and were genuinely concerned for me. During that visit F.'s mother lent me the very old and valuable embroidered velvet dress that I would wear to the party and told me that her home was always open to me. His sister R., who resided in Oaxaca City, offered to meet with me to discuss Zapotec customs. And his brother O. pledged his support to my project and offered to serve as my research assistant in F.'s place. I was hesitant to accept these offers, but in light of my deteriorating relationship with F., I would consider them. First, however, I needed to return to Oaxaca with my reluctant co-*mayordomo* and host the fiesta for our 600 invited guests. F.'s parting anger-laden words to me upon our return to the second-class bus station in Oaxaca City at 3:00 a.m. were that, in essence, we would host the party together but separately. I would do my part, which involved purchasing and preparing the food and buying gifts and, for his part, he would show up.

Guelaguetza comes from Zapotec and means the great courtesy, the custom to help one another during big events, such as weddings, births, funerals, and the planting and harvesting of crops. Community cooperation makes it possible to provide for the expenses of rites of passage and agricultural inputs. Oaxaqueños take reciprocity seriously. The state even sponsors an annual event named after this custom, a two-week long celebration of folkloric dance that takes place in Oaxaca City every July. At the end of each dance, regional delegations presents their own *guelaguetza* to the audience by throwing small fruits, hats, and sometimes even coconuts and pineapples. In the week before the fiesta of *Vinnii Gaxheé*, I thought often about this Oaxacan tradition of great courtesy. I had thought fiesta exchange created obligatory, reciprocal ties that bound people together; I had not thought about how such events could be used to cleave people apart. Had I learned nothing from Marcel Mauss about the devastating potential of the refusal to receive?

Vinnii Gaxheé 2003

Long before 14 February 2003 I realized that the fiesta I was about to host was not going to be the opening and entering of *muxe* society that I had anticipated but I rescued what I could. F. could not abide my financial contribution, nor even my presence in the lead-up to the fiesta but we were locked in obligation to the larger structure. Although F. refused to speak to me, his family and several other members of the *muxe* community did extend me several small courtesies. In the week before the fiesta, C., a member of *Vinnii Gaxheé* made numerous trips with me to the market to select the sombreros and plastic-ware gifts for the guests. F.'s neighbor S. and I spent hours in my apartment writing in black marker "*Regalo* (gift) *de los mayordomos, Vinnii Gaxheé 2003*" on the plastic bowls and plates. We later learned that the correct phrase is "*Recuerdo de los mayordomos*" – "memento" from the hosts not "gift," but C. told us not to worry since the marker would likely wear off either by spilled beer or by guests dancing with the bowls and baskets on their heads during the later hours of the party. The food was pre-pared after I made an emergency phone call to Ixtepec and enlisted the help of F.'s brother O. He arrived the day of the event at 7:00 a.m. on an overnight bus from the Isthmus seven hours away. My excellent culinary knowledge was of little use in preparing Oaxacan fiesta food for over 200 guests.[3] There is a range of foods that are potentially appropriate but none of the recipes are written. After a quick trip to the market, O. covered my kitchen floor with pans of chicken in garlic and orange marinade and spaghetti with tomato and *crema*. I set to cutting the rolls.

Other courtesies were extended throughout the afternoon. When O. and I opened the oven and found it was used to store an odd array of switches and spare pieces of wire and not attached to a source of gas, we decided it was time for a beer. How were we going to cook the nine turkey-roaster size aluminum pans of food that needed to be baked in the next few hours? After making a few telephone calls I found that no one I knew in Oaxaca had a working oven. Within an hour, however, my *muxe* friend C. from Xoxo just outside the city limits arrived to borrow my green Tehuana outfit that he would wear to the party. He knew of a bakery in Xoxo that lit a wood-burning oven each morning and might let us cook our food in the residual heat. He quickly enlisted the help of a friend with a truck and, accompanied by O., carried off the food promising to deliver it at the appro-priate hour. And, at the last minute, as I was sweating and struggling to lug the fiesta bounty down the stairs with the idea of finding a taxi, S. appeared with some friends from work to help me haul the mountain of *recuerdos* to the *Salón*.

The party went on. There were two bands. Guests filled the hall. The food was delivered on time (on Oaxacan time, several hours late) and was delicious. F. did indeed attend the fiesta but he did not speak to me most of the evening. I assumed this might be my last party and desperately jotted down contact information for anyone willing to provide me with a number or address. R., an unemployed ex-lover of F., offered to assist me with my future research plans. After glaring at me for hours, the beer loosened his reserve and F. approached to issue a warning. He squeezed my upper arm to the point of bruising and demanded that I go away and keep my distance from him and especially from R., concerned that I would replace him as an object of R.'s desire. I did not take the diplomatic route to allay tension but I had had enough. I laughed. I laughed at the sheer irony that my success in creating a place for myself in a network of family and friends became a space that F. felt he occupied. Hours later, when I was packing things up, F. saw that R. was helping me to cart serving-ware back to my house. The music had stopped so all present could hear F.'s yelling curses and accusations of my witchery. I was glad to hear it, as it forewarned the Corona missile aimed at my head. I ducked but did not need to – F. did have lousy coordination when drunk.

What a party. Aside from serving food and beer and distributing the gifts, none of the usual fiesta rituals were performed. We did not make candles together, nor dance the Zandunga, nor speak the prescribed words to our guests or to the incoming *mayordomos*. I had attended enough fiestas in Oaxaca to apprehend the sorry state of ritual at this affair. As an anthropologist, I was disappointed not to be able to participate in what I thought were the central rites of the event. No one else, however, remarked on the flubbed protocol nor on the violent concluding scene. That night I assumed that without F.'s help my research project was doomed. However, in the months after the party, and the years since, I have realized that what failed, F.'s violent reaction and the breakdown of reciprocal relationships and obligations, actually made the nature of social relationships in Oaxaca especially clear. Two days after the party, only three of the participants were still speaking with me. F., as president of the organization, had banned me from further contact with the members of *Vinnii Gaxheé*.[4] On the third day, I was officially cursed with black magic by the *Santa Muerte*[5] when F. sent an envelope containing dirt from the cemetery and a burnt twenty-peso note to my house. It was striking how short I fell from achieving my goal.

An Unremarkable Tale

As I sought a deeper understanding of my role in the event, as I examined the micro-politics of social interaction of which I had been unaware, as I dealt with my guilt of treading too heavily on foreign soil, I told my story. I spoke to F.'s family, to older Zapotec women in the Isthmus, to non-Zapotec Oaxaqueños of all ages, to *muxe* who were not associated with *Vinnii Gaxheé*, to F.'s former friends and lovers, to anyone who would listen. What emerged from these discussions formed the ethnographic substance of my research: the tales of family squabbles, imbalanced reciprocity, unrepaid loans, jealousies, manipulations, betrayals, drunken violence. Fiestas did indeed serve as the social fabric of Zapotec life; however, that fabric was not unblemished white linen. It more closely resembled a Tehuana fiesta dress – intricately embroidered designs on a dark, heavy fabric, lined with a different fabric of which only the wearer is aware, and concealing multiple layers beneath. Then add beer.

Notes

1. Names have been abbreviated.
2. *Vela* means "candle," and Isthmian fiestas are so named after the candles offered to the church in a ceremony that initiates the festivities, after which comes a procession and then an all-night party of eating, drinking and dancing.
3. Although over 600 guests were invited, we only had to provide food for those sitting in our section, to the other *socios* (members of *Vinnii Gaxheé*) and to those whom F. owed some favor.
4. My relationship with *muxe* in Oaxaca improved after F. migrated to the U.S. three months after the fiesta.
5. The *Santa Muerte* cult focuses on a set of ritual practices offered to a supernatural personification of death in expectation of the fulfillment of specific requests.

7

Arriving in Jewish Buenos Aires

Natasha Zaretsky

I arrived in Buenos Aires on a cold bright winter morning in June of 2001, ready to begin my first research trip to Argentina. Before my flight, I spent several months planning a project that explored my interests in memory, violence, and human rights. Argentina presented a compelling case, with a history fraught with rights abuses. State-sponsored terror and political repression during the last military dictatorship – from 1976 to 1983 – resulted in the torture and disappearance of an estimated 30,000 people, never to be heard from again. The mothers of those "disappeared" formed a powerful social movement, the *Madres de la Plaza de Mayo* (the Mothers of the Plaza de Mayo), which convened weekly marches around the central plaza of Buenos Aires to protest the disappearance of their children and the impunity that followed the dictatorship. Such protests, memorials and commemorations were quite visible markers of past violence but, I wondered, how does this violence shape the fabric of everyday life in other ways?

These mothers inspired my initial thinking about Argentina, but as I learned more about the country, I discovered unexpected histories of violence. Some of the mothers of the Plaza de Mayo were children of Holocaust survivors. The Mothers also stood in solidarity with those who lost their family members to other episodes of violence in Argentina, including two terrorist attacks in the 1990s: the 1992 Israeli Embassy bombing and the 1994 Argentine Jewish Mutual Aid Society (A.M.I.A.) bombing, together killing more than 100 people and wounding hundreds.

I eventually focused my project on the Jewish community of Buenos Aires, a group whose members had endured multiple periods of violence. Argentina is, in many respects, a nation of European immigrants (the vast majority of Spanish or Italian descent) and is also home to the largest population of Jews in Latin America. This community may have never come into existence, however, without the violence and expulsion they suffered in Europe. The first major wave of Jews arrived in the late 1800s and early 1900s, fleeing the pogroms in Russia and Eastern Europe; later waves included Jews escaping Nazism and the Holocaust. Although they found a refuge and a home in Argentina, they also continued to experience periods of anti-Jewish violence and came to occupy an ambiguous position in Argentine society.

The 1992 bombing of the Israeli Embassy shocked many Argentines who did not expect such terrorism to occur on their soil. Yet, because it targeted the foreign representation of the state of Israel, many did not consider it a problem that the Argentine government needed to address. The 1994 A.M.I.A. bombing, however, which targeted the largest Jewish community center in Buenos Aires, struck a more urgent chord and held a more immediate significance.

The A.M.I.A. bombing destroyed a civilian institution for Argentine citizens – killing eighty-five people and wounding hundreds – and is considered the worst terrorist attack to have taken place in Latin America. Many non-Jewish Argentines participated in large public protests and demonstrated their solidarity with the Jewish community after the attack. Others, however, no longer wished to play soccer matches with Jewish clubs and did not want Jewish institutions as their neighbors.

The response of the Argentine government only exacerbated the impression of impunity and injustice that surrounded the bombing. A botched investigation led to a trial that began in September 2001, seven years after the bombing; this trial concluded in 2004 with no convictions and came nowhere closer to the truth of what happened or who was responsible. At the time of writing, no group has claimed responsibility for the bombing and, although speculations abound, little is known for certain. In March 2005, however, the Inter-American Commission on Human Rights of the Organization of American States did determine that the Argentine government clearly failed to provide justice in the A.M.I.A. case.

This lack of justice connected this bombing to a longer history of impunity in Argentina (dating back to the political repression of the Dirty War) and ultimately led to one of the most significant consequences of the A.M.I.A. attack: a crisis of identity and belonging. Indeed, many Jewish Argentines began to question what it meant to be Jewish and Argentine and their belonging in their society and nation.

When I first arrived in Buenos Aires in 2001, almost seven years had passed since the attack on the A.M.I.A. building. Interested in the aftermath of this bombing, I went to the site of the attack – the *Once* (pronounced OHN-say) district of the city. During my first weeks there, I walked on the street, Pasteur, where the bombing took place. It had since been neatly repaved, memorial trees erected for each victim at even paces. The new building stood like a fortress, recessed from the sidewalk to prevent a future attack.

The bombing also resonated in other parts of the city. I went to the weekly *actos* (protests) of *Memoria Activa* (Active Memory), one of the social movements formed in response to the A.M.I.A. bombing. A large part of their work involved international and national advocacy efforts; but their most visible work in Buenos Aires were the weekly protests held in front of the High Courts of Argentina, where they formed an alternative tribunal, challenging the lack of justice they perceived from their state. Like the Mothers of the Plaza de Mayo, they convened every week to remember the victims of the bombing and demand justice for their deaths, fearing that if those victims were forgotten and receded into history, that justice would never be possible.

They held their protests on Monday mornings, in a downtown plaza facing the *Tribunales* – the High Courts of Argentina. They began with the blowing of the *shofar* (a ram's horn), to remember the victims of the bombing and, every Monday, they invited people to offer their testimonies, reflecting on the bombing, on violence, on impunity in Argentina. Every Monday, they called for justice, and every Monday they would leave this plaza, to return the following Monday. I stood as one of many observers at their commemorative protests. But I also wondered how this past violence mediated other aspects of life as well.

During those first weeks of research, I began contacting the few people in the Jewish community I could get in touch with, relying on the help of contacts from my department in Princeton and acquaintances in New York. Several months before my trip, I met one of those contacts, David, in a Korean restaurant in Manhattan. He was an American student who had spent time in Buenos Aires and told me about a friend, a young Argentine of European Jewish descent named Alejandro who also happened to be a former rabbinical student.

When I arrived, Alejandro graciously offered a tour of the city and invited me and my boyfriend (who traveled with me to Argentina) to go out to dinner with him and his girlfriend. He picked us up in front of the apartment building where we were staying, which I soon understood to be in one of the more expensive areas of the city, Palermo (a name that reflected the Italian influence in Argentina). Alejandro himself lived in a wealthy northern suburb and navigated the city by car. From the back seat, I leaned forward and tried to absorb as much as I could from what he was telling us while staring out at the city passing rapidly by the window. He narrated the city as we drove past different buildings and monuments and I tried to remember as many details as I could in case they would later become important to understanding life in Buenos Aires.

As we turned onto a street whose name I did not catch, he pointed out a synagogue and asked if I saw what he called *pilotes* out front. These *pilotes* were small cement pillars, shaped like truncated poles, which punctured the sidewalk in front of the synagogue. I quickly whipped my head around to look at them as we drove past. Alejandro explained that these *pilotes* were erected in front of all Jewish buildings as protection against car bombings after the A.M.I.A. attack. (I would later find out there existed a very small handful of exceptions. But, on the whole, either *pilotes* or wider cement barricades came to mark the vast majority of Jewish sites in the city and throughout Argentina in response to the 1994 bombing.) The

Jewish community installed these *pilotes* in order to make people feel safer and they continued to serve as a visible reminder of the need for security after the bombing.

Alejandro then told me that I could not take any photographs of the synagogue. I asked him if I could take photographs inside the synagogue. "Inside is fine, but never outside. It's a security measure," he explained. Luciana, his girlfriend, nodded her head in agreement, shaking her index finger back and forth to punctuate the prohibition. Although there were never visible signs to that effect, Alejandro and Luciana made it seem as if everyone in Buenos Aires knew that no photos were allowed – common knowledge for Jewish Argentines after the 1994 bombing.

Before arriving, I had read about these new security measures – *pilotes* or barricades lining the sidewalk in front of Jewish institutions (including synagogues, schools, sports clubs, organizations) and private security guards hired by the Jewish community, stationed at the entrances of buildings and events to monitor those who entered, usually checking identity documents and searching bags. Feeling unsafe after two terrorist attacks, members of the Jewish community chose to provide security for themselves, and I wondered, what did that mean about their sense of safety as citizens? What did that mean for their relationship to the Argentine state?

While I had known about these security measures before arriving in Argentina, I had never heard about the restriction against taking photographs of buildings. I made a mental note that here was another example of the rules and boundaries that defined Jewish life in the city. At high speeds, Alejandro then continued his tour of the city, pointing to buildings, neighborhoods, and other aspects of Jewish life. During that first drive, Buenos Aires, and more specifically, Jewish Buenos Aires, began to take shape for me.

Over the next few weeks, I walked the streets of the city. I stood in crowded buses as they lurched forward and made their way down the central avenues traversing the urban grid, the architecture and cafés reminiscent of Europe. During these first forays into Buenos Aires, I also noticed how the *pilotes* and barricades made Jewish buildings stand apart from other public spaces. Not only did they interrupt the physical space of sidewalks but the security guards stationed at these buildings prevented any loitering or unsanctioned use of that space – marking this as different from other areas.

Slowly, small pockets of the city took on more complex shades of meaning as I made my way into the Jewish community.

When I arrived that June, less then a month remained until the seven-year anniversary of the A.M.I.A. bombing on 18 July 2001. In the years that followed, a new building replaced the one destroyed. Walking along that street, there were constant reminders of what had taken place. In addition to the trees planted to commemorate each of the eighty-five victims, their names engraved in black stone plaques underneath, a wall of memory stood in front of the building – the first name of each victim spray-painted on a black piece of metal. During the many months after the bombing, the only thing that stood at the site of the bombing was this wall of names. Every month since the attack, the group *Familiares y Amigos de las Víctimas* (Family Members and Friends of the Victims) gathered at that wall to remember those who died and protest the injustice that followed, interrupting the normal flow of traffic and pedestrians to bring everyone back to that moment of violence.

These commemorative events (called *actos*), plaques and trees were obvious memorials to the bombing. But I also started to wonder, did these *pilotes* and the very structure of the new building – protected by a thick wall with *pilotes* and cement barricades out front – also recall the violence of the bombing? Had that moment of violence become part of the daily life in the city through the barricades and *pilotes* that arose in response?

The seven-year anniversary was rapidly approaching and in the week before the anniversary of the A.M.I.A. bombing, I tried to attend every community event that commemorated the attack. At the last minute, Alejandro told me about an *acto* that was going to take place on the night before the anniversary, on 17 July, organized by a group of Jewish youth to be held outside of the rebuilt A.M.I.A. building. He wasn't able to go with me, but at that point, I felt comfortable enough to go on my own.

I arrived alone and it was already dark when I started to walk towards the *acto* in the *Once* neighborhood. Back in New York, David described *Once* to me as a cross between the Lower East Side and the Garment District of Manhattan. It was a small, densely woven set of streets that were home to the many aspirations and difficulties of new immigrants to the city. Commerce loomed, along with community institutions. Although traditionally Jewish, the neighborhood was slowly transforming with the arrival of Korean businesses in recent years. The streets were very narrow and filled with textile shops and wholesale merchandise. During the day, a sense of constant movement pervaded the *Once* neighborhood, interrupted by the *pilotes* that lined the clusters of Jewish institutions in the neighborhood.

As I walked towards the street where the *acto* was to take place, I found *Once* to be eerily empty; the businesses were shuttered for the night and no one else seemed to be walking outside. I didn't have many things with me – just my wallet, cell phone, and a camera I brought to take photographs of the commemorative ceremony. After being asked for my identification at every Jewish building I had visited during my first weeks in the city, I also decided to bring my passport along, just in case.

At the entrance to the street of the A.M.I.A. building, a makeshift police barricade stood, haphazardly blocking off the entrance of the street to vehicles. A line of people had already formed to enter the site and were moving through the entryway after being approved by men in dark overcoats – whom I already recognized as the Jewish community's security guards. Police were scattered around the checkpoint but the security guards of the Jewish community were the ones screening us as we passed through.

These security guards seemed to mark the physical space as Jewish and the event as Jewish, representing a certain authority outside the state. They may have seemed peripheral but I would later wonder what significance they had for understanding Jewish community life in the aftermath of terror.

Most visitors came to the *acto* with a friend, or several friends. I was alone. I waited my turn in line, and got ready to answer what had already become the usual questions for me from security.

What are you here for tonight?
The *acto* organized by Jewish youth.
How did you find out about this event?
From a friend.
Where are you from?
The United States.
Can I see your passport please?
Yes.

At this point, I handed my passport over and they studied it carefully, before continuing with their questions. At no other event in Argentina was I asked for my passport in such a way.

Do you belong to the community?
Yes.

When they referred to the community, *la comunidad*, they referred to the Jewish community at large, and not just the Jewish community in Argentina. Indeed, they knew I was from the U.S., and originally hailed from Belarus, from my passport. Instead, the question itself was a further test of belonging to the Jewish community at large; if I were to ask which community, they would know I did not belong.

Although I affirmed that I did belong, they still probed further before accepting that I indeed was Jewish, asking for my credentials.

Did you go to any Jewish school, or are you a member of any congregation or organization?
No, but we do go to services for the high holidays.

That seemed to satisfy the guards. After answering the questions, they looked through my bag and allowed me to pass through. They had determined that I was not a danger to the event.

We still had twenty minutes to go before the *acto* was to begin, and I wandered around the open street, which had been emptied for the commemorative ceremony. As I proceeded towards the A.M.I.A. building, a volunteer handed me a small tealight candle, in preparation for the candle lighting. I took my candle and stood off to the side, watching everyone else. Being a youth event, it wasn't surprising to see young teenagers milling about from group to group as we waited for the *acto* to begin. Since I didn't recognize anyone there, I continued to stand alone.

The newly rebuilt A.M.I.A. building was the backdrop for the event. This night, a podium was erected in front of the wall of names, and several community members and youth gave speeches in remembrance of the bombing. The rest of the crowd gathered around while I stood back. The moment came when they began to sing and light candles in memory of the victims. I did not want to disturb the sacred nature of this commemorative moment for those who were remembering the destruction of that day or their losses but I also felt that I should take a photo and document this for my research. Torn between my desire to stand back and what I felt to be my obligation to document this event for my research, I went ahead and took out my camera. As soon as the flash went off, it seemed that everyone turned around to stare at me and I, who had been standing back and largely hidden, suddenly became acutely visible.

While I recalled that Alejandro had said that I should not take photographs of synagogues because of security concerns, I did not think that taking a photograph of a group of young people singing and lighting candles would constitute the same breach of security codes. In fact, my only concern in taking the photo was that I would interrupt what must have been a difficult moment for those gathered to remember a terrorist attack. But it turned out that the very act of taking a photograph marked me as a suspicious outsider and, thus, potentially dangerous in the eyes of the Jewish security.

As soon as I snapped the photograph, I registered the shocked look of faces turning that followed my camera flash erupting. Those eyes continued to follow us as a young man quickly approached me, abruptly taking me by my elbow and leading me off to the side of the event.

He was perhaps twenty years of age, with a clean-shaven face, dressed in a black suit, black tie, black overcoat, and black shiny shoes. Perhaps he intended to be discreet; perhaps he intended to stand out in the accepted uniform of those working as security guards for Jewish institutions. Either way, that form of dress soon became unmistakable to me.

Once we were at about twenty feet from the event, he began to question me. The unusual nature of this "conversation" was apparent from the way he stood next to me – closer than a stranger should or a friend would, in a way that did not permit me to just walk away. He then delivered his questions in a staccato voice – loud, abrupt, with a neutral facial expression – leading me to believe this to be more of a compulsory interrogation than a simple query where I was free to go at any time.

I became nervous, sensing that I had committed a transgression, a cultural error of sorts, and stepped over some invisible line. He began by simply asking for my document. I quickly handed over my passport, without questioning his authority to demand it. He inspected it very closely before taking out a small slip of paper and jotting down my information. He then put that piece of paper in his pocket and continued with his questions.

Why did you take the photograph?
I am here doing research on the Jewish community and wanted to take a photograph of the people singing and lighting candles for my thesis.
Didn't you know it is not allowed?
No, I did not.
Where are you from?
The United States.
Why do you speak Spanish so well?
I studied it in college.
Do you belong to the community?
Yes.
Who told you about this event?
A friend.
What is his name?
Alejandro.
How do you know him?
Through a friend of a friend.
How do you know that friend?
We met in the United States before I came here.

Suddenly, everything seemed suspicious. How indeed did I meet this other person who then introduced me to Alejandro? How did I end up at that event that night, all alone, taking photos when I should have known I wasn't allowed to? It wasn't posted anywhere; no one told me I could not; but if I had passed through their borders, their security checkpoints, shouldn't I have already known the rules? He continued:

Who else do you know in Argentina?

At that question, my mind went blank and I panicked. I took out the cell phone I recently purchased and scrolled through the contact information, hoping I had recorded someone's phone number who I could offer to vouch for me. I did, luckily, have Alejandro's information there. I gave the guard his number willingly, without worrying, as I should have, about the consequences for Alejandro or for me. I had never been in such a situation and did not know what to expect, or how much trouble I would be in for what I did. But *did* I do anything wrong? Everything happened so quickly that I still wasn't sure. My bewilderment only emphasized that while I felt like an expert at moving around the city, no one warned me about how to navigate these boundaries, this new Jewish Buenos Aires of security, suspicion and fear. In that encounter, it felt as if we had momentarily slipped outside the regular course of things and even outside the Argentine state, into a zone of uncertainty where the rules guiding life in the rest of the city did not operate in the same way.

Later, I would wonder about the authority this security seemed to hold at Jewish buildings and events. The Argentine police did not participate at all in my questioning, nor could they have, since taking a photograph was not against Argentine law. What right did they have to demand my roll of film? Would they have had the right to confiscate it? Did taking a photo break Argentine law or transgress the conventions and rules of the Jewish community after the bombing? Who was in charge here? I asked myself, what might this suggest about the role of the Argentine state in Jewish life in Buenos Aires? It seemed as if the state looked away at certain moments, and that indeed, they implicilty conceded that they were not capable of providing the security and safety Jewish Argentine citizens needed after the bombing.

At the end of his questions, he verified who I was and what I was doing there but still wanted my roll of film. Although I had been nervous up until that point, I simply refused to give it to him, and after consultation with his superior, he agreed to let me keep it. The young man who had just gone through the process of interrogating me then stepped back towards me, and said it was alright, politely letting me know that I may return to the *acto*; asking me to excuse the inconvenience.

Just as abruptly as it began, our encounter had ended. I walked away from him and could not stop walking. I quickly made my way out of the confines of the *acto*, my heart pounding. I couldn't just go back as if nothing had happened because I was shaken by our exchange.

In that encounter, the photograph I took momentarily rendered me as an outsider, as a potentially dangerous "other." The resulting exchange with the Jewish community's security guard positioned me in a space of uncertainty – a zone that seemed to operate outside the normal parameters of the state. While there were no further consequences that followed, in that small moment, in that interaction, I felt that much more was going on. While I was trying to figure out the boundaries of the Jewish community in Buenos Aires and how to approach my research, I had not realized that this was part of the way Jewish Argentines had come to define their own new boundaries. Through these security exchanges and encounters (products of the violence of the bombing), they positioned who was inside and outside, who was included and excluded and thus negotiated their community. During my own encounter, I was on the line, someone not to be trusted. In that process, I momentarily crossed into the space of the "other," becoming a potentially dangerous suspect for having taken a photograph they did not want me to take.

My experience signaled an important tension between the Jewish community and the Argentine state: Who was in charge of patrolling the borders of the buildings and community events? How much authority did Jewish security have? What do such details suggest about how Jewish Argentines feel as citizens, unprotected by their own state? My encounter opened up a certain kind of knowledge about living with the aftermath of violence – a violent past that continued to mediate belonging for Jewish Argentines, breaking through the surface of everyday life in moments such as these. It conditioned my entry into that world and my understanding of how the Jewish community defined its boundaries in the aftermath of a terrorist attack.

As time passed, my own encounters with security would change. They became more routine, more ordinary, less notable. I began to recognize the guards and they recognized me. I was no longer the suspicious foreigner. I even kissed some of them hello on the cheek, the common greeting between friends and acquaintances in Argentina.

Over the years, other changes also took place in Argentina – the group *Memoria Activa* ended its ten years of weekly protests in 2004. However, as of this writing, a small group of supporters continued to gather there to remember the victims. There were other signs of change: the memorial trees on Pasteur Street seemed abandoned, some of the plaques missing (presumably stolen for the value of the stone, based on what others told me). Over fourteen years have passed since the bombing and with that passage of time, inevitably, the memory of victims may fade and the struggle for that memory and for justice becomes more difficult.

However, what has remained, as perhaps another testament to that violence, are the *pilotes,* barricades, and security measures. They persist as a defining and powerful element of Jewish life in the city and throughout Argentina. They exist at almost every institution; they accompany almost all Jewish events. In a way, the ubiquitious *pilotes* and the ritual security encounters acted increasingly as an alternative site of memory for a disturbed peace; they recalled the violence of the attack and transmitted the fear from that day, now routinized, into the fissures of everyday life in the city.

These new security practices, while claiming to simply protect a pre-existing community, essentially defined the very boundaries of this community and the way its members negotiated citizenship, identity, and belonging in the wake of violence. My own encounter with the routinized security protocol launched me directly into the new ways the Jewish community defined its boundaries and created itself anew. Indeed, the violence of the 1994 A.M.I.A. bombing continued to play a role, sometimes in unexpected ways, in daily life in the city. My experience with the security that stemmed from this bombing brought me into the legacies of the violence that are not always fully visible or immediately accessible. And only after my personal encounter with the security, with this aftermath of violence, did I feel like I had begun to understand the boundaries of this community – I had finally arrived in Jewish Buenos Aires.

8

Dreamwork and Punishment in Lebanon

John Borneman

Dream Work

We often imagine countries and cities as mythical dreamscapes – cornucopias of prosperity and abundant pleasures. For much of the twentieth century, Lebanon and Beirut evoked such a dreamscape: a glorious past of cosmopolitan Phoenician traders transformed into modern French-Arabic fusion; cool mountain homes overlooking the warm Mediterranean sea; and a capital city, Beirut, that show-cased intellectual, cultural and economic surprises. But a more recent memory, of the violent civil war that raged on and off for seventeen years, between 1975 and 1992, has filled the cup of plenty with sorrows. My own dreams, as well as those of my Lebanese friends, in and near Beirut, tend to situate these recent memories, as well as our own histories of violence and its anticipation, in these dreamscapes.

On my very first evening in Beirut, in the summer of 1999, I slept fitfully, because of jetlag, I thought, until my friend, whom I will call A.,[1] called a couple of hours past midnight to reassure me that I was safe despite the loud, intermittent booms I was hearing. These sounds, he explained, were the result of Israeli planes bombing power plants around the city and it was highly unlikely they would bomb Beirut itself. Until that point I had been unable to order these sounds in my dreams and, until A.'s call, I surmised that perhaps someone was building throughout the night – the reconstruction of the downtown was proceeding full steam – and I simply wondered why the sounds were so loud.

I had a much more disturbing dream on a summer night in late August, 2001, as I was preparing to leave Beirut to do fieldwork in south Lebanon. Shortly before my first visit to Lebanon, the south had been liberated from an Israeli occupation that began in 1985 and ended, abruptly, with a complete withdrawal, on 24 May 2000. Hezbollah (Party of God), the victorious organizers of the resistance, called the withdrawal an "emancipation." It was unexpected and stunned everyone, including the Lebanese to the north, who were suddenly charged with integrating and administering a territory and a people – poorer, less educated, less skilled, less developed than them, in short, backward – for which, in the past, they had often shirked responsibility and, while under Israeli control, assumed only a representational or ideological alliance. I was trying to understand Lebanese notions of punishment, how, specifically, "collaboration with the enemy" – meaning, with Israel – was understood and punished (or not), and how this relates to the post-civil-war integration of "Lebanese society," whatever that might mean.

Before this trip to the south, I dreamt that I had been accused of improprieties – the word in the dream was "harassment" – while teaching at Cornell University, though I am now and was in the dream also a professor at Princeton. I expected these improprieties to be sexual in nature. But at the time I was unable to recollect an actual offense, and this inability to specify the wrong jarred me out of my sleep, sweaty even though the sweltering heat and humidity of the Beirut summer had already passed into a deep warmth softened by the occasional ocean breeze. I woke up because in my dream I did not know, I was unable to specify or act upon, what or to whom exactly I had done wrong, and this disturbing sense of having committed an offense of which I was unaware kept me awake for some time.

The next day, I related the dream to a friend I will call H., a Shi'a who grew up in the south, who had agreed to accompany me on this trip. He first told me of his vivid and strange dream of the previous night: He woke up dead. Then, as we drove in search of his grandfather's villa in the mountains of the south (vacated during the civil war/occupation, "occupied" by a refugee family the last fifteen years), which had a small riding stable attached below it, he offered an explication of my dream: there was a connection between my former career with horses and the word "harassment," which is related to the French word "*haras*," meaning a stud farm, a place for the reproduction of horses.

Then H. moved to the difference between the French words *manege* and *ménage*, which parallels a discrepancy between my former and present life. In the former, I was working with horses (in a riding school, *manege*), and leading a life of "floundering and lust," as in a *ménage à trois*; presently I work in the academy and lead a more restricted "life of couples." There are French expressions for this difference, "*J'ai fait mon ménage*," versus "*Je suis en ménage.*" I was bringing my domestic life from the time I worked with horses, prior to reentering academics, into a dream of the present. My past impropriety, or "harassment," is haunting me today.

H. also thought my not knowing of this "harassment" was related to the English double "no/know": both to my inability to "know" the wrong (which awakened me in the dream) and to an inability to say, or to accept, "no" from others (which constitutes the legal impropriety of harassment). I delighted in these clever observations, plausible in the Lebanese context, where conversations among those in the educated middle-class constantly switch registers from English to French to

Arabic, sometimes within the same sentence, though most often speakers digress into the language with which they are most comfortable, or which they were using at the time of an experience, usually French or Arabic. This situational linguistic competence is part of a larger emotional economy: mostly French for intellectual or philosophical topics, mostly Arabic for intimacies. English tends to be an adult language, for academic or commercial use, a language for communicating with outsiders (such as myself), while Arabic and French are learned with the affection and discipline of childhood.

H., who was working on a master's degree in philosophy, had been a news anchor for the French television station in Lebanon. With the rationalization of its workforce, he received a settlement and was most recently shaping the sales messages for some advertising companies. His control of all three languages is so playful and exceptional that it puts my own linguistic skills to shame. Hence my own explanation of the dream was more prosaic, or "flat-footed," as I said to H. It was foremost about my identification with Lebanese collaborators during the Israeli occupation, who also insisted that they were doing nothing wrong – just feeding their families, finding unskilled work as maids or day laborers in San Diego-style Israeli homes and in the irrigated green fields on the terraced hills on the other side of the frontier or, in select cases, cooperating in administration of the occupation, in the arrest and detention and interrogation, including torture, of Lebanese resisters – Israel called them "terrorists" – to the Israeli occupation.

My dream left me speechless, and anxious about the need for punishment. But whose? My dream anticipated, I suspect, failed expectations in my fieldwork in Lebanon, a conflict within my conscience, between what I should do and what I might be able to do.

Collaboration and Punishment in South Lebanon

South Lebanon, at the time of my visit, had two large memorials to the Israeli occupation, one an emptied detention/interrogation center in Khiam, the other a memorial to a massacre in a former U.N. shelter in Qana.

detention center in Khiam is now a museum of a detention center. It sits at
looking the valleys below and, indeed, much of the south. Like
in the south, it was once a fortress, dating back
by the French before the Israelis expanded and
rded, soft-speaking Hezbollah men greet H. and
a rusting military water tank left behind by the
ss, on our right, is a set of small, lacquered, hand-
ance, so glossy that they appear like the candied
nd Syria are renowned, though unusually large, as
n our left stood a man selling a children's book,

Sharon al-Shareer (*Sharon the Evil One*), camouflaged in a cover marked simply "May 25" (the date of emancipation).[2] The cover depicts a dream montage that includes a photo of Sayyed H. Nasrallah, the Hezbollah leader, a woman's eyes, a resister setting fire to a flag and the golden dome of the Dome of the Rock Mosque in Jerusalem. The book tells the story of children with stones defeating the evil Sharon and driving him from their land. I bought one.

Then we go through the actual rooms and barracks. Yellow metal plates attached to the walls state in Arabic and poorly translated English the function of the spaces: "A Typical Individual Room Before Red Cross Entry," "A Collective Room After the Entrance of the Red Cross in 1995," "A Room for Investigation with the Help of the Traitors," "The Hall of Torturing: Burying-Kicking-Beating-Applying Electricity-Pouring Hot Water-Placing a Dog Beside," "An Open Space for Sun: Ten Minutes Every Ten Days For Females." The plates intend to singularize the administrative cruelty of Israeli detention methods, to draw attention to the rationalization of all tasks and functions, this room for torture in interrogation, that for cooking, another for washing, for sleeping, for the jailers or the detained, for women or men, a space for solitary confinement, for visits with nonprisoners. My first thought, though, was that I could probably find this evil in every continent, perhaps even in a museum of a detention center in every continent. On one wall over an Israeli flag I read the graffiti: "Who are the causes for War?" On another wall: "All Jews Must Die."

The room for women's access to the sun is slightly larger than but otherwise similar to the others: a cement slab floor of about two square yards. H. dubs it a "sun deck." I laugh. But shortly after, H. feels queasy and has to leave. I walk on. The yellow plates emphasize an important distinction between rooms constructed before and after the Red Cross was granted access to the prisoners. After the Red Cross filed a report, most detainee rooms were enlarged, and beds replaced cement floors for sleeping. Most rooms have no windows and most are just large enough for a prisoner of moderate size to lie prone on the floor or to turn around in while standing up. Two special rooms are equipped for electric torture, the metal conductor grids still hanging from the ceiling, the actual machines and devices, a guide tells me, taken back to Israel. I am surprised the Israelis did not destroy more of the evidence before they left but I am told they left in a hurry. The Prime Minister at the time, Ehud Barak, simply pulled out the troops one night, an evacuation that the Israeli public seemed to expect but one that left Lebanese scrambling for positions. Hezbollah, with a large on-the-ground resistance during the occupation, was the best-organized force to step into this vacuum. They kept their weapons, despite U.N. resolutions to the effect that they should disarm, and more or less took over policing the south.

The outer courtyard replicates the recently-abandoned look, except for four paintings, unmistakably Hezbollah art: computer-generated, glitzy, painted images of doves flying above fists grasping AK-47 assault rifles and smashing through walls, of crescents, stars of Francisco, and wrecked tanks – symbols of muscular victory and cruelty, Islam and peace. Against a wall leans a large portrait of Nasrallah, Hezbollah's leader, and mimeographed photos of slain fighters are posted on the wall near the entrance. It strikes me as odd that the museum gives the names of some specific Lebanese victims, claimed as "martyrs" to the cause, but does not name any Lebanese collaborators. Only Israelis are singled out for culpability. Later, a friend who had visited within weeks of the withdrawal, in the summer of 2000, told me he remembered having seen a list of all suspected collaborators – but, then again, now he is unsure what he actually saw. Within the first several years of the Israeli withdrawal there was, except for a few isolated examples, a notable lack of local recrimination – let's call it revenge – against people who helped to inform or administer the Israeli occupation. In the late summer and fall of 2002, however, I began to hear a few rumors of local extortion practiced by Hezbollah against Christian groups.

How the south was "administered" during and immediately after the occupation is a question of perspective, and there are many. The more I ask about local details, the more fragmented the picture. During the occupation, the south remained formally a part of the state of Lebanon; its residents retained their Lebanese citizenship and were more or less free to move back and forth between northern and southern Lebanon, and some, in a labor capacity, to Israel. Although U.N. "observers" and "peace-keepers" were stationed on the border between Lebanon and Israel and had a minimal presence in some of the villages, they seemed to have little effect on how either the Lebanese or the Israelis conducted their affairs. Israel still bombed, conducted surveillance missions and made their presence known at will, the Lebanese reacted and adjusted. Hezbollah, and to a lesser extent Amal, organized the resistance. They also assumed the basic functions of the state during the occupation, providing minimal social and public assistance, primarily health care and infusions of outside capital that kept local economies from collapsing. Israel was concerned solely with its own security and military goals, to deploy the entire south as a "buffer" or "security zone" devoid of people; hence, they sought to keep the area backward educationally, culturally, and economically.

As for Israeli torture of civilians, I had already met a victim, in 1999, on my first visit to Beirut. A taxi driver, upon hearing that I am American, revealed that he is Palestinian. "America is good, a friend," he proclaimed, before stretching gnarled hand across the seat to show me a scar on his ~~gernail, which, he said, had been yanked out during~~ prisons. He then pulled his T-shirt over his right his eyes flashed more angrily, to show me a gaping got in prison – in Khiam, in fact – and he wanted me to touch it, which still has the key to his family house, in Haifa, and he gestured to show me what the key looks like. His grandfather had taken it with him when he was evicted.

"America is good," he repeated, "a friend." In response to a comment of mine, he asserted that Clinton didn't like Netanyahu, and that Ehud Barak, the Israeli Prime Minister at the time, represented some hope. "But there is no place for Jews in Palestine," he said, "they should leave." To where? I ask. "Wherever," he replied, "to Africa." This was my first exposure to a claim of Israeli torture, my first confrontation with bodily evidence, and I realized how inextricably this present episode of Lebanese-Israeli history is wound up with the Jewish-driven expulsions of Palestinians beginning in 1948.

Largely because of this Israeli policy in the south of Lebanon, between 1978 and the time of the Israeli withdrawal from Lebanon the population in the south declined from 600,000 to an estimated 65,000, with most of the refugees settling in the southern suburbs of Beirut. The long-term impact of making the south secure for Israel was to make it unsafe for local residents; Israeli demands for collaboration poisoned relations between members of the various sects. Long-term insecurity was also insured through the Israeli policy of planting approximately 70,000 land mines all over the place, which U.N. personnel (part of United Nations Interim Force in Lebanon [U.N.I.F.I.L.]), mostly Africans experienced in mine removal on their own terrain, are presently trying to find and remove.

At the end of May 2002, within a week of the "liberation," 6,000 south Lebanese, mostly members of Israel's former proxy militia, the South Lebanese Army (S.L.A.), and their families, left Lebanon – mostly to Europe via Israel, with at least half reportedly sent to Germany. Within six months of the liberation, military tribunals began to hold marathon sessions up to three times a week, and charged 2,200 Lebanese – including some of those who had already left the country—with collaboration, handing down 800 verdicts, frequently reached after two or three minutes of deliberation. Of those who had left, 202 returned within six months; others have been trickling back since.

Defense lawyers worked out a plea bargain deal with prosecutors to divide collaborators – those in "contact with the enemy" – into four categories.[3] The first was for those who had worked in Israel, the second for those who had worked in civil administration, the third for soldiers of the S.L.A., and the fourth for those who had worked in intelligence/security. Conviction for the first two categories resulted in a fine of approximately $200 and a period of detention, which, in most cases, had already been served between the time of the initial arrest and release. South Lebanese Army soldiers got six to eighteen months prison, intelligence/security employees six to fifteen years. Only one officer of the S.L.A. surrendered; most were sentenced *in absentia.* By October 2001, fifty-four high-level collaborators had been sentenced to death, all *in absentia,* meaning that they would be granted a retrial if and when apprehended. Although death by hanging is legal, it had been suspended after Lebanese President Emile Lahoud took office in November 1998.[4] Many sentences were immediately appealed, first to a supreme military tribunal, then to a civilian court of cassation, and both the tribunal and court reversed some verdicts or lessened sentences.

Israeli occupation policy had allowed one Lebanese per family to work in Israel provided that each family also offered one man to work for the S.L.A. to protect the "security zone." Most of those who did not agree with this policy either vacated their land and residence and became displaced "internal refugees" in the rest of Lebanon. Or they worked covertly with the primarily Shiite Hezbollah resistance movement. Hezbollah supported its associates, in turn, with currency from abroad, most of which likely came from Syria or Iran, or diaspora Lebanese in Australia, Europe, or the U.S. Israel enforced its employment policy across sectarian lines, so that between 50 per cent to 80 per cent of the S.L.A. members were Shiites, depending on their proportion in the local population. Consequently, some 2,000 Shiites surrendered immediately after the Israeli evacuation, knowing they had no place to flee. Muslim lawyers, under pressure not to defend the accused, were often themselves then accused of collaboration, although none, to my knowledge, was punished.

Hezbollah objected to any suggestion of a general amnesty, as had been granted following the long civil war, or wars, in 1991, insisting that individuals had to engage in "repentance" (*tawbah*) as the means for political purification before that could be considered. This term "*tawbah*" is taken from a Shiite religious interpretation of the "door of repentance" (*bab el-tawbah*), through which one must pass in order to leave the cycle of earth and enter a new cycle of time. By insisting on the applicability of this condition (purification through the door of repentance) in the military-political-jural domain, Hezbollah ended up accommodating its religious doctrine to, instead of trying to replace, the secular legal institutions of the Napoleonic tradition. Lebanon retains a legal structure similar to that the French had imposed. One official explained to me that although Hezbollah's public stance on collaborators was radical, in practice they were practical, often arguing leniency for some families, exile for others who might vote against them. In other words, for Hezbollah, a territorial displacement (exile) could substitute for a process of purification leading to a temporal metamorphosis (emancipation into a new order). Some people with whom I spoke concluded that swift legal action by the Lebanese state effectively took the place of what would have most likely been popular violence against collaborators. As most southern Lebanese who strongly wanted to condemn collaborators also shared in the difficulties of survival during the occupation, a great measure of ambivalence marked popular attitudes.

In the reckoning with Israeli occupation, equally if not more significant than legal punishment are rites of commemoration: the symbolic retribution or performative redress in cultural work, such as turning sites of Israeli torture and murder into museums, which are to be visited ritually with no foreseeable end.[5]

The Qana museum is the twisted wreckage of a massacre in museum form. As such, it is older, better financed, and more elaborate than the memorial of Khiam.

A small Shiite village, Qana was the site of a 1986 Israeli massacre of 106 Lebanese civilians (with another 120 wounded), who were killed at a shelter within a U.N. peacekeeping base by several direct hits from Israeli missiles (800 people were in the shelter). Some U.N. soldiers in nearby buildings were also killed and they are allotted a separate and large memorial on the same site, which lists their names and country of origin (most were from Fiji). At the time, Israel, caught in a war of attrition, its occupation stalled and ineffective at preventing cross-border attacks, launched "Operation Grapes of Wrath," a sixteen-day artillery and naval assault, ostensibly to wipe out Hezbollah bases. The Israeli government claimed that it was unaware of civilian presence at the U.N. base in Qana, but a U.N. investigation later suggested that, since there were several direct hits on the base, it had likely been deliberately attacked.[6] The day of the massacre, 18 April, is now an official day of mourning throughout Lebanon.

H. and I are the only guests when we arrive, and H. parks his car directly across from the site, which is on the main street of the village. A young man, dark-haired with large, alert eyes and a full mouth, immediately comes over to accompany us through the exhibit. H. says that his witnessing to visitors, like me, is considered a form of religious service. The first room contains a photo documentary of the massacre. He had memorized a lengthy story for each picture and he seems to dwell on the most gruesome photographs of the dead, with their bloody body parts strewn around the site. I tell him, "I know this story already."

"But I want to tell it to you," he replies matter-of-factly.

I am too disturbed by the graphic images to remain polite, so after a few minutes I simply abandon him while he talks and I walk into the next room, a large space with an exhibit of the artwork of college students inspired to paint the event, what the exhibit calls a "Holocaust." But the guide follows me, and I become increasingly irritated as he continues to narrate the story of the massacre, in an assured, measured, monotone voice.

To overcome this irritation, I try to eroticize him, in particular his mouth, which appears to me sensuous, but also crooked, as if some injury or birth defect was preventing the full range of movement of his lips. I think, perhaps I am projecting crookedness onto his mouth in order to distance myself from his voiceover. The pictures with small texts beneath are themselves sufficient, in my mind, to portray the enormity of the Israeli crime. I find the comparison with the Holocaust overwrought, an attempt to bestow significance on a massacre by elevating it to the crime of genocide. Nonetheless, the museum guide's demands on me follow a very correct and rigorous logic, which begins with the presupposition that the Holocaust is the *sine qua non* of modern terror and suffering. It follows that all subsequent experiences of this kind will be measured by the standard of the Jewish Holocaust.

However, I want to resist what I take to be the political instrumentalization of my empathy, an attempt to turn compassion into anti-Jewish sentiment. The Jewish

Holocaust was a German event, the Qana massacre of Lebanese Shiites an Israeli event. Separate, singular states, societies, historical eras, genealogies, sequences of events – and crimes. This young man appears to want of me not only empathy for his losses but also a revision of my understanding of the Jewish Shoa. I leave a donation and convince H. to exit the city without first having a coffee, which is our custom.

An Arab Dream

During this trip to Lebanon in 2000, I also visited the city of Aleppo, in northern Syria, accompanied by my two Beiruti friends, H. and A.. Because nothing of political significance in Lebanon could take place without at least tacit approval of the Syrians, I thought it important to include Syria as much as possible in any research on Lebanon. After our first night, A. wakes up sweating, even though the air conditioner had overly cooled our room. He relates the following dream: "I came to your place, not your home in Princeton, but a very big villa, like a suburban house, with marble floors, perhaps like our hotel, a remodeled fifteenth-century villa. You are sitting on a couch, and you are the host. You are showing a film made by Derrida."

I am puzzled: Does Derrida make films?

There are many other guests, children and families, and people of all ages, women and men. The film is extremely violent, a kind of collective violence, a massacre, people are cutting each other up. I wonder why you are showing this film to these people. It seems inappropriate. Yet I am not disturbed, for I've seen this film before. The film begins near the end, and only then proceeds to the beginning. Nothing really happens with the spectators, who just sit quietly and watch. I myself was never afraid. No one acts out; in fact, there is no shock effect. But I ask, again, why are you showing this film? Although I had seen it before, actually you and I are the intended audience; the others are an unintended audience, only spectators.

There is another scene, also in the dream, something about cruising, but the guy I am interested in goes out with you somewhere instead, he likes you.

The three of us discuss this dream. It is the memory of a traumatic event, and it brings this memory into the present. It is an encounter with this memory that invites A. to make sense of his own trauma – the Lebanese civil war that accompanied his childhood and youth. Syria prompts memory of the war, as he spent many happy summers with the family of his nanny in Syria. And perhaps Syria, being a majority Sunnite country, had seemed a respite from the sectarianism of Lebanon for A.. He had been raised in a respected Sunni family but over the course of the war Sunnis were increasingly marginalized and threatened by sectarian divisions. Unlike H., whose entire childhood was spent in Lebanon during the war, A. spent one year away, in Africa with a brother. But that escape from the war was also separation from his parents. Thus, it is perhaps propitious and more "safe" for A. to dream of the Lebanese trauma in Syria, a place he associates with childhood innocence.

The sequence of the film screening, from end back to beginning, replicates the latency inherent in trauma – that the original scene is unrecoverable and recognition possible only in reverse, after the fact. A. says the images in the film were painting-like, but still very violent. He remembers someone in the dream wearing red but in the Derrida film you could not see the actual victims. He situates me as the intellectual guide inviting others to react by screening the film. I am actively intervening, as I do in fieldwork, showing the victim's story from within the trauma, while A. is placed in the screening, having to watch others watch the slaughter, which is subjecting him to a kind of sadistic moment. But, then, I am not the author of the film. I am merely screening a film produced by someone else, by the philosopher "Derrida." Moreover, A. is not frightened by it, since he'd seen it before and he is, like Derrida, adept at reading.[7] The audience, being like a family, with mothers and kids, also seems familiar with the film's story and experiences no shock in viewing. The audience is, in fact, truly spectral because it has no apparent relation to A. and is not itself placed in the trauma. They just watch, which is perhaps the key to their culpability, the culpability of the protective Lebanese family that could merely watch and not intervene in the war.

A.'s dream was partly provoked by an encounter we had had the previous night with two Syrian-Armenians, a dentist who resides in Aleppo and an interior designer who moved with his family two years ago to Paris but visits every summer. We are sitting, at around midnight, in a café in a series of many Aleppian cafes, all of them full, across from the huge twelfth-century citadel built to defend Aleppo against the Crusaders. Men are engaged in lively conversation as well as in chess and card games and backgammon, and there is much smoking of the narguila. Everyone is pleasant and relaxed; I detect none of the tension that I associate with the dictatorships with which I am familiar from fieldwork in the communist regimes of East-Central Europe before 1990.

Conversation with the designer switches between Armenian, French, and Arabic, while the dentist speaks perfect English, as do my Lebanese friends. The dentist states that he enjoys discussing politics. I ask him why Aleppo appears to me to be such a free place when they are living under a dictatorship, in what is supposed to be a condition of unfreedom. He says that the ubiquitous pictures of Hafez el-Assad, Syria's political father who ruled for three decades, are a joke to the Syrian people. I should not take them seriously, as indicators of any behavior, or what we call "cult of personality." People put them up and ignore them. The government has no fear of public places, he says, it is only large gatherings in private that they fear. "Are there any social movements or public demonstrations here?" I ask. "The only demonstrations here are pro," he remarks and smiles.

I ask about Hama, the place where, in 1982, Rifaat el-Assad, the brother of Hafez, massacred some 30,000 to 40,000 members of the Muslim Brotherhood, who at the time were intent on toppling the secular, Ba'athist-led regime. (On our way to Aleppo, my friends and I had stopped in Hama, a bustling old city that Assad, after the massacre, had spatially reorganized: bulldozing the center and moving it to another space a kilometer away in an attempt to efface any traces of this event.) As our friend's responses were open and articulate, I risk asking him the delicate question of his reaction to this violence. I struggle to phrase a question, not wanting to use the word trauma, and there is no Arabic equivalent, but as he hears me say the word, he uses it himself in turn, making my struggle look silly. I ask, "Is Hama a trauma in Syria?" "No," he says, "the event does not at the moment exist."

He suddenly changes registers, becoming personal and emotional. As a child of five, he remembers stories of the massacre at the time, but nothing like that could be discussed, he says, and it will not be for a very long time. Along the way, he introduces the phrase, "the Syrian trauma." I sense some guilt in this admission, a guilt concerning his silence after the fact of mass murder. Then, he tells us a story of how, as a young adult, he gave directions to two German tourists. The police quickly picked him up and took him in for questioning. As he tells the story it takes on a live allegorical quality as the fact of intimidation becomes palpable. We notice a man at another table, who at first did not seem to understand English, listening intently to us.

The conversation then turns to lighter affairs – the effect of redirection by my Lebanese friends. It is likely that for our Armenian acquaintances another violent event lurks behind the Syrian trauma of Hama, the not-so-distant and still widely ignored Armenian genocide in Turkey. I dare not ask about this event unless they themselves introduce it, which they do not. Aleppo was the first stop on the exodus of those who escaped the Turkish slaughter. From Aleppo, survivors went on to Lebanon, Iraq, the West. These two families stayed.

Later I ask my Beiruti friends if they were bothered by my intervention, during which they remained unusually silent. They both admit discomfort, which leads to a discussion of how I conduct fieldwork, of my provocative questions, and of their role as mediators, friends, and informants. On this particular evening, they had agreed between themselves without telling me to let me ask people more intrusive questions, since I had not yet talked to anyone in any depth. Some of our Syrian acquaintances seemed to want to counter a common Lebanese conceit: that Syrians are less educated or sophisticated than the Lebanese, that they are not informed, not intellectual, perhaps because of political restrictions incapable of understanding what is going on around them.

My friends return to A.'s dream. A. is taking over my desire, they say, as in the cruising scene, but he ends up deserting me, or being left out, without understanding on what basis. Although I occupy the place of the phallus, it is unclear whether A. desires me or merely my roles. In the dream, A. is unaccustomedly passive. I place him in the film screening without forcing him to do anything, I set the grounds for engagement, for questions, for viewing, which in some ways parallels a deconstructive reading, hence the invocation of Derrida. In the cruising scene, A. is in a position where he wants to, and in fact should, take over the role of initiating interaction. But he is reticent, reluctant to provoke or risk improprieties, afraid of the potential consequences and responsibilities that may result. His consciousness of propriety trumps his curiosity.

My own presence as ethnographer reframes our encounter with the two Armenian men, however; it redefines them as collaborators (not to speak of the applicability of the naïve, older ethnographic term: "informant") in a way they are not when merely talking to Lebanese. My presence undoubtedly invokes the specter of police interrogation. I am, when in the Middle East, always a suspicious person; my generation, my nationality, my profession, my unmarried status – and, above all, my questions – create the profile of a probable spy. Those who speak with me are, in most cases, flaunting the rules of political censorship and thereby putting themselves under suspicion of betrayal. In fieldwork, it is marginal men, sexually, socially, politically, who mediate "culture" for me, who provide initial contacts and initial explanations. And I have seen these same men mediate for many other foreigners, irrespective of gender or sexual interest. With me they are collaborating in the dual registers of the sexual and the political, and because these registers are so fundamental to social order they are betraying the secrets of social organization. My Lebanese friends stress to me that I cannot choose in which register to operate. Neither I nor they can separate, for instance, my intellectual from purely personal interests, and this creates on the one hand excitement and intimacy but on the other discomfort because it leads them to suspect my motives for knowing about either register. It demands of them either conscious collaboration or distance.

While in Aleppo, we go to one of the oldest *hamman* (an Arab bathhouse), where I meet a Palestinian man in his early twenties, there with his father, a refugee from Israeli expulsions in 1947. The young man had arrived in Aleppo two weeks earlier, he said, freshly deported from Texas, with only a year left to complete his studies in business management. I do not know whether there was justifiable reason for his deportation, but at the very least he deserved a hearing and an explanation, which he said he did not get. My intuition, drawn largely from his demeanor, the way he tells his story without self-pity, suggests to me that he is a false suspect in the U.S.'s new war on terror, a scapegoat in the aggressive attempt to find a source external to America for its insecurities. I apologize to him, although I am no a position to make amends.

Departure

On the morning of 5 September, I wake regularly every hour, anticipating my departure. At 7 a.m., I arise and give M. a wake-up call on his cell phone, as he had requested. He shows up a half-hour later to drive me to the airport. M. drives a "service", the Beirut taxi that charges a standard 1,000 lira ($0.75) and takes you to the general area in which you are going, picking up other passengers along the way. Inevitably there is conversation with the others in the cab, and much exchange of local gossip. I jumped in M.'s service several weeks before. He ignored the other passenger and chatted with me about his daughter's local chess successes and about my research. I took down his number and employed him several times to drive me longer distances. Whereas most drivers try to charge me more than the standard fare, on my first ride with M., he refused to take a tip. On the way to the airport, a mere fifteen-minute drive from where I was staying, he surprised me by saying that he liked me. No Beiruti had done that before, at least not so directly. I like you too, I replied. He explained that I reminded him of a British man he had met, back in the early 1980s, who had taught him English. I was just like him, he said.

On the ride to the airport, he tells me about an event in 1986, which I subsequently verify. The U.S. had bombed Tripoli, the Libyan capital, looking for Gaddafi but instead killing mostly women and children, including Gaddafi's sixteen-year-old daughter. Shortly thereafter, "Arab revolutionary gunmen," as they were called in the press, abducted this man in retaliation for British cooperation in the bombing of Tripoli. At the time M.'s friend was preparing for a trip to London to visit his mother. He was held for one day, then executed.

"That's very tragic," I mumble, unable to come up with a more adequate condolence. M. does not remain silent, however. He quietly talked about other murders in the more recent past, one a Muslim man who killed several Christian coworkers, motivated, M. thought, by sectarian hatred.[8] On a trip the previous day, he pointed out to me a spot on the road where the only son of a wealthy acquaintance had been killed in a traffic accident. And on one of my other trips with M., he had told me of the murder of his sixteen-year-old nephew, another only son, in Detroit.

This accumulating confidence and intimacy began to overwhelm me, and M. slowed the car to a crawl to have enough time to complete the story of his British friend's murder. "There was a lot of violence back then," I said. "The security is much better today," he reassured me. I am still puzzled as to why M. chose this moment, the morning of my departure, to implicate me in his loss.

M. parks the car and, always gently smiling, demonstrates the hospitality for which Arabs are famous: He carries my bags to the passport control, then waits for me as guards check my identity, then waits for me as my luggage passes through the infrared sensors, then waits for me as I recede into the distance and pass through a door that blocks further vision. He worries, and he cares. *Le souci des autres*.

Postscript, 23 August 2006

During the summer of 2006, as I made final changes to this manuscript, Israel, responding both to a raid by Hezbollah forces into its territory, in which two Israeli soldiers were abducted and three others killed, and to a failed rescue mission in which five more soldiers were killed, systematically attacked Lebanon. In thirty-four days of bombings, some 1,191 Lebanese were killed, 4,490 wounded, nearly all civilians, one-third children under twelve, and 900,000 civilians were displaced. On the other side, some 159 Israelis were killed (nearly all soldiers), 997 injured, and 300,000 displaced. Estimates of destroyed Lebanese infrastructure (road, bridges, buildings) total over $3.6 billion. Much of this infrastructure had been rebuilt in the very period – four years – that elapsed since I first delivered this essay as a talk. Israel claimed that it was only trying to provide security to its citizens by destroying the Hezbollah militia and securing the release of its captured soldiers. European governments criticized Israel but did nothing more than evacuate their own citizens; the U.S. government officially approved of Israel's efforts and even expedited the shipment of additional sophisticated arms to Israel.[9]

Notes

1. Names have been abbreviated.
2. The children's book is referring to Ariel Sharon, the Israeli General (and later Prime Minister) in charge of the 1982 invasion of Lebanon. An Israeli government commission later charged Sharon with "indirect responsibility" for his role in the massacre of Palestinians in the Sabra and Shatila refugee camp in south Beirut during the invasion. For this offense, Sharon was indicted in 2001 in a Belgium court, though the Belgium parliament in 2003 changed the law, leading to a dismissal of the case. See Borneman (2004a).
3. Much of my information on the military tribunals comes from defense lawyers. I especially thank George Assaf from the Human Rights division of the Lebanese Bar Association for discussion in Summer 2003, as well as the Beirut legal offices of Chibli Mallat.
4. Lebanon has a history of opposition to the death penalty. Between 1972 and 1994, only one judicial execution was carried out. However, at least thirteen people were executed after 1994, two of them publicly, justified largely as deterrence in the aftermath of the civil war. Prime Minister Salim Hos imposed a moratorium in 1998 and thereafter refused to sign any execution orders. In

January 2004, however, executions resumed – three men, one by hanging, two by firing squad, convicted of murders.

5. For further elaboration of the different modes of accountability, see Borneman (1997, 2002, 2003, 2004b).

6. United States Major-General Franklin van Kappen conducted an official, on-site investigation three days after the massacre. His "Report dated 1 May 1996 of the Secretary-General's Military Adviser concerning the shelling of the United Nations compound at Qana on 18 April 1996," the basis for a revised report issued by former U.N. Secretary General Boutros Ghali, concluded that "while the possibility cannot be ruled out completely, it is unlikely that the shelling of the U.N.I.F.I.L. compound was the result of gross technical and/or procedural error" (see relevant documentation on the websites of Amnesty International and Human Rights Watch: www.amnesty.org/news/1996/51504996.htm and www.hrw.org/hrw/summaries/s.israel-lebanon979.html, both accessed 5 December 2008). See also the eyewitness reporting by Robert Fisk, present the day after the killing, in Fisk (2002: 673) and the summary of the case in King-Irani (1999).

7. There is another possible understanding of the reference to Derrida in the dream, brought to my attention by Gregoire Mallard, whom I thank for the following interpretation. As A. is fluent in French, he may be following a set of linguistic associations and displacements, in which he substitutes "Derrida" for *se derider,* a verb that means to relax. When somebody disturbs you, or makes an offensive or threatening comment about you, you usually react by making an "angry face," and in making that face many wrinkles appear (wrinkles translates in French as *rides*). But when you realize that the comment was not meant to be threatening or offensive, you relax and your face "de-wrinkles" (literally translated, *se de-rider*). A.'s invocation of Derrida may be about an attempt to relax in the face of the threat posed by the violent images of bodies in the film of a massacre. The other spectators in the screening are surprisingly nonplussed, but A. may feel threatened by the violence resurfacing in light of my research on the topic, which I am asking him to witness. To make the images less offensive to me and alleviate my discomfort, *Il se derida:* he relaxes.

8. Two years after M. told me this story, this very same man is one of three executed, in the first use of the death penalty in Lebanon in six years. See note 4.

9. For an analysis of why there were no prosecutions for the conduct of this war, see Borneman (2007).

–9–

Unwelcomed and Unwelcoming Encounters

Annarose Pandey

I had been to Sidi Ifni before and it had been a charming, southern Moroccan city. On my first visit I had been traveling around Morocco with the man who was my husband at the time. We have since gotten divorced, to some extent because of my experiences in Morocco. When I returned, this time to "do" my fieldwork, I was renting a small room next to a house and was living alone. My status as an available woman was thus confirmed. I hate to repeat all the clichés about having one's cultural lenses rubbed clean but I really did assume that since I had met many of the townspeople before, with a socially sanctioned male chaperone, I would experience a relatively smooth transition to becoming a member of the community. What I did not realize was that my first visit confirmed my identity as a sexually available woman whose sexuality was protected by the signifier of the "male guardian." When I returned to Sidi Ifni, I was a woman who was already sexualized and unescorted. Where was the male arbiter of my sexuality? Who would step in to fill this role? Thus began my adventures in trying to live through days of violence, depression, hateful encounters and questioning of the entire discipline to which I had heretofore dedicated my life.

Rabat has been my home for two months as I practiced my Darija, or Moroccan Arabic. I loved being in this town, which that was both relatively cosmopolitan and yet full of the same people on my walk to class every day. I bought my coffee from the same man every morning; I got my olives from the same *hanout* (small shop) owner every evening. They were the best olives I ever had and he never tired of remarking on my own remarkable ability to eat the tasty little treats. I was in the honeymoon stages of pre-fieldwork.

On 11 September, I walked to school through the same winding medina alleys that I always had. I would feed all of the stray cats little bits of egg and bread while the local kids mocked me for being one of those sappy foreigners who cared about such wretched creatures. I got to the school and met a wall of confusion and tears as some of the other students called their families in a panic. The school was a language center for visiting Americans, either on the Fulbright exchange or through various American colleges. There were two other students who lost family members that day. I went back to my room and was told to wait for news from the Fulbright Commission as to the next week's plan. At first the reactions that we, as Americans, received were of genuine concern for our families in the states who may or may not have been impacted. This supportive outreach turned to a much more aggressive and hostile reaction to our "American-ness" as the bombs began to drop in Afghanistan. Local media reported that the U.S. had begun their war on Islam. I distinctly remember one newspaper article that depicted the name "Afghanistan," written in Arabic with the tall "allif" (sounds like "ah") letters represented as minarets that were being bombed by an American plane.

Given these changes in Rabat, all of the people in my group decided to stay and continue our research and I made arrangements to head south to Sidi Ifni because I thought that given my previous visits to the town, I would be more welcomed there than I was in Rabat as an American. I truly wanted to revisit the *zwaina* (beautiful) town on the coast where Fellini would have loved to film a movie or perhaps Gabriel Garcia Marquez would have recognized an Arabic version of Macondo. I had idealized it to the extent that it presented itself as an idyllic town, ready for the anthropologist's pen. Francisco Franco had transformed the village of Sidi Ifni in 1934 to become the perfect Spanish colonial enclave. Sidi Ifni had a lovely promenade above the beach. There had been a dance hall, a glorious church, grand art deco plaza, a labyrinth for the children, an airfield and even an official building designed as a ship setting out to sea. There had been a zoo and a pool. A flood washed out the zoo along with all of its creatures one day in 1987. The pool had long been abandoned and was filled with beer cans from the men in town who were good Muslims and never drank. It was a beautiful town.

It was beautiful because while most of the buildings had been crumbling for years and the stench of the open sewers made the water fetid and the beach a place to be feared, one could easily project an image of the beauty that once was. (Here, I am aware of the classical anthropological conceit of projecting "authentic" and nostalgic images of space and time onto fieldwork "sites".) The center plaza had once served as the home for a magnificent statue of Franco. Sometime in 1969, one of the townspeople had shot off the head of the statue, leaving Franco with shards of bronze where his neck was, pointing into the dusty sky. The church remained standing but the bell had fallen to the ground decades earlier and still sat atop the various bookcases that it has crushed. I found old Bibles in various nooks and crevices of the church that were dusty but otherwise like new. The former

Spanish Consulate was empty except for the staircase that had finally started to crumble and the Spanish flag that remained in the foyer. I knew the family that had taken over the old library and were living amongst the stacks. Most of the books had been burned on the day, 30 June 1969 when the Spanish left, but there were still some original documents here and there between the family's belongings. Goats and dogs lived on the roof. Garcia Marquez really would have loved this place.

A visitor to the town would assume that it was peopled by out-of-work men who spent their days in idle discussions about the local fishing culture and week-old world events. Some people had televisions but the newspapers arrived days after publication and the men would get together to read and discuss events. The very few women with whom one might have encounters during the day were either non-Muslim Berbers or those who had not yet reached puberty or who had passed through menopause. The latter two categories of women, the pre- and post-child-bearing women were not considered highly sexual and were therefore able to move more freely through the open spaces of the town. Very few tourists ventured all the way down the coast to Sidi Ifni, but of those who did, the occasional "foreign" woman could be seen wandering the streets. Most often, these were German tourists who had driven their Winnebago-like busses down from Agadir, the nearest large city.

The official census puts the population of Sidi Ifni at approximately 20,000 but this includes the very rural Berber countryside. Having lived in Sidi Ifni, I would argue that the full-time resident population was no more than 10,000 since many of the "able-bodied men" would travel for work, either to more northern towns or off the coast on Spanish fishing fleets. Those who stayed in town earned a living by fishing in small and very dangerous, certainly not water-tight, boats. We had a very small *souk* where a handful of men and Berber women or older Muslim women would sell vegetables, fish and meats including camel, goat and chicken. The town was not prosperous nor had it been for some time.

I loved Sidi Ifni and committed to staying even after the experiences of my first days. I had arrived, with my husband who had agreed to help me settle in before returning to his own dissertation work. We moved into my apartment and were trying to figure out how to work the gas tank to boil water for dinner when a thudding knock came at the door. I expected neighbors but did not anticipate armed officials as the welcoming committee. The local *sureté nationale* (police/gendarmes) had already spoken with the people who owned my apartment. I had registered my passport and had what papers I thought were necessary to begin my work. Instead, we were asked to come to the jail and have a little talk with the officials about my reasons for being in the town, renting an apartment and plans to interview townspeople. I was clearly identified both by the local officials and the townspeople as an American woman who for some odd reason spoke Arabic. My use of Arabic was both a source of confusion and amusement because few in the town had met a foreigner, let alone an American, not to mention a woman who spoke the local Darija. My first visits to the *sureté nationale* to explain all of these unusual attributes should have been a sign of what would come. This was the beginning of what became an utter farce in which I would daily be summoned to the jail, asked my citizenship, required to provide my passport and questioned as to my motives.

I became very familiar with the local officials and at times we even got along quite well. We would joke together as they helped me with my Arabic, sometimes over very sweet tea. The weekly, if not daily trips to the jail were simply part of my routine. It was not until some weeks had passed that two other men began to follow me around town. I discovered later that they were there on orders of the Moroccan government to "protect" me as an American citizen during a very unsettling time in Morocco-U.S. relations after 11 September. When I write this, I can imagine someone thinking, how would she know that they were following her? I know because I was the only woman walking around the streets during the day and these two men were always following behind me. I had to leave my apartment unescorted so as to buy my vegetables for dinner. We had no refrigeration so the traditional practice was to send a child to the *souk* (market) for the day's rations. I had to do this for myself. These men were always just a few paces behind me. When an internet café opened in town, they came to the computer next to me and like all of the other men in the café, would watch American porn while they glanced over at me and made various sounds of air sucking through their teeth. While I can still hear the sound after years away it is difficult to describe. It sounded like a balloon that someone had just had his lips around that was releasing air through the wetness. This sound was not particular to Sidi Ifni and in fact I heard men sucking air through their teeth in many locations. It signaled to me something akin to a whistle in American culture but had a much more insidious connotation. The sound was both a performance to the other men present, a kind of machismo tactic but was also meant to signal me that the men were keenly aware of my sexuality. When I was with Moroccan women and heard this sound the women would say that the men were being *haiba,* which loosely means dirty and disgusting.

I began to develop a serious anxiety issue with going to the internet café because while the lude gestures and sounds were disturbing, other men and boys also started to follow me home. The men who were following me never tried to stop any of this and certainly did nothing to indicate that it was in their duty or desire to change the situation for the better. I have no idea if they instigated any of the harassment that came my way but they certainly participated in it themselves to such an extent that they implicitly abetted the other men's attempts to intimidate me. I would walk home quickly from any public space like the internet cafes, with my eyes and head down, but not so fast as to be seen running. I did not make this trip very often because it left me reduced to a crying panic by the time I closed my door behind me.

Sometimes the boys and men would stand outside my door, occasionally knocking and calling attention to themselves for hours. They had nothing else to do and I suppose that the whole situation was pretty entertaining for them. The local children would also be around my doorway. I befriended quite a few of them but there were two young boys in particular who took to calling me a "whore" and "prostitute." I can only assume that they had heard others use these names for me and were simply passing on the expressions. My own sexuality was open to public discussion precisely because I had arrived in town with a man and had then been living there on my own. This led to the assumption that not only was I a sexualized woman but that since the man who would traditionally be my acceptable sexual partner was not around, I was in need of another man. While most of this sexualization was a direct connection to my status of married and thus sexually available, much of it can also be attributed to my identity as an American woman. The clear and prevalent stereotype was that American women had insatiable sexual appetites that motivated their every decision. It was assumed that I was promiscuous and so the various advances made towards me were simply recognition of my implicit desires. I was desirable because I was not under any male supervision, was sexualized because I had already had a man (albeit my husband) staying in my room and I was an American woman who "obviously" needed a great deal of sex and would be open to advances. I ignored the boys and men who called to me and spent time chatting with the younger kids who loved to show me their books and drawings. This was a respite for me in many ways.

Another solace that I found was taking care of a stray cat and three puppies. I have always been an "animal person" and found my need to continue this a fundamental aspect of my sanity while the rest of my fieldwork seemed to be going so horribly awry. The cat was a local figure and while I was the only person who actually allowed him into my room, he was not a major issue. The puppies, however, were much more of an offense to people. Dogs are considered to be particularly dirty to many Muslims in Morocco and this was definitely the case in Sidi Ifni. Cats were seen as somewhat inevitable and at least a bit useful in terms of their hunting abilities. Dogs could be kept as protectors but were not to be treated kindly because of their innate meanness. The fact that I would seek out and care for these animals was completely unacceptable. On one occasion a man approached me and told me that I was a witch and should be prosecuted for feeding such dirty, dangerous creatures. In his mind, only a "witch" would be able to communicate with or even approach animals that were such a threat to people. He was genuinely angry and threatened by what seemed to me to be an act of necessity from one living species to another. The children heard this man one day and decided that they should also take action. As far as I know, two of the puppies were simply killed. The third, the one whom I even tried not to love, met a much more symbolic fate. She was skinned and thrown through my window. The children laughed and went about their play.

I have a very difficult time saying that this was simply children doing "what children do" because it seemed to me to be calculated and intentional. I do not think that I will ever forget the image. More significantly for me personally is that I cannot stop thinking that this creature was tortured because I had chosen to have our paths intersect. Sadly, this moment marked my experience and deeply affected my ability to engage in anthropological fieldwork.

Anthropology, for me, had always been a vocational calling. I loved the discipline because it was both common sense and all encompassing in its perspective. I had always spent a great deal of time traveling and learning languages: fieldwork was a natural extension of my personal and academic needs and desires. My husband, also an anthropologist, had loved fieldwork even though his closest friends robbed him on his last day in Cote d'Ivoire. Still, knowing that he loved his research so much, and fieldwork was (and is) considered a major rite of passage, I felt entirely incompetent and inept in my transition to fully fledged anthropologist. If all of these other people had been able to survive fieldwork, why couldn't I? Had all of their stories of wonderful, meaningful encounters, interviews and conversations simply been fabrications or willful projections? Were they simply perpetuating the myth? Yes, I honestly think that they were. Part of the irony is that even the standard fieldwork horror story over a drink after the weekly seminar struck me as part of the façade. The "emperor's new clothes" became my working metaphor for understanding the representation of anthropological fieldwork. People glorified both their successes and failures in such a way as to legitimate their new status as postfieldwork anthropologist. Really, what they did seem to share was a collective misrepresentation of what fieldwork was and is. The failures with fieldwork were somehow left behind when they returned "from the field." I was simply incapable of leaving these experiences behind.

I expect that a reader would say that I should have gotten over these things that happened; they could happen to anybody and weren't that bad. People have told me that I overreacted to the skinning of the dog and that "lots of female anthropologists are called prostitute and whore." To me, that doesn't mean that my reaction is inappropriate. It means that the conversations about fieldwork that should be going on over beers or coffee are simply reproducing the myths and not getting to the heart of the discipline. I am not talking about any sort of crisis of representation or problematic epistemology; I am talking about what actually happens to people when they move into new communities and experience violence and aggression that is directed specifically at them, as people, not just as anthropologists. I would hope that I am more than just this one aspect of my identity.

I say this because the violence that was enacted upon me, through the various unwelcomed appellations and through the bodies of the animals, was finally also visited on my physical and emotional body. I had been accosted any number of times, too many to count, by random men in the town. On one occasion, I was taking a communal taxi to the nearest town to buy some groceries. I was the only woman in the old Mercedes among seven men. I was dressed very modestly although in western clothing. I was wearing my usual traveling outfit of a long-sleeved, loose-fitting cotton shirt, a skirt that was also quite loose and reached the ground, a kerchief on my head, covering my hair that was pulled up and pinned away and sandals that even covered my toes. In my mind it would be difficult to be much more modest – not that it mattered in this case. Not all of the men in the car were from Sidi Ifni and it became clear that they did not realize that I could speak and understand Arabic. Shortly after we left the side of the road where people waited to fill cars for their respective destinations, the men started looking around at me. I knew that the trip would last about three-and-a-half hours and already felt claustrophobic because despite the 100-degree heat, the practice in Moroccan taxis was to leave the windows up.

I was in the back seat with three other people and there were three people up front. I kept my eyes either down or clearly looking out the window because I had long since learned that a woman does not make eye contact with a man. I heard the men up front talking and start making the sound of sucking air through their front teeth. I did not hear what they were saying until they began turning around to talk with the other men in the backseat. "How easy it would be to simply pull the car over wouldn't it?" "Nobody would know." "But maybe she is meeting someone who would tell the police." "So, what would that do?" "She would tell nobody." "Should we?" "Should we?"

I sat there, and did whatever I could to show little or no reaction on my face or in my body. I swept into a panic. Should I speak to them in Arabic and tell them that I understand what they are saying? Should I somehow ask that they pull over the car and run? Where would I run? There was nothing around except for the high desert and we were nowhere near any villages. I wasn't sure at first but then realized that the men on either side of me began feeling my legs and my back as they were pretending to adjust their seats. I did what I could to shrink my entire body and sit forward to avoid this but felt myself deepening into a complete panic.

I remembered that we were going to drive through a town, Tiznit, on our way to Agadir and usually that was where cars would stop to look for new passengers. Because our car was already full for Agadir we were not supposed to stop but I leaned forward to ask the driver if I could get out at Tiznit because I had forgotten that my brother was there to meet me and I would not want to disappoint him. I do not have a brother and certainly there would be nobody to meet me but the lie of kinship was what saved me. A male chaperone, such as a brother, was enough to make the men reconsider their plans. I felt sick. Why should I have to resort to the lie of a male protector to save myself from something that should never happen in the first place? If a male guardian of female sexuality was such as respected symbol, why weren't these men charged with protecting my dignity? I was disgusted and angry. Sadly, this anger transferred onto my husband, or rather onto his absence. If he had been there, no conversation would ever have been initiated. I thought this many times.

The only male with whom I developed any sort of relationship other than the simple and standard greeting call and response was my language tutor. I had arrived in Morocco with four years of classical Arabic training. When I arrived in Rabat, I realized that classical Arabic along with the Egyptian dialect that I spoke, were nearly unintelligible in Morocco. Furthermore, when I moved to Sidi Ifni, I realized that the Darija, or Moroccan dialect that I had learned in the northern cities of the country, were not quite the same as the dialect spoken in the south. When I moved to Sidi Ifni there was an older American woman living in town. I'd have to say that we had very different experiences of Sidi Ifni, largely because of the differences in our ages. While she did not speak Arabic and was certainly harassed on occasion, she was not propositioned sexually in the same way because she inhabited an age-grade category that was not publicly recognized as sexual. We rarely encountered one another since she spent the majority of her time working with people in the surrounding Berber villages but she did recommend a tutor with whom she had worked. I found him in a local teashop and made arrangements to work with him every other day. I asked M., a female acquaintance, if she thought this would be OK. She did not personally like the man who would be my tutor but thought that as long as we met in very public spaces, everything should be fine; this was not to mention the fact that the two men who followed me everyday would also be able to communicate that there was nothing illicit about our encounters, thereby acting as my unwitting chaperones.

We started meeting and working on Arabic. He struck me as a somewhat angry tutor who expected huge leaps and gains in my proficiency but I did my best to build on what knowledge I had. We would work on reading and speaking for at least two hours. During this time, we inevitably got to know each other and he obviously came to know right away that I was married but living on my own. Because we knew each other quite well, I assumed that he did not think of me as a whore or prostitute. He knew that I was not. I had even received confirmation from the local police one day that they had come to the decision that I was not a prostitute. They had asked enough people to know for sure. I was so relieved by this odd pronouncement that I thought it was funny to picture the police going around with a picture of me, asking if anybody thought that I was getting paid for sexual services.

My tutor would ask about my husband and we never spoke very personally about such matters but it was clear that I was away from home for a very long time. In the winter season, the sun would start going down earlier and my tutor would sometimes offer to walk me back to my apartment so that I would not be accosted. This was simply his "responsibility" he said. I saw no problem with this and was in fact grateful.

I find myself not wanting to write about this. The emperor's new clothes . . . if we all pretend that he is wearing his beautiful robes, then there are no problems, we do not see his nakedness.

The reality that I do not want to share, that reveals my own vulnerability, is that my tutor assaulted and molested me. We had been walking back to my apartment along the "promenade" above the water. There were many people around whom we both greeted although he spoke to only the men and used the local Tashelhit Berber dialect that I did not understand. I noticed that as he spoke to some of the men, they would look at me in such a way as to make me uncomfortable. The oddest part of this is that I was so used to being glanced over that I did not think anything much of it. I could not have been dressed more modestly but I honestly do not think that it mattered. As we approached the lower staircase of the "promenade", he quickly dragged me off into an alleyway. We had no streetlights and these build- ings had no electricity so nobody could see what was happening. The deeply cynical side of me thinks that even if somebody had happened by, they would not have done anything to help me. I am a strong woman and had taken a fair number of self-defense classes but these never prepare you for the shock of the moment. I know this man and he knew me. I found it difficult to believe that any of it was happening at all. I resisted as much as I could and know that my struggles defi- nitely protected me to some extent but not enough. I remember thinking that calling for help or trying to get the police would be even more dangerous. Who knew what they would do to me? All I wanted was to go home and I wanted it with a kind of desperation that is still difficult for me to imagine.

My tutor knew that most people already thought of me as an available sexual- ized being and took advantage of this. That I did not think of myself or present myself as available meant nothing to him. Not only did he know what he was doing to me, I think that in his mind, he was simply acting on what he imagined my own desires to be. After months of being subject to police inquiry, hostile encounters on the street and even outside my own doorway, ugly sounds and looks, I had finally become sexualized in the way that people had been treating me all along even if I did not have a say in the matter. I had learned to walk with my head down, to deny my own sense of body and space in order to avoid and subvert the treat- ment to which I was subjected. The irony was that this kind of modesty made me even more like the Moroccan women who did not leave their houses without male chaperones because they knew what it meant to be a woman alone and outside of the family's supervision and control. Afterwards, when I felt compelled to talk with M., she was understanding but also said, "well, what did you expect? You spent time with a man. What else was going to happen?" This, to me, was a way of blaming me and vindicating him. M. was well aware of how painful my life had become but could only support me to a certain point. To really get angry and try to help me would be to recognize the ways that she herself had been treated all her life. She knew, ultimately, that I could leave and that she could not. We all know the "blame the victim" model all too well. That I am yet another one of many who have become part of this parable is not surprising. What I most resent is that when I returned from fieldwork and began to think through my experiences through writing, I felt that I could not and in fact refused to pretend that I had experienced such terrible events during my fieldwork; the violence that was part of my fieldwork *had* to be part of my dissertation. To do anything else would be a lie.

I had always had a very convoluted and jargon-laden academic writing style. I could string together recursive and complex ideas like the best of them. When I returned, I found that my writing was much more narrative and personal. I could write no other way. How could I write about what happened to me and around me in the typical obfuscating, opaque way that has become a hallmark of the discipline? Why bother? My dissertation did not go over well. I am still working on revisions and understand that a dissertation is not a personal diatribe. I do not think that it was and was actually quite proud of myself for being able to write a dissertation on "projections of history and spatio-temporal representations of colonial imaginings." I was supposed to remove myself. But isn't fieldwork all about putting yourself *right there*?

This piece is not cathartic. I do not believe in "closure." My goal in writing is to communicate, to think through writing. I have no conclusion and in fact feel tempted to cite a former professor's conclusion to an 800+ page book, "in conclusion, inconclusion." The fact is however, that I have mocked this wordplay for years. Instead, what comes to mind are the words of my greatest mentor, "onwards and upwards." For me "upwards" has been becoming a high school teacher, which most of my peers in graduate school would see as being "downwards." It isn't. It took me a very long time to write even these short pages because I care so much about them. My mentor would see that what I have written represents my own version of "onwards."

Guide to Further Reading

Parvis Ghassem-Fachandi

This guide to further reading is intended to introduce students to anthropological literature and theorizing on violence. It is not an exhaustive survey, nor does it summarize the individual works in detail. Instead it offers interested readers *important axiological points* for further inquiry suggesting an array of theoretical possibilities for interpretation in juxtaposition to the narrower focus on individual experiences with violence in the contributions. The guide will begin with some theoretical works, not presented purely chronologically but as an introduction into several general theoretical frames of analysis. Although the focus of the volume is on ethnography, we hope to inspire students to read widely across disciplines. Finally, we offer readings for regional ethnographic studies on violence for a deeper investigation into concrete violent realities. Most works are available and thus referenced in English translation, but to contextualize the work historically we give dates in square brackets of the original date of publication in the original language written.

The empirical phenomena that have prompted scholars to define and develop theories on the nature and origin of violence are immensely complex and diverse. This fact has led some commentators to doubt the heuristic value and validity of subsuming diverse empirical phenomena under the rubric of "violence." Are violent phenomena in question related in significant ways only in the mind of the researcher? We say no, and in contradistinction to such a positivist view, we claim that the conceptual difficulties of the notion of violence derive largely from its essential nature: violence never simply appears or disappears as a fixed thing but remains in flux in processes of transformation, such as sublimation, inscription, substitution, displacement, denial and repression. The German word *Gewalt* is helpful here – it combines semantically three essential characteristics of violent transformation: power, force, and physical violence, which in English are rendered into separate concepts.

The fact that violence is extant in diverse mediated forms is an insight that lies at the foundations of modern philosophy and social science and has left an imprint in sociology, history, and anthropology. It is implicit in Hobbes' state of nature and Hegel's master-slave dialectic, in Marx's history as class struggle and in Nietzsche's resentment as a vital force of history, as well as in Freud's speculation on the origin of civilization in the guilt of primal murder. It is expressed in Durkheim's analysis of the social as a coercive force, in Simmel's identification of conflict as a form of sociation (*Vergesellschaftung*), and in Weber's ideal-type distinction of forms of domination and authority. This list could be extended to include almost every major theoretical thinker of our time. The following guide concentrates mainly, but not exclusively, on modern political violence.

First, however, we mention a series of useful collected volumes to which we are deeply indebted, which bring together a wide array of historical, philosophical, psychoanalytical, and ethnographic material: *The Anthropology of Violence*, edited by David Riches (1986); *Fieldwork under Fire: Contemporary Studies of Violence and Survival*, edited by Carolyn Nordstrom and Antonius C. G. M. Robben (1995); *Violence, Identity, and Self-Determination*, edited by Hent de Vries and Samuel Weber (1997); *Meanings of Violence*, edited by Göran Aijmer and Jon Abbink (2000); *Anthropology of Violence and Conflict*, edited by Bettina E. Schmidt and Ingo W. Schröder (2001); *Violence: Theory and Ethnography*, edited by Andrew Strathern and Pamela J. Stewart (2002); *Annihilating Difference: The Anthropology of Genocide,* edited by Alexander Laban Hinton (2002); *Violence in War and Peace: An Anthology*, edited by Nancy Scheper-Hughes and Philippe Bourgois (2004); *Death of the Father: An Anthropology of the End of Political Authority*, edited by John Borneman (2004); *Violence*, edited by Neil L. Whitehead (2004); *Terror and Violence: Imagination and the Unimaginable*, edited by Andrew Strathern, Pamela J. Stewart and Neil L. Whitehead (2005). These collected works cover much of the range of research and are therefore an apt introduction to the teaching of violence in anthropology.

Axiological Readings

The catastrophic experience of the World War Two, as well as the growing consciousness about the devastating effects of European imperialism, has produced a lasting and impressive body of scholarly work that tries to map, explain, and understand human expression of political violence within modernity. It seems evident that it is in relation to these two axial experiences – and their many avatars in wars of expansion, decolonization, and partition – that all current work on violence has to be located. A student of the anthropology of violence would be wise to begin with Hannah Arendt's *The Origins of Totalitarianism* (1951), an encyclopedic work that bridges the analysis of modern anti-Semitism, the formation of the modern nation state, continental imperialism, racism and their culmination in totalitarianism.

Shadowing and directly informing the events of the World War Two are the experiences of World War One, as significant as ever today, as many scholars have pointed out. Sigmund Freud's *Thoughts for the Times on War and Death* (1915) and Walter Benjamin's *Critique of Violence* (1921) remain important interventions. Freud expressed his own shock when confronted with the re-emergence of lustful expenditures of hate in World War One, but then concluded that violence denied and no longer expected is precisely what allowed for such a sudden eruption. Benjamin, by contrast, thinks through the utopian possibilities of a "violence of pure means," which might suspend the endless cycles of violence once and for all. Written in the immediate aftermath of the fall of the Habsburg and German monarchies, and during the Russian revolution's more "innocent" phase, Benjamin's challenging text carries palpable influences of authors such as Georges Sorel and Carl Schmitt. Despite these divergent perspectives, there is a strange air of timelessness in these two alternatives: the utopian vision of Benjamin and the cautionary, reflexive note by Freud. Both perspectives seem applicable to events with which we are more familiar today, such as massacres in Bosnia and Rwanda in the 1990s, or the post-9/11 U.S.-led War on Terror.

The immense ramifications brought about by revolution and war led Freud to complete a key study of violence, *Group Psychology and the Analysis of the Ego* (1921), in which he deals with the socio-psychology of the masses (Freud called it not group but more specifically *Massenpsychologie*) and diagnoses the double identification of the individual: with the leader of the group (or its ideological principle) and with the other members of the collective. For Freud these identifications are fundamentally libidinal and akin to a sort of love: in the absence of any possibility for sexual union they become the substituted deferral of impossible libidinal desire. Freud's insights hark back to his speculations on primal murder of the father figure in a forgotten stage of human development that he elaborated in *Totem and Taboo* (1912/13), which identifies the origin of civilization with a violent act of murder and incorporation as well as the guilt engendered through it.

The negative and potentially destructive character of mass action poses important questions that were visited earlier by another Austrian scholar, the sociologist Georg Simmel, whose short text *The Negative Character of Collective Behavior* (1908) makes for a valuable but remarkably unacknowledged reading on the modern urban crowd. Simmel theorizes that the cumulative nature of negativity is able to unify divergent groups, be it by abnegation or by destruction – two forms of negation at work in sacrifice. Simmel's thought contains the seed for much later work on nationalism, which places national sacrifice and abnegation at the center of an analysis of modern forms of political violence. Georges Bataille's *The Psychological Structure of Fascism* (1933/34) is another early and neglected text, written during Hitler's rise to power in Germany, and Mussolini's political tenure in Italy. Bataille attempts to analyze the collective upsurge of fascism as a revolt against the social relations of capitalism and thus an effect of the political failure of socialism. Taking off from Marx's assertion of *Mehrwert* (surplus), he argues, that that part, which was not reintegrated into the productive process was channeled into symbolic and collective form. Fascist leaders were able to co-opt, manipulate, and channel these collective forces into militarism. As political mass movement, fascism manifested the "reality of the affective and symbolic dimensions of social experience" (Brenkman 1979), which the Anné Sociologique (mainly Émile Durkheim and Marcel Mauss) had discovered in their analyses of religion and society. In this suggestive, if somewhat unbalanced, attempt, Bataille creatively blends the work of early French anthropology with Freudian psychoanalysis.

Freud's understanding of processes of identification and outward projection of unconscious emotional impulses had tremendous influence on other subsequent studies, such as Theodor W. Adorno's (et al.) *The Authoritarian Personality* (1950), a socio-psychological etiology of violent characters, and Hannah Arendt's *Eichmann in Jerusalem: A Report on the Banality of Evil* (1963b), an analysis of the disturbingly unexceptional character of perpetrators of genocide. The ordinary nature of victimizers and the largely voluntary nature of their reprehensible actions are issues that have been revisited recently in Christopher R. Browning's *Ordinary Men: Reserve Police Battalion 101 and the Final Solution in Poland* (1992) and Daniel Goldhagen's *Hitler's Willing Executioners: Ordinary Germans and the Holocaust* (1997). The latter two disagree mainly about the role of "German culture" in the anti-Semitism of Weimar and Nazi Germany and thus in how to explain the personal motivations of soldiers who carried out atrocities.

Arriving at similar conclusions, Jan Gross's *Neighbors: The Destruction of the Jewish Community in Jedwabne, Poland* (2001) additionally stresses the accusations of ritual murder against Polish Jews by their Catholic neighbors, mythological and folkloric themes prevalent in Europe since at least the eleventh century. Their persistence is connected to the significance of Abrahamic sacrifice in Judeo-Christian traditions (cf. Poliakov 1974, Dundes 1991, Horowitz 2006), validating Freud's assertion that violent acts are often fed by a resentment kept latent and repressed. Jacques Semelin's *Purify and Destroy: The Political Uses of Massacre and Genocide* (2007) systematizes these approaches and offers a valuable comparative perspective looking at the Holocaust, Bosnia Herzegovina, and the Rwandan genocide.

A theme running through many contemporary analyses of violence is the connection between modern political violence in the context of nationalism and elements of custom, culture, and folklore, which are either forgotten and then rekindled as resentments or consciously exploited in mass actions and festivals. Another theme is the role of aesthetics and symbolic form in relation to violence. Nazi Germany has remained a fertile field for examining both sets of questions.

Compare for example George Mosse's *The Nationalization of the Masses: Political Symbolism and Mass Movements in Germany from the Napoleonic Wars through the Third Reich* (1975) and Theodor W. Adorno's "Theses against Occultism" in his reflections of *Minima Moralia: Reflections on a Damaged Life* (1950). Written in exile during World War II, Adorno's text proposes a perceptive relation between forms of occultism and fascism.

Further examination of the intimacy between religion, sexuality and violence might begin with Roger Caillois's *Man and the Sacred* (1939) and Georges Bataille's *Eroticism. Death and Sensuality* (1957). While Caillois reflects on transgression, festival, and war and their relation to sacrality in pre-modern societies, Bataille, building on these insights, asks why in ritual sacrifice that which has previously been consecrated is destroyed. Through the institutionalization of transgression, Bataille argues, man's search for a lost intimacy is expressed through the expenditure in violent destruction – the production of death. Bataille thus elucidates an important communicative aspect of violence with general utility for all violent contexts. René Girard's *Violence and the Sacred* (1977) building on Sir James Frazer (1890), Henri Hubert and Marcel Mauss (1899), Sigmund Freud (1912/13), and Georges Bataille (1957, 1967, 1973), focuses on a scapegoat mechanism that lies at the foundation of culture and society. Giorgio Agamben in *Homo Sacer: Sovereign Power and Bare Life* (1995) critiques Bataille's and Caillois' notion of the sacred and, by revisiting Carl Schmitt, Michel Foucault, Walter Benjamin, and Hannah Arendt, formulates a critic of the legal and institutional force of the juridical-politico domain of modern state power.

On the question of nationalism, perhaps the most influential work has been Benedict Anderson's *Imagined Communities: Reflections on the Origins and Spread of Nationalism* (1983). Identifying in nationalism an eminently cultural element, Anderson suggests analyzing images that communities adhere to like anthropologist do kinship and religion. He poses the question on the outset of how modern forms of identification can foment a loyalty that is willing to embrace death and war in national sacrifice. This theme of national sacrifice is further explored in *Sacrifice and National Belonging in Twentieth-Century Germany*, edited by Greg Eghigian and Matthew Paul Berg (2002), and *Blood Sacrifice for the Nation: Totem Rituals and the American Flag* (1999), edited by Carolyn Marvin and Francisco W. Ingle, two political scientists who apply Durkheim rigorously to contemporary American political form.

The cataclysmic events of the two world wars, culminating in the Holocaust, found perhaps their most profound examination in Max Horkheimer and Theodor W. Adorno's *Dialectic of Enlightenment: Fragments of Philosophy* (1944), a work that attests the obvious return to savagery in the most advanced civilizations, the subversion of enlightenment ideals in the context of modern mass culture, totalitarianism and capitalism. The book is in a deep dialogue with the German philosophical tradition of Georg Friedrich Hegel, Karl Marx and Sigmund Freud.

Much as World War One preceded World War Two, the violent experiences of colonization preceded those of colonialism. This narrative drives Joseph Conrad's *Heart of Darkness* (1902), a meticulous description of the realities of the rubber boom in the Congo, and Frantz Fanon's *The Wretched of the Earth* (1963), in which Fanon calls for acts of emancipation, including violence against internalized forms of authority, which have become nested in the colonial subject's sense of self. Jean Paul Sartre wrote a preface to Fanon's famous book and took up these questions in his subsequent work. Michael Taussig's *Shamanism, Colonialism, and the Wild Man: A Study of Terror and Healing* (1987) picks up ethnographically on Fanon, Benjamin, Bataille, and Horkheimer/Adorno, stressing the strange mimesis between the savagery attributed to the colonial subjects and the savagery of the colonists.

In contradistinction to Sartre, Fanon, and Benjamin, Hannah Arendt criticizes the utopian usages of violent means in *On Violence* (1970), a book written during the 1960s student unrest, amidst new left identification with anti-imperialist movements in the "Third World." She defines violence not as a way to assume or resist power but as a sign of utter *Ohnmacht* (powerlessness – a German word denoting loss of control and of consciousness, a fainting with the sense of "castration"). Hans Magnus Enzensberger's more recent meditations in *Civil Wars: From L. A. to Bosnia* (1990) carries this further, taking issue with attempts to render rational and comprehensible what he identifies as utterly self-destructive and autistic forms of contemporary violence. The distinction that Arendt draws between violence and power, distinguishing one form of *Gewalt* from another, is a vital one, especially for the current discussion of violence in the U.S. It also indirectly addresses the question of legitimacy of political form and legal structure, which Arendt explores in *On Revolution* (1963a), where she uses the American and French revolutions to study the principles that underlie all revolutions.

A series of works in the French structuralist and poststructuralist tradition parallel the German tradition above. Similar to Horkheimer/Adorno's dialectic of enlightenment, which remains fundamentally suspicious of the achievements of modernity, Michel Foucault's *History of Sexuality: An Introduction* (1976) identifies in the modern subject an internalization of state power through administrative technologies and new forms of knowledge. This process is characterized by a strange simultaneity of increased concern for life accompanied by invasive forms of state violence. In *Discipline and Punish: The Birth of the Prison* (1975) Foucault reverses the progressionist logic of an enlightenment narrative, which understands the development of the modern state as an improvement over the arbitrariness of the sovereign's power, a theme that is later picked up by Agamben (1995).

In contemporary forms of state knowledge/power, he claims, the state has gained a more comprehensive power over governed subject populations. Violence, then, is power over life (*bio-power*) and *gouvernementalité* (a play on the French words for "government" and "mentality"). Foucault's approach, influential in analyses of post-colonial societies, insists that the colonial and post-colonial state's technologies of administration of large subject populations created new forms of identity, concepts of personhood and divinity, religion and secularity, belonging and territory, all forms of knowledge with devastating effects in many parts of the post-colonial world.

Pierre Bourdieu's *Outline of a Theory of Practice* (1972) develops the influential concept of symbolic violence, a violence that has been euphemized and disguised, rendered internal and corporeal in mental and bodily dispositions. Through *doxa,* the practices structuring the social world are concealed, taken-for granted, hiding the conditions of their emergence along with the conditions that might enable their proper perception. This leads individuals to misconceive of their own actions and hence their positions within the social worlds they inhabit – ultimately a misrecognition anchored in the individual's "sense of self." What has been rendered invisible, however, is externalized and thus ultimately generative, active, and reproduced in daily praxis – for example through a bodily *hexis* applied to the world. Attentive to mental and bodily dispositions, Bourdieu's approach skillfully amalgamates insights from Weber's sociology of *Verstehen,* Durkheim's coercive nature of classificatory systems, Marx's analysis of society as class struggle, and Merleau-Ponty's phenomenology of the corporeal.

Bourdieu's insights have influenced many subsequent sociological studies on violence and the body, such as Loïc Wacquant's *Body and Soul: Notebooks of an Apprentice Boxer* (2004), which elucidates the links between the institution of the American inner-city ghetto as an "ethnoracial prison" and the métier of boxing, a kinetic sport in which participation comes at the price of physical self-destruction. Unlike Foucault, Bourdieu's approach is supposed to be emancipatory – in handing back to the social actors the "real sense" of their actions by elucidating the genesis of social visions and divisions as well as the categories that make them less apparent. Both approaches, by Foucault and Bourdieu, share with ethnographic work that they attempt to understand the way in which people participate in their own subjugation through the way they think and act in the world. Simultaneously, both thinkers keep a conscious distance from psychoanalysis – Foucault by dismissing it outright and Bourdieu by replacing it with what he calls a socio-analysis, a "psycho-analysis of the social."

Less averse to psychoanalysis, the philosopher Jacques Derrida enters into a more difficult terrain in relation to violence. In *Of Grammatology* (1967), Derrida addresses, by way of a critique of logocentrism, the violence of the sign itself and its inscription in language. He looks to language itself (in writing/reading) for the trace of an originary violence, and draws attention to the erasure of this origin at the moment of its inscription. Influenced by a wide array of thinkers, including Spinoza, Hegel, Husserl, Freud, Heidegger, and Bataille, Derrida's critic of logocentrism is at the same time a critique of metaphysics. Derrida simultaneously acknowledges and resists the violent heritage of ideas and subverts the concern of prior thinkers with purity, interiority, origins, chronology, exteriority, and authority. As Etienne Balibar (1993) has pointed out, this approach makes Derrida less prone to a certain type of naïveté vis-à-vis contemporary claims to non-violence. In *The Gift of Death* (1992), Derrida meditates on the Abrahamic sacrifice that underlies both Judeo-Christian and Islamic traditions through a close reading of Kierkegaard. In *Force of Law* (1992), he works through Benjamin's *Critique of Violence* on the mystical foundations of authority, and seems to concur with some of Arendt's concerns.

Ethnographically Informed Work on Violence

Informed by the texts and authors mentioned above, contemporary anthropological projects have focused increasingly on violence, not conceived as a freak occurrence interrupting cultural and social processes but rather as constitutive of society and everyday life, expressing either change or continuity in oppressive political and social forms. More recent studies on violence deal with cosmology, ritual, folklore, symbolic form, language, identity, and belief in relation to economy, and nationalism. They provide significant new perspectives on the phenomena in a variety of ethnographic settings, and are particularly important in combining genuinely anthropological insights with the need to understand the complex dynamics of particular places.

Influenced by the work of Derrida, Michael Meeker's *Literature and Violence in North Arabia* (1977) relates poetry and voice to inter-tribal warfare and political violence. Abdellah Hammoudi's *The Victim and its Mask: An Essay on Sacrifice and Masquerade in the Maghreb* (1988) shows the subversion of Moroccan sacrifice from within itself through the bacchanalian excess of masquerade, a theme that revisits Victor Turner's work on ritual (1969). Also influenced by Turner, Maurice Bloch's *Prey into Hunter: The Politics of Religious Experience* (1992) reveals how violence is built into the way societies deal with death, and with the ritual technologies employed to access immortality, which he terms "rebounding violence." Through an oscillation between the experience of vital life and transcendence of life, the existential drama between transformation and permanence is played out in an attempt to ritually control violence.

Allen Feldman's *Formations of Violence: The Narrative of the Body and Political Terror in Northern Ireland* (1991) and Liisa Malkki's *Purity and Exile: Violence, Memory, and National Cosmology among Hutu Refugees in Tanzania* (1995) are ethnographies that seek to understand violence as a modern political phenomena shaped by cultural and economic dynamics (cf. Krohn-Hansen 1997). While Malkki worked with Hutu refuges in Tanzania and the construction of memory and cosmology, Feldman analyzes the relation of state and paramilitary violence in urban Belfast to space and body symbolism; both explain how violence becomes corporeal. In a similar vein, Christopher Taylor's *Sacrifice as Terror: The Rwandan Genocide of 1994* (1999), elucidates how the symbolic form of violence acted out in the present are influenced by traditional rites of sacred kingship and medicine—transfigured and transposed in modern genocidal violence. Fernando Coronil and Julie Skurski's *Dismembering and Remembering the Nation* (1991) complicates the relationship posed between violence, myth, and political form postulated by typological approaches that posit correspondences between types of societies and forms of violence.

Emulating Malkki's work on the indeterminacy of distinctions between Hutus and Tutsis, and Feldman's Foucaultian analysis of how the body becomes the site of sacrificial violence during interrogations, Arjun Appadurai (1998) argues that many violent acts proceed as if they attempted to create a kind of certainty of the identity of the victim through vivisection, a violent inspection that strives to concretize and clarify through perverse surgical procedures. In other words, in modern ethnocidal violence, what globalization has rendered increasingly unstable and precarious is sought in somatic stabilization—an interesting and suggestive contribution to the study of contemporary violence. Mahmood Mamdani's *When Victim become Killers: Colonialism, Nativism, and the Genocide in Rwanda* (2001) links an analysis of the Rwandan genocide with the racialization of ethnic difference under colonialism and the devastating consequences for ethnic relations between Hutus and Tutsis, whereas Johan Pottier in his *Re-Imagining Rwanda: Conflict, Survival and Disinformation in the Late Twentieth Century* (2002) critics the systematic erasure in media analyses of the class aspect of the conflict as well as the post-genocidal leader's acquiescence to this fact. This points is also made by Catharine and David Newbury's work on the genocide in Rwanda (1999). Influenced by Bataille, Benjamin, and Taussig, Alan Klima's *The Funeral Casino: Meditation, Massacre, and Exchange with the Dead in Thailand* (2002) interprets mass-mediated violence through funeral gambling and Buddhist meditation on death.

Influenced by Bourdieu, Philippe Bourgois's *In Search of Respect: Selling Crack in El Barrio* (2002) documents the brutal street culture and crack economy of East Harlem, indicating the ways in which scarce symbolic resources such as "respect" are part of a larger economy of violence. The author unravels ethnographically how in the context of poverty and racism, violence and self-violence – abuse through addiction or penal institutionalization for assault – are fundamentally linked. The humiliation and desperation that causes drug abuse can only be managed by turning self-destruction into the destruction of others, a process that is systematically encouraged and sustained by a neglectful state and its ideological scaffolding. While the self-destruction of the poor is ultimately useful for the state, the projection of violent effectiveness is essential for staying on top of things in El Barrio.

Gananath Obeyesekere's *The Work of Culture: Symbolic Transformation in Psychoanalysis and Anthropology* (1990) takes up Freud's foundational theme of how primal murder (parricide and filicide) relates to patriarchal values in Hinduism and Buddhism respectively. Abdellah Hammoudi's *Master and Disciple: The Cultural Foundations of Moroccan Authoritarianism* (1997) explores the relation of authority to political form and Islam and in *Lords of the Lebanese Marches: Violence and Narrative in Arab Society* (1996), Micheal Gilsenan shows the subversion of violence and ideal masculinity through the use of irony.

James T. Siegel's *A New Criminal Type in Jakarta: Counter-Revolution Today* (1998) investigates the emergence of new imaginative forces such as "criminality" and ghosts in mass media and rumors during Suharto's New Order in Indonesia. In *Naming the Witch* (2006), Siegel continues this project by analyzing the persecution and murder of citizens accused of being witches and he interprets these accusations as attempts to control new emergent social forces that cannot be named, for which there is no recourse in culture. Becoming marked by that which has no name, they become the carriers of all that has to be destroyed. This work is significant in that it departs from the analysis of violence as symbolic or cultural form and proposes, rather, that violence erupts when culture fails, namely through the breakdown of signification, the inability to locate death and thus control the anxious address of death. If the identification of a witch causes fear, it also suggests the existence of a fabulous power that murder is supposed to control, while the act of killing is never really able to put it to rest.

Marguerite Guzman Bouvard's *Revolutionizing Motherhood: The Mothers of the Plaza de Mayo* (1994) describes the brave struggle of Mothers for information about the whereabouts of their disappeared sons and husbands, who were abducted, tortured and killed by paramilitaries of the junta regime in Argentina in the 1970s. Daniel Goldstein's *Spectacular City Violence and Performance in Urban Bolivia* (2004) investigates vigilante lynching and street festivals as the effects of democratization, which engender new forms of violence among indigenous migrants in Cochabamba, Bolivia. Alexander Laban Hinton's *Why Did they Kill? Cambodia in the Shadow of Genocide* (2005) focuses on how emotionally resonant forms of cultural knowledge are employed in the context of the devastation under the Khmer Rouge in Cambodia. John Borneman's *Settling Accounts: Violence, Justice, and Accountability in Postsocialist Europe* (1997) explores legal attempts to address violence following the end of the Cold War. Following Hannah Arendt in *Origins* (see above), Borneman opposes forms of forgiveness that substitute for establishing systems of accountability. The sociologist Orlando Patterson (1998) analyzes the symbolic economy of American lynching after the Reconstruction period where the sacrificial killing of the "Negro" was assimilated by perpetrators and participants alike to the crucifixion of Christ, while in his more recent work on the South Africa, Feldman (2002) shows how torture under apartheid was consummated as performance of culinary images and practices of food consumption.

A series of works on ethnic and religious violence in South Asia deserve particular attention as they try to combine insights of postcolonial studies and the analysis of ritual and religion in the context of nationalism. Bruce Kapferer's *Legends of People, Myths of State* (1988) juxtaposes Australian nationalism to Sinhalese nationalism and the role of ontology, hierarchy, and ritual. Stanley Tambiah's *Buddhism Betrayed? Religion, Politics and Violence in Sri Lanka* (1992) interrogates Buddhism in the context of politically motivated violence, and his *Leveling Crowds: Ethnonationalist Conflicts and Collective Violence in South Asia* (1996) explores the role of masses and crowd behavior in violence; Sudhir Kakar's *The Colors of Violence* (1995) elaborates on unconscious aspects of violence such as mimetic identifications between Hindus and Muslims in India.

In the volume *Violence/Non-Violence: Some Hindu Perspectives,* edited by Denis Vidal, Gilles Tarabout and Eric Meyer (1994), the reader is introduced to diverse aspects of traditional and contemporary *ahimsa* (non-violence), inclusive of how this culturally salient concept relates to war, conflict, or stigmatization of minorities. Other important works include Valentine E. Daniel's *Charred Lullabies: Chapters in an Anthropography of Violence* (1996) dealing with Tamil workers in Sri Lanka's highlands in the context the nationalist violence; Urvashi Butalia's *The Other Side of Silence: Voices from the Partition of India* (2000), an attempt to reckon with the partition of India and Pakistan and Thomas Blom-Hansen's *Wages of Violence: Naming and Identity in Postcolonial Bombay* (2001), an analysis of the Shiv Sena and Hindu nationalism in Bombay.

Recently Veena Das's *Life and Words: Violence and the Descent into the Ordinary* (2007) as well as Roma Chatterji and Deepak Mehta's *Living with Violence: An Anthropology of Events and Everyday Life* (2007) both employ detailed ethnographic material in order to investigate how violence works itself into quotidian life, shattering a social world and a sense of self, while by that very fact also opening a space for reworking the limits of the social (cf. Martin 2007). Jonathan Spencer's *Anthropology, Politics, and the State: Democracy and Violence in South Asia* (2007) focuses among other things on the agonistic energies released in such phenomena as elections, and poses programmatically an "anthropology of the counter-political." This strategy tries not to deny, but to defuse the effects of the political. Finally, Arjun Appadurai's *Fear of Small Numbers: An Essay on the Geography of Anger* (2006) tackles the question of why the age of globalization – with its liberal ideas, financial flows, expansion of human rights – simultaneously remains so arrested in mass violence.

It is disturbing to realize, how much these later questions suggestively mirror the ones posed by an older generation of authors mentioned at the beginning of this Guide to Further Reading. We have highlighted some key texts selectively: theoretical approaches and key ethnographic works on modern political violence.

However, as the authors of this volume have shown, even if we focus only on political violence, it can take peculiar forms in different places and at different times, always in excess of analytical possibilities. The experience of and the encounter with violence, in their individual or collective apprehensions, are never equal to analyses. Yet, while on the one hand the movement from experience to conceptual language (*Begriff* – notion) must be a cautious one, it on the other hand can never be elided if our goal remains one of understanding (*begreifen*).

Bibliography

Adorno, T. W. (1974), *Minima Morali: Reflections from a Damaged Life,* New York: Verso

Adorno, T. W., Frenkel-Brunswik, E. and Levinson, D. J. (1974 [1950]), *The Authoritarian Personality,* London: Norton.

Agamben, G. (1998 [1995], *Homo Sacer: Sovereign Power and Bare Life.* Stanford: Stanford University Press.

Aijmer, G. and Abbink, J. (2000), *Meanings of Violence: A Cross-Cultural Perspective,* Oxford: Berg Publishers.

Anderson, B. (2006 [1983]), *Imagined Communities,* London: Verso.

Appadurai, A. (1998), "Dead Certainty: Ethnic Violence in the Era of Globalization," *Public Culture,* 10(2): 225–46.

Appadurai, A. (2006), *Fear of Small Numbers: An Essay on the Geography of Anger,* Durham: Duke University Press.

Arendt, H. (1951), *The Origins of Totalitarianism,* New York: Harvest.

Arendt, H. (1963a), *On Revolution,* London: Penguin Books.

Arendt, H. (1963b), *Eichmann in Jerusalem: A Report on the Banality of Evil,* New York: The Viking Press.

Arendt, H. (1970), *On Violence,* New York: Harvest.

Balibar, E. (1993), "Some Questions on Politics and Violence," *Assemblage,* 20: 12–13.

Bataille, G. (1979[1933/1934]), "The Psychological Structure of Fascism," *New German Critique,* 16: 64–87.

Bataille, G. (1986 [1957]), *Eroticism. Death and Sensuality,* San Francisco: City Lights Books.

Bataille, G. (1991 [1967]), *The Accursed Share,* New York: Zone Books.

Bataille, G. (1992 [1973]), Theory of Religion. New York: Zone Books.

Benjamin, W. (1966 [1921]), "Critique of Violence," in Demez, P. (ed.), *Reflections, Essays, Aphorisms,*

Autobiographical Writings, New York: Schocken Books.

Bloch, M. (1992), *Prey into Hunter: The Politics of Religious Experience,* Cambridge: Cambridge University Press.

Blom-Hansen, T. (2001), *Wages of Violence: Naming and Identity in Post-colonial Bombay,* Princeton: Princeton University Press.

Bourdieu, P. (1977 [1972]), *Outline of a Theory of Practice,* Cambridge:

Cambridge University Press.

Bourgois, P. (2002), *In Search of Respect: Selling Crack in El Barrio,* Cambridge: Cambridge University Press.

Borneman, J. (1997), *Settling Accounts: Violence, Justice, and Accountability in Postsocialist Europe,* Princeton: Princeton University Press.

Borneman, J. (2002), "Reconciliation after Ethnic Cleansing: Listening, Retribution, and Affiliation," *Public Culture,* 14(2): 281–304.

Borneman, J. (2003), "Why Reconciliation: A Response to Critics," *Public Culture,* 15(1): 197–206.

Borneman, J. (ed.) (2004a), *The "Case of Ariel Sharon" and the Fate of Universal Jurisdiction,* Princeton: Princeton Institute for International and Regional Studies.

Borneman, J. (2004b), *Events of Closure, Rites of Repetition: Modes of Accountability,* Conference on Settling Accounts: Truth, Justice and Redress in Post-Conflict Societies, Harvard University, 2–3 November. Unpublished manuscript.

Borneman, J (ed.) (2004c), *Death of the Father: An Anthropology of the End of Political Authority,* New York: Berghahn Books.

Borneman, J. (2007), "The State of War Crimes following the Israeli-Hezbollah War," *Windsor Yearbook of Access to Justice,* 25 (2): 274–89.

Bouvard, M. G. (2002 [1994]), *Revolutionizing Motherhood: The Mothers of the Plaza de Mayo,* Wilmington, DE: Scholarly Resources Inc.

Browning, C. R. (1992), *Ordinary Men: Reserve Police Battalion 101 and the Final Solution in Poland,* London: Harper Perennial.

Bunsha, D. (2006), *Scarred. Experiments with Violence in Gujarat,* New Delhi: Penguin Books India.

Butalia, U. (2000), *The Other Side of Silence: Voices from the Partition of India,* Durham: Duke University Press.

Caillois, R. (2001 [1939]), *Man and the Sacred,* Champaign: University of Illinois Press.

Chatterji, R. and Deepak, M. (2007), *Living with Violence: An Anthropology of Events and Everyday Life,* London: Routledge.

Conrad, J. (1993 [1902]), *Heart of Darkness,* New York: Random House.

Coronil, F. and Skurski, J. (1991), "Dismembering and Remembering the Nation: The Semantics of Political Violence in Venezuela," *Society for Comparative Study of Society and History,* 33(2): 288–337.

Daniel, V. E. (1996), *Charred Lullabies: Chapters in an Anthropography of Violence,* Princeton: Princeton University Press.

Das, V. (2007), *Life and Words: Violence and the Descent into the Ordinary,* Berkeley: University of California Press.

De Vries, H. and Weber, S. (eds) (1997), *Violence, Identity, and Self-Determination,* Stanford: Stanford University Press.

Derrida, J. (1974 [1967]), *Of Grammatology,* Baltimore: Johns Hopkins University Press.

Derrida, J. (1992), "Force of Law: The 'Mystical Foundation of Authority'," in Cornell, D., Rosenfeld, M. and Carlson, D. G. (eds), *Deconstruction and the Possibility of Justice,* New York: Routledge.

Derrida, J. (1995 [1992]), *The Gift of Death,* translated by David Willis, Chicago: University of Chicago Press.

Dundes, A. (ed.) (1991), *The Blood Libel Legend: A Casebook in Anti-Semitic Folklore,* Madison: University of Wisconsin Press.

Eghigian, G. and Berg, M. P. (2002), *Sacrifice and National Belonging in Twentieth-Century Germany,* Arlington: A&M University Press.

Enzensberger, H. M. (1994), *Civil Wars: From L.A. To Bosnia,* New York: The New Press.

Fanon, F. (2005 [1963]), *The Wretched of the Earth,* New York: Grove Press.

Feldman, A. (1991), *Formations of Violence. The Narrative of the Body and Political Terror in Northern Ireland,* Chicago: University of Chicago Press.

Feldman, A. (2002), "Strange Fruit: The South African Truth Commission and the Demonic Economies of Violence," in Kapferer, B. (ed.), *Beyond Rationalism: Rethinking Magic, Witchcraft, and Sorcery,* New York: Berghahn Books.

Fisk, R. (2002), "The Massacre," in *Pity the Nation,* New York: Nation Books.

Foucault, M. (1990[1976]), *History of Sexuality. Vol. 1: An Introduction,* New York: Vintage Books.

Foucault, M. (1995 [1975]), *Discipline and Punish: The Birth of the Prison,* New York: Vintage Books.

Frazer, J. G. Sir (1960 [1890]), *The Golden Bough. Abridged Edition,* London: Macmillan & Co.

Freud, S. (1950 [1912/13]), *Totem and Taboo: Some Points of Agreement between the Mental Lives of Savages and Neurotics,* London: Routledge & Kegan Paul.

Freud, S. (1959 [1921]), *Group Psychology and the Analysis of the Ego,* London: W.W. Norton & Company.

Freud, S. (1953 [1915]), "Thoughts for the Times on War and Death", in Strachey, J. (ed.) *The Standard Edition of the Complete Psychological Works of Sigmund Freud,* vol. 14, London: Hogarth.

Gilsenan, M. (1996), *Lords of the Lebanese Marches: Violence and Narrative in Arab Society,* Berkeley: University of California Press.

Girard, R. (1977 [1972]), *Violence and the Sacred, translated by Patrick Gregory,* Baltimore: Johns Hopkins University Press.

Goldhagen, D. (1997), *Hitler's Willing Executioners: Ordinary Germans and the Holocaust,* New York: Random House.

Goldstein, D. (2004), *Spectacular City: Violence and Performance in Urban Bolivia,* Durham: Duke University Press.

Gonzalez, R. J. (2007), "We Must Fight the Militarization of Anthropology," in *The Chronicle of Higher Education*, see http://chronicle.com/ temp/email2.php?id= qqrpZjJnmtG8rjmgnkbwrSnJqThjM3yZ, accessed 30 January 2007.

Gross, J. T. (2001), *Neighbors: The Destruction of the Jewish Community in Jedwabne, Poland*, Princeton: Princeton University Press.

Gusterson, H. (2006), *The Cultural Turn in the War of Terror*, paper presented at the American Anthropological Association Meetings, 17 November 2006.

Hammoudi, A. (1993 [1988]), *The Victim and its Masks: An Essay on Sacrifice and Masquerade in the Maghreb*, Chicago: University of Chicago Press.

Hammoudi, A. (1997), *Master and Disciple: The Cultural Foundations of Moroccan Authoritarianism*, Chicago: University of Chicago Press.

Hinton, A. L. (ed.) (2002), *Annihilating Difference: The Anthropology of Genocide*, Berkeley: University of California Press.

Hinton, A. L. (2005), *Why do they Kill? Cambodia in the Shadow of Genocide*, Berkeley: University of California Press.

Horkheimer, M. and Adorno, T. W. (2002 [1944]), *The Dialectic of Enlightenment: Fragments of Philosophy*, Stanford: Stanford University Press.

Horowitz, E. (2006), *Reckless Rites: Purim and the Legacy of Jewish Violence*, Princeton: Princeton University Press.

Hubert, H. and Mauss, M. (1981[1899]), *Sacrifice: Its Nature and Function*, Chicago: University of Chicago Press.

Isbell, B.-J. (1985[1978]), *To Defend Ourselves: Ecology and Ritual in an Andean Village*, Austin: University of Texas Press.

Isbell, B.-J. (1994), *Public Secrets from Peru*, available at http://isbellandes.library.cornell.edu/, accessed 5 December 2008.

Isbell, B.-J. (2005), *Para defendernos: una reflecion*, Cuzco: Centro Bartolome de las Casas.

Isbell, B.-J. (2008), *Finding Cholita*, Champaign-Urbana: University of Illinois Press.

Kakar, S. (1995), *The Colors of Violence*, New Delhi: Viking Penguin India.

Kapferer, B. (1988), Legends of People. *Myths of State*, Washington: Smithsonian Institution Press.

King-Irani, L. (1999), "Petition Charges Israel with War Crimes: The Case of the Qana Massacre Survivors," *Middle East Report*, 8 December.

Klima, A. (2002), *The Funeral Casino: Meditation, Massacre, and Exchange with the Dead in Thailand*, Princeton: Princeton University Press.

Krohn-Hansen, C. (1997), "The Anthropology and Ethnography of Political Violence," *Journal of Peace Research*, 34(2): 233–40.

Malkki, L. (1995), *Purity and Exile: Violence, Memory and National Cosmology Among Hutu Refugees in Tanzania*, Chicago: University of Chicago Press.

Mamdani, M. (2001), *When Victims Become Killers: Colonialism, Nativism, and the Genocide in Rwanda*, Princeton: Princeton University Press.

Martin, E. (2007), "Violence, Language, and Everyday Life," *American Ethnologist,* 34(4): 741–5.

Marvin, C. and Ingle, D. W. (1999), *Blood Sacrifice and the Nation,* Cambridge: Cambridge University Press.

Meeker, M. E. (1977), *Literature and Violence in North Arabia,* Cambridge: Cambridge University Press.

Mosse, G. L. (1975), *The Nationalization of the Masses: Political Symbolism and Mass Movements in Germany from the Napoleonic Wars through the Third Reich,* New York: Howard Fertig.

Newbury, C. and Newbury, D. (1999), "A Catholic Mass in Kigali: Contested Views of the Genocide and Ethnicity in Rwanda," *Canadian Journal of African Studies,* 33(2–3): 292–328.

Nordstrom, C. and . Robben, A. (eds) (1995), *Fieldwork Under Fire: Contemporary Studies of Violence and Survival,* Berkeley: University of California Press.

Obeyesekere, G. (1990), *The Work Of Culture: Symbolic Transformation in Psychoanalysis and Anthropology,* Chicago: University of Chicago Press.

Pandey, G. (2006), *Routine Violence: Nations, Fragments, Histories,* Stanford: Stanford University Press.

Patterson, O. (1998), *Rituals of Blood: Consequences of Slavery in Two American Centuries,* New York: Basic Civitas Books.

Poliakov, L. (1974), *History of Anti-Semitism: From the Time of Christ to the Court Jews,* New York: Schocken Books.

Pottier, J. (2002), *Re-Imagining Rwanda: Conflict, Survival and Disinformation in the Late Twentieth Century,* Cambridge: Cambridge University Press.

Riches, D. (1986), *The Anthropology of Violence,* Oxford: Basil Blackwell Publishers.

Scheper-Hughes, N. (1992), *Death Without Weeping: The Violence of Everyday Life in Brazil,* Berkeley: University of California Press.

Scheper-Hughes, N. and Bourgois, P. (eds) (2005), *Violence in War and Peace: An Anthology,* Oxford: Blackwell Publishing.

Schmidt, B. E. and Schröder, I. W. (eds) (2001), *Anthropology of Violence and Conflict,* London: Routledge.

Semelin, J. (2007), *Purify and Destroy: The Political Uses of Massacre and Genocide,* New York: Columbia University Press.

Siegel, J. T. (1998), *A New Criminal Type in Jakarta: Counter-Revolution Today,* Durham: Duke University Press.

Siegel, J. T. (2006), *Naming the Witch,* Stanford: Stanford University Press.

Simmel, G. (1950 [1908]), *The Negative Character of Collective Behavior,* in Wolff, K. H. (ed.), The Sociology of Georg Simmel, New York: The Free Press.

Smith, R. W. (1914[1889]), *Religion of the Semites,* London: Adam & Charles Black.

Spencer, J. (2007), *Anthropology, Politics, and the State: Democracy and Violence in South Asia,* Cambridge: Cambridge University Press.

Strathern, A. and Stewart, P. J. (eds), (2002), *Violence: Theory and Ethnography,* London and New York: Continuum.

Strathern, A., Stewart, P. J. and Whitehead, N. L. (eds) (2006), *Terror and Violence: Imagination and the Unimaginable,* London: Pluto Press.

Tambiah, S. (1992), *Buddhism Betrayed? Religion, Politics, and Violence in Sri Lanka,* Chicago: University of Chicago Press.

Tambiah, S. (1996), *Leveling Crowds: Ethnonationalist Conflicts and Collective Violence in South Asia,* Berkeley: University of California Press.

Taussig, M. (1987), *Shamanism, Colonialism, and the Wild Man: A Study in Terror and Healing,* Chicago: University of Chicago Press.

Taylor, C. (2002), "The Cultural Face of Terror in the Rwandan Genocide of 1994," in Hinton, A. L. (ed.) *Annihilating Difference. The Anthropology of Genocide, Berkeley: University of California Press.*

Turner, V. (1969), *Ritual Process: Structure and Anti-Structure,* Ithaca: Cornell University Press.

Tyrrell, M. W. D. (2007), "Why Dr. Johnny Won't Go To War: Anthropology and the Global War On Terror," *Small Wars Journal,* 7, February, available at www.smallwarsjournal.com, accessed 5 December 2008.

Verkaaik, O. (2004), *Migrants and Militants: Fun and Urban Violence in Pakistan,* Princeton: Princeton University Press.

Vidal, D., Tarabout, G., Meyer, E. (eds), (2003 [1994]), *Violence/Non-Violence: Some Hindu Perspectives,* New Delhi: Manohar.

Wacquant, L. (2004) *Body and Soul: Notebooks of an Apprentice Boxer,* Oxford: Oxford University Press.

Whitehead, N. L. (2004), *Violence,* Oxford: School of American Research Press.

Index